CONFRONTATION

Confrontation

THE STUDENT REBELLION AND THE UNIVERSITIES

Edited by

DANIEL BELL and IRVING KRISTOL

□

BASIC BOOKS, Inc., Publishers

New York □ London

DANIEL BELL, co-editor of *The Public Interest,* is Professor of Sociology at Columbia University. His book, *The Reforming of General Education,* was a study of Columbia College in its national setting. He is currently a member of the Executive Committee of the Joint Faculties at Columbia.

JOHN H. BUNZEL is Professor of Political Science and chairman of the department at San Francisco State College.

NATHAN GLAZER is Professor of Sociology at the University of California at Berkeley and currently Visiting Professor of Sociology at Harvard University.

IRVING KRISTOL, co-editor of *The Public Interest,* contributes frequently to *The New York Times Magazine, Fortune,* and other periodicals.

SAMUEL LUBELL is Director of the Opinion Reporting Workshop at Columbia University's School of Journalism.

SEYMOUR MARTIN LIPSET is Professor of Sociology and Government at Harvard University. In recent years, he has concentrated his attention on youth movements and is the editor of *Student Politics* (Basic Books, 1967).

TALCOTT PARSONS, Professor of Sociology at Harvard University, is at present working on a major study of the academic system.

ROGER STARR is Executive Director, Citizens' Housing and Planning Council of New York, Inc.

NATHAN TARCOV, a recent graduate at Cornell, is pursuing graduate studies in political philosophy.

INTRODUCTION

The past five years have been, for American universities, the most dramatic in their history. The drama, indeed, is so flamboyant that sober contemplation is exceedingly difficult. Still, by now one can see fairly clearly through the fog of controversy and discern the structural changes that have transformed the American University in the quarter of a century since the end of World War II. They are five in number.

The first is the rise of mass higher education. An implicit commitment has gradually emerged to offer every American student who can meet minimal standards some amount of higher education. Already some 40 per cent of 18- to 22-year-olds are in college, and the proportion is increasing. In the process, the campuses of the major State Universities—Berkeley, Los Angeles, Wisconsin, Michigan, Minnesota, Ohio State, *et al.*—have been transformed into educational megaliths; at the same time, there has been an extraordinary proliferation of junior colleges, community colleges, branches of major campuses, and the like. With the expansion of the student body has come the growth of a professoriat that now constitutes a large occupational class. Inevitably, it has all the characteristics of such a class: a keen sensitivity to status distinctions, aspirations toward upward mobility, resentments at each and every sign of "relative deprivation," and so on.

The second change is the burgeoning of research. Research may or may not divert first-class minds from teaching, but there can be no doubt that it is integral to the advance of a scholarly field, whether it be biology, physics, or economics. There is also no doubt that when a university faculty lacks men who are engaged in such research, the quality of instruction will suffer. One can see this, for example, in the Soviet Union, where all research is detached from the university and is concentrated in an Academy system. In consequence, the Soviet universities are second-rate institutions so far as educating scholars is concerned. In the United States, scholarship and education are intertwined. Largely because of the emphasis on research, the American graduate school has become a central feature of the university—often, it must be admitted, to the detriment of the undergraduate college. Whether this detrimental effect is necessary or accidental is a key question in American education today.

The third feature is the multiplication of scholarly fields and the differentiation of subjects into newer and smaller specializations. Today, a university that wishes to be a center of scholarship requires a specialist in the politics of North Africa, East Africa, West Africa, South Africa, in African history, economics, linguistics, geography, sociology, and the like; and the same multiplication of area studies holds as well for Latin America, the Far East, Southeast Asia, Eastern Europe, the Soviet Union, and so on. The differentiation of subjects—the rise of microbiology, econometrics, neuropsychiatry—is itself a function of the development of research and the emergence of distinct and necessary sub-specializations.

The newer emphasis on research and the advances in the frontiers of knowledge bring the university squarely into the areas of public service and public policy involvement. Such involvement is not completely new. The major land grant universities in the country transformed American agriculture as a result of the research carried out in their experimental stations. But this research was marginal to the major political and social issues of the time. Today, scholarly research—technological, military, economic, social services, urban affairs, and health—impinges directly on major policy decisions. In consequence, the university is today a major resource of our "knowledge society." Its leading members move in and out of government. It has become integral to the development, if not the execution, of public policy in almost all fields. It has also made the university system more dependent on the federal government for financial support.

Finally, as part of an emergent *national* society, there has arisen a national university system. This has meant that the profession, rather than the particular school, has become the focus of a professor's attention and chief concern. This, in turn, has resulted in an unprecedented geographical and social mobility of the professoriat in the United States. It has also created an unprecedented gap between faculty and students. The older, "local" intimacy is much less common.

All these structural changes have imposed crushing burdens on the university. And the response has not been adequate. One of the chief deficiencies has been a failure of awareness that a change of scale—both of numbers of students and number of subjects—becomes necessarily a change of institutional shape. The university of 1969 is not simply the university of 1945 writ large. The failure of the past twenty-five years is therefore, first of all, a failure of anticipation, a failure of planning, and at bottom a failure of imagination. One cannot simply take a university—Berkeley, say—and triple its student body, quadruple its faculty, and expect it to resemble the pastoral idyll overlooking the Bay it once was. And it was equally a failure of imagination not to realize that, when Berkeley became the eruptive focus of student discontent in 1964, it would become a model for students elsewhere.

The great task before the educational planners of this nation is not simply to figure out "where the money will come from" in the next two decades but the desirable shape of the university system itself. Should one link graduate schools and their research preoccupations with large undergraduate colleges? Should one not have, perhaps, two kinds of graduate schools, one training an individual broadly for a research function, the other for education and service? What is the optimal size of any single campus? What kind of division of labor can be created between different kinds of universities so that each is not compelled, for illusory competitive reasons, to "cover all fields." These are the necessary questions which face the university and it is astonishing how rarely they are asked, let alone considered.

It has been student resentment which has, with dramatic suddenness, forced the university to examine itself, its inherited structures of governance, its archaic system of administration, and its jumbled curriculum. And it is a commentary on the unreflective nature of the university system that the rude awakening had to come in this way.

The generalized sources of student resentment are not mysterious. To begin with, there is the fact that, increasingly, an "organizational harness" has been dropped on the student at an early age. There is the competitive anxiety to get into a "good" college, a high status college, which can serve as a springboard for gaining a superior position in the society. Once in college there is the pressure to choose a career and choose a major, with the ever-present fear that a change in intention can mean the loss of valuable time. For most of the students in the better schools, there is also a continuing pressure for grades in order to get into a "good" graduate school. The university has gained a quasi-monopoly in determining the future stratification system of the society; like any monopoly, it generates distrust and antagonism.

Within the university itself there has been a sense of neglect among the students, in part because professorial attention has now obviously shifted to the graduate school, in part because of the sheer multiplication of numbers. Much of the curriculum has come to seem to be "without relevance"—by which most students mean that it does not speak to their personal or emotional concerns. (But one wonders: Did any university ever presume to do so?) A smaller, more acute minority has perceived that what passes for general education in most colleges is usually little more than an intellectual antipasto made up of bits and pieces of "classic" writers. The real problem is not that college education is "irrelevant" but that it has lost its coherence.

Two other elements, largely political, conjoin with these sociological factors to explain student discontent. One, of course, has been the Vietnam war, a war which has been seen, increasingly, as morally dubious and politically muddled. For the troubled student, Vietnam has become a crucial symbol of the deceit of government and, by extension, of the rottenness of the society.

Along with this has been a sense of the failure of American liberalism, a sense shared by the liberals themselves. For the liberal, however, the failure to mount effective social programs during these past years was seen as arising out of the inherent complexity of our social problems, the lack of detailed social science knowledge as to how to "cut" into them, and the shortage of trained administrators. For the young student, in contrast, with a temperament more moral than political, it appeared that the government had "copped out" of its responsibilities. And when many turned to politics from their moralism, they found—as generations have in the past—a set of ready-made formulas in a stilted and primitive Marxism. But since even Marxism has lost much of its explanatory power, these students have been led to think in such amorphous terms as "the system" and "the establishment," and to rely heavily on a conspiracy theory of history.

The upshot has been that what was originally concern over a specific set of identifiable and specific political issues (e.g., Vietnam, civil rights) has been overwhelmed by an onrush of anger, rancor, and a generational rage born of seeming impotence. And what began, often, as an attack against the way in which authority has been exercised turned into an attack against all existing authority. Here, that mood merges into a historic cultural tendency that, in the name of attacking "repression" and "taboos," has been anti-institutional and even antinomian. And this leads to a paradox, for the most important aspect of student behavior is that, while its sociology and politics are easily ridiculed in intellectual terms, its temperament and its style are actually "legitimated" by the culture of the society. This schizophrenia has often made it difficult for professors, themselves the products of that culture, to oppose the student style.

And that style has evolved into the style of "confrontation." It is the style of symbolic gesture, the style of expressive action. It provides an emotional satisfaction in mobilizing a collective resentment. It fits the moralism of student politics in that it puts issues in either/

or terms, and demands a resolution on a "total" level. It is a major historical irony that a style which may fit extreme existential situations should be regarded as appropriate to a university campus where extremity is the scarcest of human conditions.

The style of student protest which has emerged from all this— its ends and its means—is no longer a political style, properly speaking, but a "happening" or drama, conformable to the lineaments of an esthetic mode. Politics has never wholly eschewed violence, but what defines politics is a set of ideas about goals or ends, and what defines rational politics is the question whether the means used are proper or proportionate to the ends. Means which are inadequate render a movement feckless; means which are ends in themselves become grotesque. But for the radical student body, circa 1969, there is no authentic interest in such rational politics, for there is really no conception of clear goals which can be fought for, negotiated, or compromised. For the "politics of confrontation," the goal is not really the satisfying of grievances but the destruction of authority itself. Sometimes this is put into the language of democracy or populism, i.e., the desire of students to have a voice in the decisions that affect them. (And the question of what voice a student should have is, in and of itself, a genuine one.) But more often this is simply preliminary to the demand for a voice in everything, as a "right," with little willingness to consider the question of differential responsibilities and obligations, questions of technical competence and the like. This sweeping demand for "participation" usually masks, simply, a desire to disestablish and render illegitimate all existing authority.

The situation of the blacks, at least of the more militant among them, is different. Though they use the style of confrontation, their anger rather than being diffuse is specific; their goals rather than being moral are highly political. They are openly and directly seeking to carve out for themselves, right now, a special enclave within the university which will concede to them a measure of self-governing power, and which will allow them to enlarge the number of blacks in the university system with little regard to the traditional criteria of competence. In a psychological sense, it is a surge for identity through self-assertion; it is the "put down" of the white. In a sociological sense, it is the cool reckoning that, if what is emerging is a meritocratic society based on achievement, then what they want is a ticket into that society, written on their terms. What is involved here is a clear bid for status and power, in which education becomes the medium of the demand. But it has little to do with the problems of education as they have been conceived in traditional terms, and one consequence of such a demand for power may easily be the destruction of the idea of education. All of this, however, is problematical and it risks confusing the rhetoric of black militants with their practice once they have had to face up to concrete responsibilities.

The chapters in this book, with one exception, appeared originally in the Fall, 1968, issue of *The Public Interest*. (The exception is Irving Kristol's chapter, which was published in *The New York Times Magazine*.) They were written largely in the spring and summer of that year, and in only a few cases has it been felt necessary to update them. They provide, we believe, a fairly comprehensive picture of the student movement, one of the most significant sociological movements of the 1960's; and together they also provide material for an analysis of one of the most troublesome areas that will confront the United States in the 1970's, the definition of the idea of a university.

In addition to containing reportage and analysis, the chapters reflect a set of values which infuses the magazine in which they first appeared. This is, first of all, the commitment to dispassionate inquiry as the ground of understanding. But also there is commitment to the idea of rational authority: to the view that opinion is not knowledge, that intellectual qualifications are a condition for judgment, and that some judgments are more worthwhile than others. It is thus a commitment to reason and to its mode of discourse, the mode of civility. We believe that without rational authority and civil discourse, a civilized society—and that is the ultimate model of the university—is impossible.

January 1969

DANIEL BELL
IRVING KRISTOL

CONTENTS

CONFRONTATION

1

"Student power" in Berkeley

NATHAN GLAZER

WHATEVER students may be doing to change the world—and they are clearly doing a good deal—it could turn out that, in the end, it is rather easier to change the world than the university. This, it seems, is the inference to be drawn from four years of student rebellion at the University of California at Berkeley, where the present wave of student disorders— which has had such phenomenal impact in Italy, West Germany, and France—first began.

Four years after the Free Speech Movement exploded in autumn 1964, the world does look very different, and the FSM looks like a prophetic turning point; but the University of California looks very much the same, and it is this paradox that concerns me in this essay.

It may appear a case of distorted institutional loyalty to give Berkeley the primacy as the point of origin of the present wave of student civil disorder, and yet I think that what started at Berkeley in 1964 was rather different from the student violence of the years before—whether the student demonstrations of Japan in 1960, the endemic student violence of India, or the student rebellions of South Korea and Turkey that helped overthrow governments. There were five key differences:

1. The Berkeley student uprising occurred in an affluent country that, whatever the case with uneducated Negroes, treated the educated well. There was no problem of unemployment for the educated (as there was in India, South Korea, and other developing nations). Thus the student uprisings could not be related to such

issues as livelihood and status for the educated. It was new, then, in that it could find issues that were crucial to students despite their assurance of affluence.

2. It was new in that it was not directed against an oppressive national, local, or university regime—as "oppression" had been generally understood until that moment. In time, the student movement was so successful that the civil government of local communities (such as Oakland and Berkeley), and of the nation, and of the universities could be cast in an oppressive role, though they had generally not been seen in that light before. In contrast, much of the student disorder in developing countries was directed against military or dictatorial regimes; in Japan, the regime was democratic, but was nevertheless not considered so by many students and intellectuals. The new student movement that began in Berkeley was able to discover or create new issues pertaining to the basic constitution of a democratic government and the institutions within a democratic society.

3. It was new, too, in that it exploded at a time when there were relatively few great burning issues on the national agenda. One could still hope, in the autumn of 1964, that civil rights legislation and social legislation would rapidly enough satisfy the demands of American Negroes (white backlash seemed a more urgent problem then than black militancy), and Vietnam was not yet the overwhelming issue it was to become. But just as in Germany and France in 1968, student activists in Berkeley were able to create big issues on what most people felt was a relatively placid political scene.

4. It was new in its tactics. It found means of dramatizing its rebellion against an affluent and democratic society by forcing it to respond in ways that could be cast as repressive and authoritarian. The politics of "confrontation" was not original with the Berkeley students, but they nevertheless elaborated it in new and startling ways.

5. But perhaps the most striking novelty in the Berkeley student revolt was that the two ideologies which had played the largest role in sparking student uprisings around the world, Marxism (in democratic countries) and liberalism (in dictatorial and Marxist countries), played a minor role in Berkeley. Marxists of various persuasions, and liberals too, were of course involved, but neither the classic demand for socialist revolution by the first, nor for civil liberties and democratic reform by the second could fully encompass the main thrust of the Berkeley student revolt. Marxism and liberalism were rather two wings of a movement whose center was poorly defined—though "participatory democracy" thoroughly carried out in every institution and social process was perhaps its clearest feature. It is revealing that, when the Berkeley student rebels paused after their victory over the administration, and cast about for repre-

sentative figures who might express their philosophy and help them
to define their positive aims, they chose Paul Goodman, who is not
a Marxist, and invited him to the campus. Goodman considers himself an anarchist, and the dominant theme in his voluminous writings
is specific and detailed attention to the small social structures and
institutions that immediately affect people and their lives—predominantly the school, but also housing, the neighborhood, local
government, the work setting. In radical contrast to the Marxists,
who had banned as "utopianism" all consideration of the details
of how to reconstruct society, Goodman's main achievement is to
analyze and propose means of refashioning those details. If Marxists
traditionally wait for the revolution, and in the meantime radicalize
people by demonstrating that no change but the largest can help
them, Goodman does quite the opposite—he hopes to show them
that many small changes can help them.

Revolt against whom?

In summary, Berkeley to my mind is the first example of a student
rebellion that occurs in conditions where students are privileged,
their future is assured, where liberal, parliamentary democracy
prevails, and where the principal ideology of the student rebels is
neither Marxism nor liberalism but rather the effort to create a
participatory and somewhat communal democracy. It is the first
student rebellion to have considered what is still wrong in a liberal,
democratic, and permissive society, and by what tactics and
strategy revolutionaries can bring larger and larger numbers to
agree with them that a great deal is wrong.

It is, of course, not easy to escape from the past, particularly
when so many problems of the present resemble those of the past.
Thus Vietnam permitted and enabled Marxism again to become
more prominent in the radical student movement—but let us recall
that the Berkeley revolt precedes any large concern with the issue
of Vietnam, and with the associated pressure of the draft, though
these soon became the dominant issues of the movement. Moreover,
the means of "revolutionizing the masses" inevitably are never entirely new. Thus it is known that when the police attack, one gains
recruits and strength, and a good deal of attention must be devoted
to the tactics that get the police to attack.

But what *is* new are the means of casting a liberal polity in the
role of an oppressive one. Thus, the student activists place great
emphasis on the constraints of organization and government (any
organization and government), and as a corollary emphasize the
importance of participatory democracy, which concretely tends to
mean that any mob is right as against any administrator, legislature, or policeman. (Fortunately, up until now we have had left-

wing rather than right-wing mobs, and they are milder.) In the thinking of the radical students, the IBM card that facilitates student registration can be cast in the same role as the police control cards of the tsarist state or the Soviet Union.

So the line that leads from Berkeley to Columbia, through the universities of Italy, West Germany, France, and England, marks something new. What is happening in Eastern Europe and Spain, in Brazil and Argentina, is easier to understand—it is the fight for freedom. But what then do the student uprisings of the affluent world represent? The answer isn't easy or clear. For from the beginning there was a central ambiguity in the student disorders here (as there are in those of other affluent countries). Were students protesting primarily against their *universities*—the institutions of higher education, with their special constitutions, rules, requirements, culture? Or were they protesting against their *societies*, with their unresolved problems and their "hypocrisies"?

The primacy of politics

It is not easy to disentangle the two sorts of issues, in practice, but they are clear in theory. On the one hand, we have issues that stem directly from the concrete institutional setting of higher education—relations among administrators, students, and teachers; roles in setting rules for the three groups; power to exercise discipline, and to define the actions that call for discipline; power to determine curriculum, criteria for admission and graduation, faculty appointments, and the like. On the other hand, we have the two great issues of American life in the late 1960's—the race issue and the Vietnam issue, and what they may be taken to reflect in society: racism, the dominance of the military, middle-class fears of Communism encouraged by the mass media, the power of corporations, etc.

From the beginning, in 1964, the university issues have played second fiddle to the political issues, even though this was often hard to see—for the actual battleground was generally the university and the representatives of "the establishment" under siege were the university officials. But the university, in effect, was standing in for the world and its problems—which made for dilemmas in knowing how to handle student rebellion, but which also meant that the central structures and institutions of the university were really not the chief target. According to the radical students, the university had to be reformed—but mainly in order to permit the political resistance or intervention of students in a corrupt society to become more effective. Thus, one reason why the impact of the student revolt on the colleges and universities has been moderate up to now was that issues of educational reform came up later and were secondary to the political issues.

In the thinking of the student radicals and their leaders, the primary problem was the society, not the university. How then does the university get involved so prominently in the act? The university gets involved because (1) the radical students demand that it offer a refuge and base for political action in the community; (2) they treat it as a surrogate for society in general—whether out of frustration, or because it was a nearer target, or in order to practice tactics and strategy for the larger offensive against the stronger institutions; and (3) they eventually hope actively to enlist it in their efforts at political education and mobilization. The university thus serves three possible functions for student radicals: as refuge and base, as surrogate for and representative of an oppressive society, and finally as potentially active ally in the attempt to transform society.

In the first case, the university simply—to use the language of the student radicals—"gets in their way." This was the origin of the Free Speech Movement: the students wanted the right to meet freely on campus, to raise funds, to recruit supporters, and to discuss the whole range of issues that concerned them, including the use of unlawful tactics in their political activities. This last was the sticking point in the first major Berkeley climax in December 1964, and it was left somewhat unresolved, with the faculty voting that only considerations of "time, place, and manner" should limit student political activity on campus, and the regents of the university insisting that considerations of legality should still limit the right to political activity on the campus. In the end, a kind of *modus vivendi* has emerged in which the radical students feel relatively unhampered in discussing the full range of present-day political issues and tactics, including of course a good deal that is unlawful, but in which the administration does not limit them unless major publicity is given to their actions—and even then it simply works out a compromise to demonstrate to the regents and to the governor that it can exercise some power over political activity on campus. Thus, when a "Vietnam Commencement" was proposed last spring to honor those who refused to be drafted, there was a good deal of negotiation between the organizers of the commencement and the university administration as to where and when it should be held and just what its content would be. But it was held.

The university as surrogate

More significant has been the university's role as a surrogate or representative of society. Here, some of the chief issues have been whether the university should give special placement exams or report grades to draft authorities (when standing in class was a factor in drafting students), whether the university should permit

representatives from such government agencies as the armed forces
and the CIA and from Dow Chemical to recruit employees on campus, and the role of the university in classified and weapons research.
Here the university is acting as part of or as agent for society —
and the radical students have had the convenience of an agent of
society being near at hand and also being more vulnerable to attack
than some of the institutions it may be taken to represent. While
in the first case — where the university serves as base and refuge —
the radical students have insisted that the university make no judgment as to the legality or illegality of their actions and that it leave
it to the civil arm alone to determine whether they have broken
the law and should be limited in their political activity, in this
second case the radical students insist that the university *must* make
a judgment as to the morality of the activities it permits on the
campus — and among those it must ban are any that serve the
interests of the armed forces or the foreign policy of the government.

At Berkeley, the role of the university as a surrogate and representative of those forces in society that radical students oppose has
been, for the latter part of the last academic year at least, in eclipse.
The radical student movement has moved on from an attack on university practices in connection with Selective Service and military
and government recruiting to a direct attack on Selective Service
stations. The university has been superseded, first by the Selective
Service headquarters in Oakland, and then by the police, with whom
the radical students have clashed in Oakland in their efforts to
surround and close the Selective Service station. Radical student
antagonism to the Oakland police is now heightened by the alliance
with the militant and armed Negroes of the Black Panther party,
who have been harassed by the police. In addition, the city government of Berkeley and its police have been added to the list,
since the police opposed, with tear gas, the efforts of radical
students to close a major street ostensibly in order to hold a rally
supporting the French students and workers. In addition, the radical
students have been active in helping organize the Peace and Freedom party, which ran the writer Paul Jacobs for U.S. Senator, the
former student leader Mario Savio for state legislator, and a variety
of leaders of the Black Panther party for Congress and other posts.
In all this, the university role as surrogate and representative
of society has for the moment been eclipsed — the Selective Service
authorities, the police, the local civil authorities, the state government, and the national government have for the time being at least
taken its place.

But, after one gets the university to move out of the way, and
after one prevents, through the manufacture of disorder, the representatives of government agencies from recruiting on campus and
cuts the universities' ties with defense research (not that this has

been fully accomplished, but the mechanisms for doing so have been well developed)—then what? The rules as to political behavior in a university are after all fairly incidental to its chief functions—unless matters come to the point where unpopular (that is, nonradical) opinion is intimidated. (While that has happened at Berkeley and elsewhere, it is owing less to the new rules, which are on the whole good, than to the attitude of the New Left to the expression of dissident opinion, which is bad. It also owes something to the ease with which people allow themselves to be intimidated.) Similarly, just who recruits on campus and how much classified research is permitted or exists is to my mind incidental to the central functions of the university. Classified research has in any case never loomed large. The huge laboratories that various universities direct for the Atomic Energy Commission have been cut off from the university, administratively and sometimes physically. It is hard to see that they have had a major impact on the university—which is perhaps one reason why it has been hard for the radical students at Berkeley to launch an attack on the university's relationship with Livermore and Los Alamos. These relationships could in any case be cut without any significant effect on either the university or the laboratories—just as relationships with IDA are now being cut by a number of universities.

The question remains: what about the heart of the university—the teaching of undergraduate and graduate students, the day-to-day research of faculty and graduate students? How are they affected by the student rebellion? The answer is that, up to now, there has been little effect. The structure of the university and its normal activities go on, suffering only minor impact from the events that have made student activism a major political issue in the state, the nation, and now in the world.

The "free universities"

We have suggested one reason for this—that the radical students have really not been primarily interested in educational reform. During Paul Goodman's visit, for example, the radical students were more interested in him as a radical social prophet than as a radical educational reformer. Yet there has been a section of the radical student movement that, together with some nonradical students and a few members of the faculty, has been interested in educational reform for a long time—this group began its activity even before FSM. FSM gave the reformers potentially much greater influence and a much larger audience. In the past, this group had run meetings which attracted little attendance and little interest. Meetings on educational reform after FSM attracted somewhat more student interest, though nowhere near the number that became involved in protest on the great political issues and in the confrontations with the university administration that the tactics chosen always seemed to lead to. And, revealingly enough, not one of these major confrontations with the administration since FSM has ever dealt with an educational issue. But if radical student interest in educational reform was not great, administration interest was. For it is natural and understandable for educational administrators to assume or hope that student unrest and disorder must reflect and must be curable by institutional reform. Acting Chancellor Martin Meyerson in 1965 and Chancellor Roger Heyns who succeeded him were eager to sponsor changes in the university. The question was, what changes?

The first expression in education of the student rebellion was the student-run free university. One was organized at Berkeley (it bears the unfortunate initials FUB), another at Stanford. At San Francisco State, owing to the greater strength of student radicals, or the greater acquiescence of administration and faculty, the free university seems to have been in effect organized within the college, under the control of students, but giving credit for work. There are three points to be made about the free university as a means of revolutionizing the university. First, it is not new. Radical and other ideological groups have always organized courses outside the university in order to push some specific outlook or to present material that they felt the university was slighting. Long before the free university, one could take courses off campus on "Revolutions of Our Time and Why They Failed," "Basic Principles of Marxism-Leninism," or the like. (Today's free university will generally have a course in guerilla warfare, picking up from Mao and Ché, and on the ideologists of Black Power.) There were other free, off-campus, noncredit courses that were and still are generally available around a university, often in the religious centers catering to students. Naturally, these courses would try to pitch themselves to student interests and could show a flexibility and rapidity in responding to current issues that the regular university departments could not. I imagine Kierkegaard was being taught in off-campus religious student centers before he got into the curriculum of many university philosophy departments; the off-campus pastors had a greater incentive to find something that might reach and excite students.

I mention this background only because it is my impression that the free universities are not so different from these previous efforts to supplement university education, though they are on a somewhat larger scale. But of course the ambition of the free universities is greater than this, as their name implies; it is to teach new areas of learning and experience, by new means, all of which would not be allowed in an "establishment" university. The problem is that almost anything that the law allows—and a bit more—is to be found in an establishment-run university, and you get credit for it besides.

I would guess that the summer universities now being launched in the wake of the May days in France will have a greater impact—simply because their universities have been more conservative.

There is a second factor that limits the effectiveness of the free universities for revolutionary purposes. Just as the off-campus religious centers have to offer courses that are responsive to student interests and fashions, so too must the free university. Perhaps the organizers would like to give courses in urban guerilla warfare—and they do—but there is nothing they can do to make them more popular than courses in drug experience, meditation, sensitivity training, new forms of sexual and interpersonal relations, film-making, and a variety of other present-day youth interests. The free university, then, is limited in its effect, not only because it gives work in areas that other extra-university groups have already covered, but precisely because it is so responsive to its clientele and their shifting interests.

Finally, another reason for its limited effect is that the faculty, many of them young and only recently (or still) student radicals themselves, are by no means backward in adding to the curriculum those new ideas that the radical students feel the university is suppressing. Frantz Fanon, Paul Goodman, Herbert Marcuse, and Ché Guevara get into regular courses of the university as fast as they get into the free university. This is perhaps one reason why drugs, meditation, and sex, which admittedly are handled in a more academic way, if at all, in the establishment university become a major stock-in-trade of the free university. And this, in turn, helps to explain why the phrase "repressive tolerance" is now so popular on the Berkeley scene—it is Marcuse's explanation of how the establishment draws the teeth of revolutionary ideas by spreading them through university courses and the mass media.

Experiments at Berkeley

When the free university—the student-run university—gets within the fold of the university, its effects are greater, but still not revolutionary. I have spoken of the student-run courses at San Francisco State College, given for credit. The same development has occurred at Berkeley, as part of a number of experiments in education that flowed from the FSM. One of the results of the movement was the establishment of a faculty Select Committee on Education at Berkeley (the Muscatine Committee, as it became called after its chairman, Professor of English Charles Muscatine), which issued a large and substantial report.[1]

---

[1] This report, *Education at Berkeley* (University of California Press, 1966), has been brilliantly analyzed in an article by Martin Trow, "Bell, Book, and Berkeley," *The American Behavioral Scientist,* June 1968.

The Select Committee reviewed the student rebellion at Berkeley, recognized it had many causes and that many were beyond the reach of the university, and then went on to urge reforms in education at Berkeley. It proposed no new and large sweeping transformation of the university, though some of the faculty reacted as if it had. What it did propose was very many small changes, and one major institutional change, all designed to support experiments and innovations in education. In effect it proposed escape hatches for specific student and faculty interests, while the rest of the university was to go on its accustomed ways. Not clear as to how the curriculum of a huge university could be reorganized, it proposed a new institution—the Board of Educational Development—that would have the power to approve courses and courses of study outside the regular departments and would not require their approval or the approval of other faculty committees.

These courses could be initiated by students or by faculty. If initiated by students, they required a faculty sponsor, though his role could be minimal. The board has been established, has been in operation now for two years and has sponsored quite a number of interdisciplinary and nondisciplinary courses (twenty in the Spring 1968 quarter[2]). There is as yet no new curriculum that has been proposed to it—though if one were, it could be approved. One of the most imaginative and unconventional of the courses it sponsored was one which sent some forty students to Washington in spring of 1968 to live with and observe the Poor People's Campaign. Students wrote papers and received credit, and were supervised by a faculty member. This course perhaps expresses best the kind of change the radical students would like to introduce, a course in which one becomes somewhat more expert in political activism and its understanding. However, even here the faculty sponsor imposed an academic discipline that was very likely felt as external and irrelevant by some of the activists who took the course.

There is also now a student-run Committee on Participant Education, which will develop courses that students show interest in. (These do not give university credit unless the student makes a special arrangement with a faculty member, but in view of the number of acquiescent faculty members, this is not hard.) These courses involve a few thousand students a year. The most popular this past year was a course on (or in) meditation. They can be best considered something of a cross between extra-curricular activities and course work. Once again, despite Board of Education courses and Committee on Participant Education courses, and the popularity of some of them, the university—that is, the departments and the

---

[2] Perhaps 1,500 courses are given on the Berkeley campus during a regular quarter.

research institutes, the faculty, the course work, the students—proceeds on its regular way, rather unaffected.

There have been other changes. Even before FSM, Professor Joseph Tussman of Philosophy and some faculty colleagues of various departments had been urging an experimental college, to conduct for some students the first two years of their college education, replacing the normally disparate collection of courses they take by a single unified curriculum, based on the treatment of four major periods of civilization. This program was approved experimentally, and about 120 students and five faculty members plus graduate assistants were provided with a former fraternity house and full freedom. The program has graduated one class, and has completed the first year of work with another. It is not easy to come up with an unambiguous verdict as to its success. One thing is clear however: having begun with five regular faculty members deeply involved and committed, it is now down to one, plus visitors brought specifically to teach in the experimental college. And rather than serving as a model for other experimental colleges, it seems questionable whether it can continue. This is no profound verdict on it—it merely confirms what everyone who has had some experience with experiments in higher education knows, that the departments and the disciplines define the greater part of college education, and it is very difficult to establish anything outside the regular departmental lines.

But having said this, one must also add that it is not at all clear that what would or could be established outside the regular departmental and disciplinary lines would be better than what exists within them. We should also add that the Tussman experiment, aside from the fact that its establishment was facilitated by the desire of the administration to encourage experiment as a result of FSM, has only loose connections with the student rebellion at Berkeley. It is not student initiated or student run, nor does the curriculum particularly reflect the new student interests. Although there is a great deal of faculty and student freedom in how to handle the curriculum, it still consists of fixed readings in fixed periods of civilization.

The passing of general education

The main thrust of student activism, in contrast, has been to further diminish the appeal of the notion of any fixed or required liberal arts curriculum. Here a good part of the faculty, with its specialist interests, agrees with the student radicals. One might say the educational ideal of both, at this point, if they have any, is better expressed by President Eliot of Harvard and his pure elective system than any available alternative.

While the Muscatine Committee Report, which moved somewhat

in this direction, was approved by the faculty, with the unenthusiastic support of student radicals, another educational report, which tried to move in the direction of a more coherent curriculum that would reflect the ideal of a broadly accepted liberal arts education, was defeated by the faculty. At the time the Muscatine Committee was appointed, a second special committee (called the Herr Committee, after the historian Richard Herr who chaired it) was formed to review the undergraduate program in the College of Letters and Science, the largest unit on the Berkeley campus. The committee proposed that the undergraduate program should be more coherent. Instead of the common arrangement whereby each undergraduate was required to take some work in a number of fields which supposedly defined the well-educated man (science, social science, humanities, mathematics, languages, etc.) and was free to select what he would out of the wide range of courses offered in each field, the hope of the committee was that a more relevant undergraduate education could be structured, in part by developing special undergraduate courses attuned to the interests of students in other fields (science for literature students, and vice versa). Of course, this would mean either getting the faculty to agree to develop such courses and programs or recruiting new faculty. In effect, it meant breaking the pattern of organization that is so well suited to a faculty committed to disciplines and research and is organized in powerful departments. In such a situation—which characterizes Berkeley and most universities—the undergraduate curriculum is arranged by treaties between groups of departments in the various major areas, rather than by any agency reviewing undergraduate education from a nondepartmental perspective, and the introductory courses and the courses designed for those from other fields, the so-called "service" courses, generally get little attention. The Herr Committee proposals meant that a faculty gathered on the basis of research interests and capacities and disciplinary orientations would now have to devote more attention to undergraduate teaching and nondisciplinary concerns. In this case, the interests of the faculty coincided with the interests of politically activist (and other reform-minded) students, who wanted as little restriction and limitation as possible in getting through their four years in college. The Herr Committee report, as a result, did rather poorly, and its major proposals were voted down by the college faculty (only a small minority of whom in any case were interested enough to attend the meetings at which the report was discussed), in favor of a simpler student-formulated proposal.

The movement of the university toward greater fragmentation, greater specialization, strong independent departments, a weakening concern with general education, was either endorsed or at any rate not interfered with by these changes.

Toward participation

Another major report came under consideration by the faculty, *The Culture of the University: Governance and Education.* This is the report of a faculty-student Commission set up in January 1967, after another major blow-up at Berkeley. This one was occasioned by radical students blocking military recruiters. When the administration called in the police, the predictable results occurred—the radical students gained a great deal of support, including that of liberal students and faculty, there was a student strike, and a faculty-student commission on governance was set up. The majority report of this commission is the first of the three I have discussed that expresses in some central way the ideas of the radical students.

The majority report, like the two reports before it, eschews any detailed discussion of the content of a desired education—who knows what that should be? But it does know what is wrong with the present education.

It argues:

> Some of the most thoughtful and serious students have come to repudiate many of the social goals and values they are asked to serve in the university and upon graduation. That repudiation is directed in part at the conditions of technological society which seem to threaten human dignity. The new world emerging seems to exact greater conformity, more routinized lives, more formalized relationships among individuals. . . .

Faced with the crises of race, urban violence and decay, environmental degradation, war,

> many students express intense dissatisfaction with the university, since it provides much of the knowledge and most of the trained personnel required by the technological and scientific society. . . . It is little wonder, then, that many students are no longer content to spend their college years preparing to "take their place" in such a society. Nor is it surprising that many students regard as irrelevant the miscellany of superficial, uncertain choices and professional training which often passes as the curriculum.
>
> Such discontent is deepened by the degree to which the university's atmosphere reproduces the characteristics of the society. The university is large, impersonal, and bureaucratic. The acquisition of specialized skills has often been substituted for education of persons, instead of supplementing it. . . .

The two crucial failures of the university, the majority report argues, are first, "its failure to develop a student body which respects the value of the intellect itself," and students therefore suffer from "passionless mind and mindless passion" (as well as mindlessness and passionlessness, on the part of the majority of the students, who are characterized by apathy and careerism), and second, its domination by "service." The "function of providing useful knowledge and expert consultants to assist society in its effort to satisfy human needs, has somehow gotten out of hand."

And the university is not well organized to deal with these problems: "Inertia and discouragement have combined to produce a situation in which fundamental educational problems are discussed only sporadically and then in so prosaic a fashion as to make education seem a dreary affair when compared with the drama of campus politics." The university *should* be an educational community, but it sees itself as if it were "any other pluralistic society populated by diverse interest groups and lacking a common commitment to anything more than the bargaining process itself."

This is roughly the majority report's analysis of the problems of Berkeley. In the light of all this, it is somewhat disappointing to discover that the major recommendations of the report, spelled out at elaborate length, are, first, an extensive decentralization of all the functions of the university to the departmental level, together with a great increase in the role of students in educational policy-making at every level, from the departmental up and down; and second, an elaborate system for exercising student discipline through various courts and panels and appellate bodies, whose aim is to ensure the fullest due process, but which strikes me as something only a lawyer could have written, and one suspects only lawyers can read or understand.

The majority report, despite the varied character of its writers and its strong commitment to a traditional view of higher education, has gained the support of the student radicals, because it does offer them a greater field of action. The report has been sharply criticized by a Commission minority of two faculty members.[3] It has been presented to the faculty, where there is a good deal of dragging of feet at undertaking its detailed and extensive suggestions on decentralization, student participation, and new forms of handling student discipline.

The majority report reflects to my mind many illusions: that the university can and should remain fully separate from the state, criticizing it and training its self-proclaimed enemies but nevertheless gaining generous support from it; that service and practical knowledge are inferior to other kinds of education; that it is administrative arrangements that primarily prevent the kind of education that will involve radical students in their education rather than in transform-

---

[3] Sociologists of knowledge will perhaps be interested in knowing that the dissenting minority consisted of a statistician and an economist; the majority of a lawyer, a political scientist, a historian, and a Professor of Public Health, and all six student members of the Commission.

ing the world; that the modern university can or should be changed
into a coherent educational community devoted to common ends
(aside from its general ends of education, research, and service,
which the majority finds inadequate); that the endless elaboration
of due process and its required apparatus of courts, hearing officers,
transcripts, appeals bodies, etc., will solve some basic problem of the
university; that extensive decentralization and student participation
can be introduced without adding to the burden of a faculty that
even now tries to escape duties of all kinds, aside from research and
graduate teaching. One has the feeling that the university that would
emerge from these proposals would be a delight to student politicians, but to hardly anyone else.

One outcome of the report, supporting a trend that was already
strongly evident, will be more student participation in academic
matters at Berkeley. But what is not clear is the extent to which
this will, or can, affect the general structure of university education.
After all, we have had a good deal of experience with student participation, at colleges such as Antioch and Bennington, and in various graduate departments and professional schools on the Berkeley
campus itself. I think student representation on a greater range of
university, college, and departmental committees may introduce
valuable points of view. But it does not transform education—it only
demonstrates that the dilemmas of contemporary higher education
are not simply of the making of conservative professors or administrators. And if students can be taught that by participation in faculty
and administrative committees, well and good.

Left and right, black and white

The radical student rebellion has not yet affected the central
functions and character of the university. It is still dominated by
departments, and by a specialist-minded faculty. Research and publication are still the chief means by which faculty members gain
status. Undergraduate teaching gets less attention than either graduate teaching or research and writing. Most students are interested
primarily in jobs, careers, and credentials in colleges and universities,
and no one has suggested how to change this, short of reversing the
entire trend to mass higher education. The increasingly large support universities need comes from states, the federal government,
parents, corporations, and alumni, on the assumption that they
are a good thing for society, and help increase its wealth and solve
its problems. Out of this massive support, the functions of the university that traditionalists and radicals alike would like to see
increased—social criticism and the liberal arts—gain resources on a
scale they have never known up to now. But one can see little

prospect that the modern university can be transformed into the school of the revolution, though one sees a rather greater possibility that some universities will be destroyed in an effort to do so.

Interestingly enough, in a relatively brief period the rebellion of black students has had much greater impact on the universities than the years of disorder by white student radicals. The explanation is simple. As I have suggested, the student radicals don't quite know what they want to do with the university, and many of their demands (for student participation, for example), can be accommodated without major upset. Radicals are to be found on many faculties, as they always have been, and Marx and his successors are in the curriculum. All this does not make them happy, because the academic tone changes all, but they have found no means to affect this, and their major thrust has been to such peripheral matters as to who recruits on campus and the university's formal relation with defense institutions.

On the other hand, the demands of the black students have been concrete, and have gone directly to curriculum and university organization. They want specific courses on American Negro history and culture, and African history and culture. They want programs to recruit more black students, tutor them, and support them. They want more Negro faculty. Whereas the impact of the white student radicals has been met by administrators as that of an external invading army, which they have tried to appease with educational changes which scarcely interested them, the attack of black students has been directly on educational issues, and can be met to some extent by changes in curriculum, and by student and faculty recruitment. Not that there are not critical dangers to the university developing in the black demands—there are. They are the implicit demand for quotas of students and faculties, the sometimes voiced demands for separate living quarters and separate and exclusive courses for black students, and involved in both is a potential attack on the ability of the university to maintain standards. But whereas the white radical students have fundamentally been interested in the university as a base for an attack on society, or as a surrogate for their attack on society, the black students, whatever their rhetoric, are fundamentally interested in changing it so it can do a better job of getting them *into* society. The university has to fight the first, but it can respond positively to the second. The problem here is the illusions of many black students as to just what is involved in getting into society. White radical students have convinced a good number of them that it is all or only a game unrelated to ability and effort.

There is a second reason why white radicals have not been able to change the university: their faculty allies on political issues have been split and on the whole, have been conservative on university issues. Even Herbert Marcuse has partially exempted the university, or at any rate the San Diego Campus of the University of California where he teaches, from the devastating critique to which he subjects the rest of society. Many a faculty member who has said "yes" to getting out of Vietnam or getting military recruiters off campus has said "no" to greater student participation in the shaping of the curriculum, or in the advancement and selection of faculty members.

But there is a third reason why the radical students have not reshaped the university: there is no image or vision, no outline or guide, no philosophy available, that tells us how to shape the university. The traditional liberal arts curriculum is dead. It can excite little loyalty from anyone, except for academic deans and the humanities faculty. Those parts of the university that prepare people for the more concrete and obviously meaningful tasks in the world remain relatively unaffected by student disorder—engineering, the sciences, the law and medical schools. Their students and faculty generally do not get involved, and do not see that the university needs reforming—or, if they do, they have rather positive and manageable proposals as to who and how to reform it.[4] It is the social sciences and the humanities that supply the rebels, student and faculty, and of these it is the "softer" rather than the "harder" fields, sociology rather than economics, English literature and history rather than foreign languages. The crisis of the university is a crisis of those areas. How should students in these fields be educated, for what functions, what resources should be devoted to education in these areas, to what ends? It is the traditional liberal arts areas of the curriculum that are the sources of discontent and unhappiness —and here sociology, which provides by far the most student militants, is no exception, for it is not the technicians that sociology trains, but rather the social critics it forms, who become the rebels. Nor can the radicals be appeased, either by the university or the society. They insist that both must be overturned and transformed—to be replaced by what, remains vague, and to most people frightening.

---

[4] David Riesman has reminded me that this is beginning to change and that law schools and, to a smaller extent, medical schools—though not yet engineering or the sciences—are now contributing a good share of student radicals, and in particular they are being deeply affected by the growing movement to involve more lawyers and doctors directly in service to the poor and to the ghetto dwellers. However, it is still my impression that the kind of nihilism that is so common among social science students when they consider the university and its functions is scarcely to be found among law and medical students—they want to change their schools, hardly to destroy them, and I believe the discipline of professional education and the higher status their ordeal gives them within the university will prevent the radical alienation from their education that is now so common among social science graduate students.

A scorched earth policy?

Perhaps the most serious current radical effort to define a program for radicals in the universities is the Radical Education Project of Ann Arbor, which publishes the Radicals in the Professions Newsletter. All the dilemmas of student radicals in higher education are there exposed. The newsletter reports on the little triumphs of academic radicals—such as how, through "a little planning and initiative," the American Society for Aesthetics was persuaded to take a stand on Vietnam.

But when it comes to what radicals can do to transform the university into a truly radical institution, matters get vaguer. One mathematics professor, writing on "Teaching Mathematics Radically," reports that he is still far from knowing how to do it—he has gotten as far as emphasizing the concepts behind the formulas, which one imagines is the kind of thing conservative mathematics teachers might well agree with. There is a report on having students grade themselves. There are proposals for research projects and community projects that are not very different from others for which one gets credit or gets paid. But one asks, are they truly capable of creating that totally different and transformed world that now excites the imagination of student radicals? And if they disappoint in achieving such an objective, as they must, will it not begin to appear more attractive to destroy the university rather than reform it?

It is rather ominous—for one concerned for the universities—to read a lengthy analysis in the Radicals in the Professions Newsletter of why universities and university faculties are really no places for radicals after all. It is also ominous, to me, that a growing proportion of students feels a fundamental alienation from the university administration and the faculty. In 1964, Robert Somers, a Berkeley sociologist, conducted a poll on the campus—which was conducted during the excitement of FSM—and 56 per cent of the students agreed that the campus administration can "usually be counted on to give sufficient consideration to the rights and needs of students in setting university policy." In 1968, after four years of moderate academic reform, with an administration far more responsive to student desires, the proportion agreeing with this formulation had dropped to 32 per cent. Only a slightly higher proportion in 1968 thinks that faculty can "usually be counted on," etc.—48 per cent. There is no question as to the increasing alienation of a very substantial part of the students. One finds the same phenomenon among Negro Americans—and in both cases I would argue strongly for greater participation, student and community. Not that I think it will solve the basic problems particularly faster, but it may con-

vince those who now think of themselves as oppressed classes that
the problems are not easy to solve.

In any case, there have been bombings and fires and window
smashing on the Berkeley campus, which had not happened in the
earlier years of intense student activism. Conceivably the student
radicals may decide on a scorched-earth policy before they
withdraw.

In the end, one must judge whether the student radicals fundamentally represent a better world that can come into being, or
whether they are not committed to outdated and romantic visions
that cannot be realized, that contradict fundamentally other desires
and hopes they themselves possess and that contradict even more
the desires of most other people. I am impressed by Zbgniew Brzezinski's analysis of the student revolution:

> Very frequently revolutions are the last spasms of the past, and thus
> are not really revolutions but counterrevolutions, operating in the name
> of revolutions. A revolution which really either is non-programmatic
> and has no content, or involves content which is based on the past but
> provides no guidance for the future, is essentially counterrevolu-
> tionary.[5]

The student radicals come from the fields that have a restricted
and ambiguous place in a contemporary society. They remind me
more of the Luddite machine smashers than the Socialist trade
unionists who achieved citizenship and power for workers. This is
why the universities stand relatively unchanged—because despite
their evident inadequacies the student radicals have as yet suggested nothing better to replace them with.

---

[5] "Revolution and Counterrevolution (But Not Necessarily about Columbia!),"
The New Republic, June 1, 1968.

2

Black Studies
at
San Francisco
State

JOHN H. BUNZEL

O<small>N</small> college campuses across the country today, black nationalism, still only in its earliest stages but emerging with considerable force and purpose, comes in many different sizes, shapes, and even colors. (It is no accident that in many quarters Negro is "out" and Black is "in," or that the NAACP is sometimes referred to as the National Association for the Advancement of Certain People.) Yet one thing is clear: just as one finds black artists in the existing theater calling on one another to stop assimilating and imitating white standards, and instead to begin building cultural centers "where we can enjoy being free, open and black, where," as actress and director Barbara Ann Teer put it, "we can literally 'blow our minds' with blackness," so one also finds black students in our existing academic institutions demanding a program of Black Studies — one that will not only lead to the affirmation of their own identity and self-esteem, but will recognize the new needs of the black community and thereby help to define the concept of "black consciousness." Black Power, black nationalism, a black society — whatever meaning these terms will come to have for the whole of American society in the years ahead, the curricular idea of Black Studies will become the principal vehicle by which black students will press their claim for a black "educational renaissance" in colleges and universities throughout the nation.

Although it is still too early to tell how the demand for Black

Studies will ultimately be incorporated into different undergraduate instructional programs, it is already evident that the idea itself represents a formidable problem for American educators. For one thing, the concept of Black Studies, at least on many campuses, is as much a political consideration as an educational one. At San Francisco State College, the demand for inclusion of black courses in the curriculum has capitalized on an atmosphere of student militancy, black and white, real and potential. Privately, it is acknowledged that one of the reasons the blacks did not participate in the sit-in demonstrations organized in May 1968 by the Mexican-American students (and supported in full force by the Students for a Democratic Society) was that the president of the college had already appointed a man — chosen by the Black Students' Union — to develop and coordinate a Black Studies curriculum, a job for which he had been specifically recruited and on which he was hard at work. It is also worth noting that the appointment of a Black Studies Coordinator was made by the president alone — that is to say, without the knowledge of, or consultation with, the Vice President for Academic Affairs, the Council of Academic Deans, or the faculty. The president, characteristically, was candid about what he had done: this college is going to explode wide open, he said, if the blacks do not get what they want soon. (In the fall semester, he had suspended four members of the Black Students' Union after they had pushed their way into the office of the campus newspaper and physically attacked the editor.) Yes, the man he had asked to be the Coordinator of Black Studies had recently been fired from Howard University for what the *Negro Digest* called "his militant pro-black activities"; but, said the President, he had a Ph.D. in sociology from the University of Chicago and was anxious to come to San Francisco State. No, he had not spoken with any one in the sociology department about the appointment, because he felt he had to move quickly "if we are going to keep the lid on this place."

The point is that the President had reacted to what he felt to be a critical situation. His response was a political one, in the most practical and urgent sense of that term. He may very well have been right; no one will ever know. However, in terms of the acutely difficult academic problems involved in developing a curriculum of Black Studies and its implications for the educational program as a whole, his interest and concern was something less than visible. In point of fact, the President was soon to resign and leave the college.

Yale, Harvard, and elsewhere

Many of the major universities in the United States have already taken steps toward developing their own form of Black Studies. At

Yale, a faculty-student committee has proposed the creation of an undergraduate major in Afro-American studies that, according to Robert A.
Dahl, professor of political science, will involve "an interdisciplinary
approach to studying the experience and conditions of people of African ancestry in Africa and the New World." Students would be
provided a broad view of the African experience, but would be required to concentrate on one of the relevant disciplines by way of
enlightening their understanding and knowledge of the cultural,
economic, political, social, artistic, and historical experiences of
Africans and Afro-Americans. Beginning this September, Harvard
will offer a new full-year course in "The Afro-American Experience,"
and is considering a degree-granting program in Afro-American
studies for the not-too-distant future. The new course will begin with
the African background and the Negro experience in American
history through 1945 and, in the second semester, will consider issues
of race relations, psychology, civil rights, housing, employment, and
education from 1945 to the present. A faculty group of four will be
headed by Frank Freidel, professor of American history and biogra-
pher of Franklin D. Roosevelt. He will be joined by another historian
with a professional interest in poverty studies, a political scientist
who specializes in African and American Negro studies, and an
expert on American and Latin American history. As a a social science
offering, it is comparable to the Introduction to Western Civilization
and will be limited, at least initially, to 200 students. Parallel to this
course, Harvard's Institute of Politics of the John F. Kennedy School
of Government will offer a series of lectures on the Afro-American
experience by visiting scholars, required of students taking the
course and open to others. In addition, the Association of African
and Afro-American Students will offer a series of films and television
tapes.[1]

Other colleges and universities around the country are similarly
engaged in considering the direction their program of Black Studies
will take. The problems to be resolved are as difficult as they are
numerous, but they are significantly different depending on the
institution involved. An Ivy League university, for example, will be
very much concerned with the academic substance and soundness
of any proposed Black Studies curriculum. Given its educational
tradition and philosophy, the heavy research emphasis of its faculty,
and the particular undergraduate constituency it attracts and admits
(virtually no "underclass minorities" of the slums), a Yale or a
Harvard can insist on and expect a considerable measure of intellectual discipline in all of its academic programs. Or consider a university such as Stanford. Comfortably located in the white suburban

---

[1] The information here on Yale and Harvard is from a report by Fred M. Hech-
inger, *The New York Times*, June 23, 1968.

area of Palo Alto, it has little or no sustained involvement with the poverty environment in general (San Francisco-Oakland) or the core-city minorities in particular, and therefore has not had to deal with the problem of large numbers of militant blacks renouncing, not only the normal curricular offerings, but their whole college experience for being totally irrelevant to their own perceived needs and the needs of the larger black community.

Understandably, the way a college or university approaches the problems of its minority students will depend in part on the view it holds of its mission as an academic institution. Thus, a Black Studies program that is geared primarily to the needs of black students will follow one set of tracks if it is designed primarily to develop future academicians, but will move in a very different direction and at a very different pace if its major purpose is to equip and train its students to present "the black perspective" when they return to the black community to help transform it.

San Francisco State College, a microcosm of the diverse and polyglot urban and suburban society of the Bay Area, has seen more and more of its energy in the past few years converge on the needs and demands of its black students. It may be illuminating, therefore, to consider the recent proposal for a Department of Black Studies in what has generously been designated "this tumultuous educational scene."

The Black Students' Union at SFS

The academic year 1965–1966 has been called the year of the student revolution at San Francisco State, for it was during this year that changes in the attitudes of a small but influential number of students were consolidated and expressed in new functions of student government and new forms of faculty involvement. The most important of the Associated Students' programs were channeled into three major activities: (1) the Experimental College, which offered a diversity of courses never before seen in a college bulletin; (2) the Community Involvement Program, which placed students in neighborhoods throughout the city to help support them in their efforts to work in the communities, principally the ghettos and slums; and (3) the Tutorial Program, which concentrated on helping children learn to read, to do arithmetic, and to want to stay in school. The programs were regarded as successful, and in the words of a later report, 'The experience was earned, the price was paid, and our point was made, the point being that students on this campus wanted forms of education that the institution was not providing." It was the same point that would be made over and over again, reflecting the growing disaffection among black and other minorities on the campus.

In the summer of 1966, the Black Students' Union emerged and almost immediately became a major force in the student government.[2] During the following year, it turned its attention to the educational problem of black and other minority students on the campus, which they saw in its broadest terms as the problem of relevance, estrangement, and identity. The high drop-out rate, low grades, and general lack of motivation among large numbers of these students was due, they said, not only to a general feeling of separateness, but to the more compelling fact that education from kindergarten through college under the authority of the white community fails to focus on subject matter that is germane to the life experiences of the people in the minority community. Specifically, the charge was repeatedly made that black and other minority students have little opportunity to place themselves in an identifiable historical and personal context in the traditional curriculum. Disregarding the question of its intellectual worth and value, some of the perceptions and feelings of a leader of the Black Students' Union on why the present college curriculum is inadequate are revealing:

> One Black student told us of sitting in an Anthropology class for an entire semester and being interested in the class on only two occasions —once when the instructor offered a lecture on the Negro in America, and again when there was a lecture on Africa.

> Few Black students are really interested in the western, "classical" music which characterized entire departments of music. Black students have no fundamental cultural understanding of western music. And since a part of many beginning music classes is spent instructing students that the only legitimate music is that of Beethoven, Mozart, Stravinsky, etc., this is seen as a denial of Black students themselves. For example, a Black student interested in music theory spent his first semester arguing with his instructor for the legitimacy of Black musicians, Charles Parker and John Coltrane. He lost the argument by receiving a "D" grade and is now out of college.

> Black people are not western; they are "westernized," made to be western. So basically their psychology is not Freudian, Adlerian, or Jungian, only so far as they have accepted westernization. Students find themselves enchanted by the schools of psychology, but as they probe deeper they find less and less in an association with their lives. Other Black students pretend they can relate to western psychology by "becoming" Freudian. They psyche themselves out as we say, by trying to describe manifestations of every desire by description directly from the psychology textbook.

> When Black students begin to describe themselves in real situations,

---

[2] It should be kept in mind that out of a total college enrollment of 18,000, a good turnout for student government elections each spring is about 3,000–4,000. One other point worth mentioning: the annual budget of the Associated Students, derived from student fees, is over $300,000.

they are at times put down. A Black woman student wrote a paper on Marxism and alienation in which she said that she could not be alienated from a society of which she had never been a part. She had recently joined the Black Students' Union. The instructor attacked the student's basis of thought and gave her a low grade. She soon afterwards had a nervous collapse and has been out of the school for more than a year.

As perceived by the Black Students' Union, their educational problem at San Francisco State is clear and unambiguous: they read *white* literature, study *white* families, analyze *white* music, survey *white* civilizations, examine *white* cultures, probe *white* psychologies. In a word, the college curriculum is white-culture-bound.

An improvised black curriculum

To remedy the situation, which in concrete terms meant attracting the interest and enthusiasm of the black student, the Black Students' Union quickly set its sights on the development of a black curriculum. The Black Arts and Culture Series was instituted in the fall semester (1966) as a part of the Experimental College. The purpose was to introduce a positive focus on the life experiences of black people in America. Classes covered the areas of history, law, psychology, humanities, social science, and dance. One year later the first Black Studies was enacted, with a total of eleven classes for which thirty-three units of college credit were given. Several hundred students, black and white, enrolled in the courses, which were taught on a voluntary or part-time basis either by members of the faculty or graduate students sympathetic to the program. Among the classes listed in the Black Studies Program for the spring semester (1968) were the following:

ANTHROPOLOGY: *Historical Development of Afro-American Studies* (3)
DRAMATIC ARTS: *Improvisations in Blackness*
EDUCATION: *Miseducation of the Negro*
ENGLISH: *Modern African Thought and Literature*
HISTORY: *Ancient Black History*
PSYCHOLOGY: *Workshop in the Psychology of, by, and for Black People*
SOCIOLOGY: *Sociology of Black Oppression*

The improvisation of a black curriculum during the past two years at San Francisco State has reflected a growing feeling among members of the faculty and student body that educational innovation starting at the college level be given a chance to remedy the perceived ills of the past and create a model for other levels of education as well. By the end of the 1967–1968 academic year, it was taken for granted that there would be a Black Studies program. The question was no longer whether it would happen, but what direction it would take and how the administration, faculty and students would choose to react.

Nathan Hare's proposal

Meanwhile, the newly appointed Special Coordinator of Black Studies, Nathan Hare, has circulated a proposal for a degree-granting Department of Black Studies that deserves careful study. The document is his and his alone, and for this reason his particular angle of vision, indeed his basic assumptions and attitudes, are especially pertinent. He has been described as "a man seething with anger about the path of Negro leadership, the duplicity of whites, and the fallibility of many Negroes who 'follow' both." A sample of his remarks made in a public speech at Stanford University does not belie the description:

> I had expected to speak to a black audience. You can build a wall a mile high, but white people will always climb up and peer over at what you're doing. [He added that he was glad white students were interested in black culture and history, in spite of the environment of the "white brainwashing factory," the university.]

> The bourgeois nationalists (among pre-Civil War Black Power groups) were more interested in personal gain and mobility within their group than freeing the slaves. The main difference between them and the revolutionaries was in their outlook on the world in which they lived. The revolutionaries had lost faith in the routine means of righting wrong. They were crippled, though, by a feeling of powerlessness against the white power structure. It's like today. They say we are too few to fight. We should vote. But I can kill 20 (white) men. I can cut one's throat, shoot another, drop a hand grenade in the middle of a whole bunch. I get only a single vote, and that's between the lesser of two evils.

> *On white historians:* It is anachronistic for white men to teach black history to black militant students. The white man is unqualified to teach black history because he does not understand it.

> *On black historians:* Black people must declare void what the white slave masters have written and must begin to write their own history and direct their destiny. Black historians, presenting other than the white viewpoint, are forced into copious footnoting and must accept the conventions of the white academic overlords in order to make our history valid and get it published in white journals.

> *On the draft:* I was asked if I am an American first or a Negro first. I said I'm a black man first and not an American at all. Since most Americans do not consider me an American, I see no reason to fight for them. I said that before it was fashionable. I did serve six months

in the Army, but that was in peacetime. And I said I couldn't fight for them, and if I did I would shoot as much as possible at the whites around me.

I don't believe in absolutes, so I do not categorically reject all white men, only 99 and 44/100ths of them.

The importance of Hare's pronouncements is not that they are angry or bitterly anti-white. This, after all, is part and parcel of the militant black rhetoric today that derives its own satisfaction in constantly putting down "whitey," including those who have a "hunger for humiliation." What is important is that they provide a backdrop against which his "conceptual proposal" for a Department of Black Studies can be more clearly understood and evaluated in terms of its basic rationale and philosophy.

Hare acknowledges at the outset that the whole idea of Black Studies is "more far-reaching than appears on the surface." His conversations with academicians across the country on the education of black Americans leave no doubt in his mind that even those who have accepted the idea of Black Studies do not fully understand its need. "They see the goal as the mere blackening of white courses, in varying number and degree," he writes. "They omit in their program the key component of community involvement and collective stimulation." Their program is individualistic, aimed at "rehabilitating" individual students by means of pride in culture, racial contributions generally, and regenerated dignity and self-esteem. "They fail to see that the springboard for all of this is an animated communalism aimed at a Black educational renaissance." Thus many well-intentioned efforts, Hare says, are doomed to inevitable failure. "They comprise piecemeal programs that, being imported, are based on an external perspective." Put simply, they are white, not black.

Nor will Hare accept any form of "tokenism." He cites the example of "an eminent Negro professor" who proposed increasing drastically the ratio of Black — "by which he meant 'Negro,'" Hare adds — students and professors. "The students for the most part would be admitted with the expectation that, excepting those salvaged by tutorial efforts presently in vogue, they would eventually flunk out, the merrier for having acquired 'at least some college.'" This approach, Hare says, is not the answer to the problem. Although he is willing to "endorse the professor's suggestion in fact though not in theory insofar as to do otherwise would appear to condone current tokenism," he dismisses the approach on the grounds that it may be used "to appease the black community while avoiding genuine solutions."

When a representative from a foundation proposed giving full financial assistance to the "talented tenth" and hiring black persons to recruit such students and inform them of the availability of such aid, Hare responded by saying that this is only slightly better than providing no aid at all. "A talented-tenth approach is largely superfluous to the educational needs of the black race as a whole," Hare writes. "Talented-tenth students, for whatever reason, have escaped the programmed educational maladjustment of the Black race, just as some trees survive the flames of a forest fire." Such a program, "though noble on the surface, offers super-tokenism at best, but neglects the important ingredient of motivation growing out of collective community involvement. It is individualistic in its orientation and only indirectly, therefore, of collective consequence."

"Separatism?"

Of concern to many members of the faculty and student body at San Francisco State is the question of "separatism" — specifically, will a Department of Black Studies result in "a college within a college"? Hare's comments on this point deserve to be quoted in full:

> Even if it be so that Black Studies would ring more separatist in tone than Latin American Studies, Oriental Studies, and the like, this is not the issue. The question of separatism is, like integrationism, in this regard essentially irrelevant. The goal is the *elevation* of a people by means of one important escalator—education. Separatism and integrationism are possible approaches to that end; they lose their effectiveness when, swayed by dogmatic absolutism, they become ends in themselves. It will be an irony of recorded history that "integration" was used in the second half of this century to hold the Black race down just as segregation was so instituted in the first half. Integration, particularly in the token way in which it has been practiced up to now and the neo-tokenist manner now emerging, elevates individual members of a group, but paradoxically, in plucking many of the most promising members from a group while failing to alter the lot of the group as a whole, weakens the collective thrust which the group might otherwise muster.

A related question is whether or not white students would be admitted into the program. The answer, Hare says, "must be ambivalent inasmuch as the program has to be aimed primarily at the Black student, particularly in its motivational activities involving the Black community." Hare is concerned that white students will flood Black Studies courses.

> One way to draw white students off (or/and care for the surplus) is for existing departments to increase their offerings in blackness as they are doing now under the guise of "dark" (or, as sociologists say, "color-compatible") courses. This would probably result in greater benefit to the white students' needs anyway and most certainly would offset the apparent sense of threat in the minds of conventional departments.

Hare then makes an important admission:

> It may be necessary eventually to distinguish Black education for
> Blacks and Black education for whites. There is no insurmountable
> incompatibility or mutual exclusiveness between Black Studies and
> ethnic group courses in other departments. Indeed they are easily re-
> inforcing and could make a major contribution to better "race rela-
> tions" or, as politicians are fond of saying now, "the effort to save the
> nation" in decades ahead.

The principle of inclusion

In a section of the proposal called "Redefinition of Standards,"
Hare offers some singular observations. He begins by saying that
current standards evolved in large part from a need to restrict the
overflow of recruits — what he calls "the principle of exclusion" —
into existing professional niches.

> This gave rise to occasionally ludicrous requirements. The late social
> theorist, Thorstein Veblen, author of *Theory of the Leisure Class,* might
> hold that the liberal arts approach grew out of the leisure class men-
> tality, where it was prestigious to be non-productive and to waste time
> and effort in useless endeavor. Hence footnoting minutiae and the like.
> When middle class aspirants began to emulate these codes, the prin-
> ciple of exclusion evolved. However, now we are faced with the
> educational enticement of a group conditioned by way of the cake of
> time and custom to being excluded. How do we transform them into
> an included people? For example, a law school graduate with high
> honors might fail the "bar" exam (pun intended) because of political
> views, or fail the oral exam for teacher certification because of an un-
> popular approach to teaching. . . . Or pass everything required except
> the "language" exam. It is widely known that languages studied for
> graduate degrees are quickly almost totally forgotten and are rarely
> of any use after graduation. Much of the motivation for the retention
> of this and even more useless requirements apparently stems from the
> "leisure class" origin of the "liberal arts" approach where, as Thor-
> stein Veblen explained, prestige was attributed to "non-productive" or
> wasteful useless endeavor.

What Hare is saying is that requirements were devised "to
serve the functions of exclusivity rather than recruitment" and that
now "we are facing the necessity for collective recruitment from a
group victimized as a group in the past by racist policies of exclusion from the educational escalator." While the two most "salient
'qualifications' " for professorial rank today are a Ph.D. "and a string
of 'scholarly' publications," Hare wants the freedom "to depart from
those criteria without risking the suspicion of 'lowering standards.'
That the Ph.D. is not necessarily synonymous with teaching effectiveness," he adds, "is accepted by most persons confronted with the
question." Less understood is the question of publication.

Consider two candidates for a position in history, one qualified a la conventional standards, the other not. Never mind the fact that articles outside the liberal-moderate perspective have slim chances of seeing the light of day in "objective" scholarly journals. More ludicrous is the fact that the Black historian, in adhering to the tradition of "footnoting," is placed in the unenviable position of having to footnote white slave master historians or historians published by a slaveholding society in order to document his work on the slavery era.

When it comes to recruiting a faculty, Hare believes that a Black Studies program would want to redefine the notion of a "qualified" professor "by honoring teaching effectiveness and enthusiasm more than qualities determined by degrees held and other quantifiable 'credentials.'" Is there to be a role for the white professor? "Their participation," Hare states, "at least during the early, experimental stages of the program, must be cautious and minimal." He admits, however, that the impracticality of recruiting a sufficient number of black professors may force a relaxation of this principle. But on one point there is no compromising: "Any white professors involved in the program would have to be Black in spirit in order to last. The same is true for 'Negro' professors."

Central to Hare's whole proposal for a Department of Black Studies is the component of community involvement. To bring about this development it is necessary "to inspire and sustain a sense of collective destiny as a people and a consciousness of the value of education in a technological society. A cultural base, acting as a leverage for other aspects of Black ego development and academic unit, must accordingly be spawned and secured." Students and other interested parties "will be organized into Black Cultural Councils which will sponsor cultural affairs (art, dance, drama, etc.) in the Black community and establish Black holidays, festivities and celebrations." For example, a Black Winter Break could begin on February 21, the day they shot Malcolm X, run past George Washington's birthday and end with February 23, the birthday of the late Black Scholar, W. E. B. DuBois. "This," Hare says, "could approximate the Jewish Yom Kippur." There are many other suggestions: Black Information Centers "to increase communication, interpersonal contact, knowledge and sociopolitical awareness"; a Black Community Press, put together by "members of Black Current Events clubs and students taking courses in Black journalism"; a Bureau of Black Education "to provide Black scholars mutual aid and stimulation, and to organize Black textbook and syllabi writing corps."

The new curriculum

Finally, Hare outlines his plan for the Black Studies curriculum. The initiation of the program is to be accomplished in two stages:

(1) Phase I, involving the pulling together of some of the currently experimental courses into a new department; and (2) Phase II, the inauguration of a major "consisting of an integrated body of black courses revolving around core courses such as Black history, Black psychology, Black arts, and the social sciences." (See Table 1.) In addition, as part of the course requirements, there will be student field work in the black community, involving an effort to transform the community while educating and training the student. (This,

TABLE 1.   *Tentative Black Studies Major for Fall, 1969*

CORE COURSES	UNITS
Black History	4
Black Psychology	4
Survey of Sciences: Method & History	4
Black Arts and Humanities	4
	16 units
BLACK ARTS CONCENTRATION	
The Literature of Blackness	4
Black Writers Workshop	4
Black Intellectuals	4
Black Fiction	4
Black Poetry	4
Black Drama	4
The Painting of Blackness	4
The Music of Blackness	4
Sculpture of Blackness	4
	36 units
BEHAVIORAL AND SOCIAL SCIENCES CONCENTRATION	
Black Politics	4
Sociology of Blackness	4
Economics of the Black Community	4
The Geography of Blackness	4
Social Organization of Blackness	4
Development of Black Leadership	4
Demography of Blackness	4
Black Counseling	4
Black Consciousness and the International Community	4
	36 units

observes Hare, is the key ingredient which "Yale's program omits.") Although the Black Studies Program "would not preclude electives outside the Black curriculum, even for majors, it would seek to care for a wide range of academic training in the humanities, the social and behavioral sciences." Although most persons enrolled in Black Studies courses would not be majors,

those graduating as such could become probation officers, case workers, poverty workers, or enter graduate or professional schools in preparation for careers as lawyers, social workers, teachers, scholars, professors, research scientists, businessmen, administrators, and so on.
They would, other things being equal—we feel certain—quickly
emerge and predominate in the upper echelons of the Black community.

The specific content of the curriculum as proposed by Hare
follows below. "Although much of it is expressive" (geared to ego-
identity building, etc.), concludes Hare, "the utilitarian function has
by no means been omitted. . . . The Black race woefully needs concrete skills . . . both for individual mobility and community development."

Some problems

The proposal outlined above will get a full hearing this coming
year before an academic program of Black Studies is recommended
for adoption at San Francisco State and sent to the State College
Board of Trustees for its final approval. The range of opinion and
reaction will be wide, from those who see no reason to make special
curricular provisions for black students to those who believe that
whites are not competent to pass judgment on an educational program for blacks. Some members of the faculty will rush to support
whatever the most militant black students want simply to show that
they are not up tight about militant black students. (These faculty
members are never up tight, except about being up tight.) Others
will oppose Black Studies with the question: why not a Department
of Jewish (or Indian or Chinese or Mexican-American) Studies?
Still others will propose alternate plans — for example, that existing
academic departments increase the number of minorities on their
teaching staffs and develop course offerings that will meet the different ethnic needs on the campus. Predictably, however, the great
majority of the faculty, the "silent middle," will choose to be uninterested and uninvolved. They will have nothing to say.

Any proposed program of Black Studies will inevitably produce
a flood of questions. The trouble is that dispassionate answers are
difficult to come by. Perhaps the most that can be done, in keeping
with the commitment of the academic community to the use of
reason in the resolution of problems, is to suggest a number of issues
that deserve consideration and analysis.

1. It was not too long ago that the battle was fought to dis-
suade college admissions offices from requiring a candidate to submit
a photograph or to state his race or religion. In many colleges and
universities the specific target was the so-called "quota system,"

which had a special application to Jews. Today the "new-liberal" position is that Negroes must not only be identified but admitted to college by special quotas. Race and color are no longer to be ignored. (When Nathan Hare was asked if he believed the admissions office at San Francisco State should require a photograph with each student application, he replied, "Of course. How else are we going to identify the blacks?") At a number of universities, militant students have demanded the admission of specific numbers of Negroes, which increasingly is being translated into quotas roughly equal to the proportion of Negroes in the total population of the locality or of the nation.

Daniel P. Moynihan, speaking for many who subscribe to the "old-liberal" position, has warned that quotas for one group inevitably turn into formulas against another. "Let me be blunt. If ethnic quotas are to be imposed on American universities . . . Jews will be almost driven out. They are not 3 per cent of the population." (This, said Professor Moynihan, would be a misfortune for Jews, but a disaster to the nation.) According to a report in *The New York Times,* undergraduates at Harvard enthusiastically endorsed ethnic representation, if not exactly quotas, on the faculty, but had misgivings about applying the same principle to student enrollment. As Professor Moynihan pointed out, if such quotas were to be applied, seven out of eight Jewish undergraduates would have to leave, and much the same exodus would be required of Japanese and Chinese Americans. "America," Professor Moynihan said, "has known enough of anti-Semitism and anti-Oriental feeling to be wary of opening that box again."

Virtually everyone is agreed that special efforts should be made to increase the enrollment of Negro students in our colleges and universities. The problem is to find a way to open the doors "without going from the assumption of color-blindness to the extreme of forcing on every institution quotas of racial and religious membership."

2. Many whites have not yet fully understood the psychological meaning and force of an issue that, to many blacks, is even more critical than white racism — namely, pride and personal identification. More than any other component of the racial question, it pervades every discussion of a black curriculum. Its importance and enormous power cannot be minimized. The fact is that black students do respond directly and positively to a black instructor. The relationship is clear, personal and effective. It is a potent consideration, and is at the heart of every argument in support of a Department of Black Studies.

On another level of analysis, however, many in the academic community are concerned about its ultimate meaning and implication. At issue, at least for some, is the matter of standards. Is the color of a professor's skin more important than the substance of the course? The Black Studies Coordinator phoned the Chairman of the Political Science Department to inquire about a course in *African Government and Politics* scheduled for the fall semester. "What color is the instructor?" was his only question. "White," he was told. He was not interested in the fact that she was writing her Ph.D. dissertation in the area of African politics and had received her training under the supervision of a leading authority in African problems at the University of California. His single concern was color. Thus a fundamental professional question is raised: is color the test of competence? It has only been recently that colleges and universities have succeeded in removing *politics* as a test for hiring and firing. Now is it to be color?

A Department of Black Studies, it should be said, would make such questions unnecessary. All personnel in Black Studies would be black, with the sole and avowed purpose of concentrating on blackness.

"Collective stimulation" and academic propriety

3. At a time when educators throughout the United States are trying to devise new ways to reach their students on a more personal, individual basis, it is significant that Hare's proposal for a Department of Black Studies is aimed at "collective stimulation" — that is, to get black students to stop thinking individualistically and to begin thinking collectively. Put another way, the black curriculum is not explicitly designed to encourage black students to develop qualities of independence, skepticism, and critical inquiry — in a word, to think for themselves — but rather to intensify the motivation and commitment of all who enroll in the program to return to the black community and translate everything to which they have been exposed into black leadership and black power. As a political program for community action it is not to be faulted. As an academic program — or, perhaps more properly, as a program in academic surroundings — it poses some different problems.

For those whose total educational philosophy and concern is contained in the penetrating nugget, "Let them do their own thing," there will, of course, be no problems at all. Others, however, will have some questions. Will those who teach in the Department of Black Studies be of the same political and ideological persuasion, or will efforts be made to recruit a black staff that purposely reflects different and opposing points of view? Would Black Studies hire a black undergraduate to teach one of its courses for credit? Will the Department of Black Studies mirror the views of the Black Students' Union, thereby reinforcing the Union's political goals and purposes on campus?

4. Nathan Hare has said that "Black people understand black problems better than anyone else. We are determined to solve our own problems and the important first step is education." Few will dispute the first half of the statement. There may be some question, however — in an academic community it could not really be otherwise — as to what is meant by education. It is certainly not to be confused with indoctrination, any more than tales of heroism, white or black, can pass for genuine history. It is true that for many students in this country the history of man has too often been treated as though it "started in Athens and ended in California," with the Afro-American story simply left out. The question now is whether a Department of Black Studies would substitute propaganda for omission, or, as some have said, new myths for old lies. For example, many highly respected historians view black history in the United States as a problem of deciding where and when the question of race or religion, or any particular characteristic or trait, has historical significance. Would this approach, this form of intellectual discipline, be acceptable to Black Studies? Would Black Studies look on a course in African history as an opportunity simply to venerate the great achievements of cultural forebears, or would it also lay stress on, say, the historical fact that the more advanced African peoples and energetic leaders were often the very ones who sold other Africans to slave traders, thereby helping to bring about Negro slavery in America?

Or consider Hare's own book, *The Black Anglo-Saxon*, published three years ago. Writing as a sociologist, he argues that black, would-be Anglo-Saxons are forgetting or denying their "Negroness." However, Professor Troy Duster, a social scientist at the University of California (Riverside), points out that much of E. Franklin Frazier's scholarly life was spent documenting the fact that the Negro in the United States was stripped of almost every vestige of his African culture, and that his primary substantive culture is an American one. In discussing one type of black Anglo-Saxon, Hare states that "their pathetic pursuit of white values is an effort to elude their true personal and social identities." But, asks Professor Duster, "do Negroes really have a separate set of ethical and moral precepts, or separate standards for evaluating themselves and others? If so, what is the well-spring of this distinctly Negro culture if it is not that of the whites who brought Negroes to this country in the chains of slavery?" Would this intellectual position be fully recognized and discussed in a Department of Black Studies? Would open and sharp disagreement over the nature and substance of an American Negro culture be encouraged?

Martin Luther Kilson, Jr., assistant professor of government at Harvard and advisor to Harvard's Afro-Americans, has asked some pointed questions: "What community or segment of Black peoples should be used as representative of whatever the Black Experience is or has been? Should it be the Republic of Haiti where Black Power has been oppressive of the black masses? Or black fratricide in Nigeria? Or the black experience with 200 years of white racism in the United States?" Professor Kilson does not hesitate to say that all men, black, white, yellow, and red, are capable of oppressive abuse of power, without gaining from such experience any special will or capacity to rid human affairs of oppression. "Indeed," he concludes, "it is a common fallacy to believe that what is momentarily politically serviceable is ipso facto intellectually virtuous."

EPILOGUE

[Editors' Note: This Epilogue was written in December 1968 to take account of developments during the Fall 1968 semester.]

BLACK STUDIES was a controversial issue at San Francisco State throughout the 1968 fall semester.[3] On September 13 the President announced that he had created a Black Studies Department for which he hoped a curriculum, faculty staffing, and the necessary funds would soon be forthcoming. But in the weeks and months that followed, the Black Students' Union repeatedly charged that "the racists in the administration have been and are destroying the whole concept of Black Studies" and that "all Black student and Third World student programs and achievements face extermination on this campus." The accusation was untrue, but that mattered little to those

---

[3] In the first week of the semester the Vice-President for Academic Affairs at San Francisco State called me into his office to tell me that, as a consequence of my having written "Black Studies at San Francisco State," I was now a "target" of the militant blacks on campus. (It should be pointed out that during September I had circulated dittoed copies to a number of my colleagues on the faculty, including Nathan Hare, for their comments and criticisms.) On September 25 the campus newspaper printed a long essay entitled "BSU States Its Philosophy, Goals, and Achievements" in which it was stated that "Dr. Bunzel's article was the cause of the Black Studies Department losing grants totalling up to a half-million dollars. This money would have been used to provide jobs and grants for Black students, and at the same time as salaries for Black faculty." The statement, of course, was false and preposterous, not only because the article had not even been published yet (it was not to appear in print until November) but because there were no such funds to be lost, as members of the college administration, including the President, quietly assured me. It was not long thereafter that I heard myself being denounced as a "racist," a "faculty mandarin," and "a lackey of the CIA and the Democratic Party." (I had been a member of the Kennedy delegation from California and had attended the Democratic National Convention in Chicago.)

who were heady on the fare of black liberation and revolutionary bombast and for whom the real need was the dramaturgy and psychic release derived from a powerful symbolism. It was not long before Black Studies was caught up in the mythic language of black pride and identity, of "soul" needs, of black rage and violence. Passionate and explosively charged rhetoric, calculated to mobilize sentiments and generate emotive responses, obscured the elements of reality and made all the more difficult, if not impossible, any serious and sustained examination of the proposed Black Studies program, including consideration of curricular options and outcomes. In early November, at the invitation of the Black Students' Union, Stokely Carmichael came on campus and told an audience of over 800 Third World students that "white people have the luxury of being revolutionary, but for us it is a necessity." In helping to give cohesion and direction to the impending strike, he made it clear that "when you are talking about Black Studies you are not talking about course content, you are talking about methodology and ideology." For someone like myself (and many others on the faculty), who has been committed for three or four years to the development of a program of ethnic studies at San Francisco State, it was not difficult to see that the concern for some measure of academic substance and integrity had long since been swept away in the flood of symbolic arguments seeking symbolic solutions.

There was great pressure to adopt the program of Black Studies authored by Nathan Hare, although 95 per cent of the faculty had neither seen it nor knew anything of its character and content. So pervasive was the sense of urgency and the fear of an imminent explosion on campus that the paramount thought was to get Hare's curriculum through the necessary committees as rapidly as possible. There was no time (or, as some preferred to say, it was not the time) to be concerned with its quality or direction.

On a Thursday noon in late October the Undergraduate Curriculum and Instructional Policies committees met jointly to consider for the first, and only, time Hare's concept of Black Studies. The members of the two committees sat around a rectangular table. Standing directly behind them two and three deep were members of the Black Students' Union who had packed the room to give visible evidence of their strength in numbers. The final draft of the proposed curriculum was given particular attention. (See Table 2.)

Members of the two committees spent most of the time asking Hare to explain certain features of the curriculum. "What is Black Statistics?" "Will only black people be hired to teach in the Department of Black Studies?" "Will white students be admitted into the program?" In little more than an hour and a half they completed their work, quickly voted support of the Black Studies pro-

posal (the Dean of Academic Planning abstained), and forwarded
it to the Academic Senate with the recommendation that it be
adopted immediately. There were no surprises. The two faculty
committees charged with the responsibility of examining and thereby giving college-wide approval to new academic programs had
officially met and deliberated. The scenario had been played out.

But at what cost? A number of profoundly important questions
having to do with the planning of any Black Studies program were
not considered. For example, a fundamental assumption was made
from the outset and virtually accepted without challenge or debate
— namely, that if the college is creating a Department of Black
Studies it should place the task in the hands of Blacks or, perhaps

TABLE 2.   *Proposal for a Department of Black Studies*

Major Pattern:

12 units	(core, required)
24 units	(electives in area of concentration)
9 units	(electives from throughout the college, on advisement)
45 units	total

CORE COURSES   UNITS

Black Studies 601	Black History	3
Black Studies 602	Black Psychology	3
Black Studies 603	Survey of Sciences: Method & History	3
Black Studies 604	Black Arts and Humanities	3
		12 units

Clarification of number and types of electives, if any, under the
proposed degree program including special options:

BLACK ARTS CONCENTRATION

Black Studies 605	The Literature of Blackness	3
Black Studies 606	Black Writers Workshop	6*
Black Studies 607	Black Intellectuals	3
Black Studies 608	Black Fiction	3
Black Studies 609	Black Poetry	3
Black Studies 610	The Painting of Blackness	3
Black Studies 611	The Music of Blackness	3
Black Studies 612	Sculpture of Blackness	3
Black Studies 613	Black Radio, Television, Film	3
Black Studies 614	Black Journalism	6*
Black Studies 615	Black Oratory	6*
Black Studies 616	Black Philosophy	3
Black Studies 617	Black Classics	3
		48 units

TABLE 2.   (*continued*)

BEHAVIORAL AND SOCIAL SCIENCES CONCENTRATION

Black Studies 618	Black Politics	6*
Black Studies 619	Sociology of Blackness	6*
Black Studies 620	Economics of the Black Community	6*
Black Studies 621	The Geography of Blackness	3
Black Studies 622	Social Organization of Blackness	6*
Black Studies 623	Development of Black Leadership	6*
Black Studies 624	Demography of Blackness	3
Black Studies 625	Black Counseling	6*
Black Studies 626	Black Nationalism and the International Community	3
Black Studies 627	The Anthropology of Blackness	6*
Black Studies 628	Black Consciousness	3
Black Studies 629	Black Statistics: Survey & Method	6*
Black Studies 630	Black Economic Workshop	6*
Black Studies 631	Black Political Workshop	6*
		72 units

Recommended patterns of electives in both emphases will be available for guidance.

* Field work and/or off-campus work required.

more exactly, in the hands of Black Studies specialists who are black. There is a deceptive simplicity in this argument which obscures a basic fallacy. A college or university never places the task of creating a new department (or any significant administrative or academic entity) solely in the hands of those who advocate its creation. The reasons are eminently sound: every self-respecting institution of higher learning recognizes that although there are segments of the academic community that pursue their specialized interests, there is the even more compelling idea and concept of community which must mean that certain values and concerns are held in common. There is, in other words, the larger collegial reality and distinctness-of-being of which everyone is part and to whose standards of excellence and to whose long-established expectations about intellectual and administrative rigor and clarity they are presumed to be committed.

But there is still another and perhaps even more significant consideration implicit in the original proposition which deserves some attention. Black Studies, it is argued, makes a unique claim for acceptance, with perhaps pro forma or only negligible review, because only blacks can judge the proposals of blacks or because black students can relate only to black teachers. Thus, the argument runs, only black teachers or black specialists can legitimately pro-

pose Black Studies courses. It should be made clear that to state
these arguments is neither to validate nor invalidate them out of
hand. The point is that at San Francisco State, unlike many other
colleges and universities presently considering Black Studies, these
arguments were never seriously examined in any college-wide
faculty review committee. For example, no discussion was ever
focused on the critical premise that being black is not in itself an
absolute qualification for being an expert, any more than being
white is in itself a qualification for being an expert. Nor was there
any attempt to separate the different educational contexts in which
being black might have meaning. A black statistician cannot by
definition be a more expert statistician qua statistician than a yellow or white statistician. Either the college or university is a single
community with standards of scholarship that make Black Statistics
as repugnant as Lysenkoist Biology or it begins a piecemeal transformation into a cockpit of ideologues and fanatics who have abandoned the search for knowledge. The same is true of a black biologist, physicist, or chemist. However, in every one of these and
other instances, a black teacher who is a biologist or physicist will
presumably be able to relate significantly better to black students
than a white biologist or physicist. But even this last point might
need to be qualified: presumably black teachers relate significantly
better to black students when blackness is the prime subject matter. Acceptance of any broader principle might mean that the college would have to provide a black and a white teacher for every
course in every department on the grounds that to do otherwise
would be to disadvantage black students. Not only is such a policy
pragmatically impossible but many if not all observers would regard
it as pedagogically, philosophically, and politically indefensible.

Among the ten demands of the Black Students' Union for which
the members went on strike in November (they were all declared
to be "not negotiable") five related specifically to Black Studies.

1. That all Black Studies courses being taught through various
   other departments immediately become part of the Black
   Studies Department and that all the instructors in this department receive full-time pay.
2. That Nathan Hare, acting Chairman of the Black Studies Department, receive a full professorship and a comparable salary
   according to his qualifications.[4]

---

[4] Nathan Hare had been an assistant professor at Howard University and was
appointed a lecturer at the salary of associate professor when he came to San
Francisco State in the spring of 1968. Thus the demand that he be promoted to
full professor was made only nine months after he joined the staff. Regarding
this particular matter, three other points should be made: (1) promotion of a

3. That there be a Department of Black Studies granting a Bachelor's degree in Black Studies; that the Black Studies Department, chairman, faculty, and staff have the sole power to hire faculty and control and determine the destiny of its department.
4. That 20 full-time teaching positions be allocated to the Department of Black Studies.
5. That all black students wishing so, be admitted in the fall of 1969.

This is not the time or place to discuss all the demands. However, the third one above is one of the most important in that it raises some serious and difficult questions. The nub of the issue is the insistence that those in the Black Studies Department have the "sole power" to run it in any way they choose — in short, the kind of autonomy and control not given to any other department in the college. At San Francisco State, departments enjoy a high degree of independence, but their decisions are subject to review by appropriate faculty bodies and administrative personnel. Furthermore, the college and all of its departments are legally responsible to the Office of the Chancellor, the Board of Trustees, and the Legislature of the State of California. And there's the rub, at least so far as the militant blacks are concerned. As one of their spokesmen on campus put it, "That's the white power structure, and all it means is more white double talk and white racism. What we want is very simple: we want to be left alone to do our own thing."

As of the time I am writing (December 1968) there is no way of knowing how this demand and all the others will be settled. Perhaps the Department of Black Studies will be grafted onto the rest of the educational program with no difficulty at all. Perhaps it will take its place with the other departments at San Francisco State, which is to say separate but equal but not "more separate" or "more equal" than others. Perhaps the new curriculum, which many regard as essentially one course in blackness flattened out into 72 units, will develop into a highly-respected degree program. Many people are hoping. But no one is placing any bets.

Black Studies is a new venture. One would have thought it plausible, therefore, to suppose that a number of different ideas would have been given at least cursory attention since the forms of organization, methods of analysis, curricular possibilities, and

---

faculty member to another rank is the responsibility of the promotions committee; (2) at San Francisco State there is no necessary relationship between the rank a faculty member holds and the administrative post to which he may be assigned; (3) at the present time there are at least eight departmental chairmen and one associate dean who have not attained the rank of full professor.

the like are still very much in the process of discovery. But on this subject the political environment at San Francisco State had already been polarized: one either supported in its entirety the specific proposal as outlined in these pages, which reflected essentially the views of one man working alone or one was summarily defined and dismissed as an "enemy" of Black Studies. It was as if the academic universe had been divided into the "moral" and the "perverse." It should have been possible in principle to accept the notion that alternatives are feasible and that criticism and skepticism are both legitimate and essential in the search for the most viable option. The same principle should apply to specialists in Black Studies. It may be unfortunate though it is still true that the credentials of such specialists are not as readily identifiable as those of scholars in other well-established fields. All of us must learn to live with this uncertainty without seeing in it the malevolent workings of a power-crazed and intransigent racist majority.

3

The
activists:
a profile

SEYMOUR MARTIN LIPSET

ANY effort to account for the rise of student activism in the United States during the 1960's is faced with the fact that we are obviously dealing with a worldwide phenomenon. This, in turn, suggests that the sources of political activism among students must essentially be found in politics itself—in the changing world-wide climate of political opinion. Students as a stratum are more responsive to political trends, to changes in mood, to opportunities for action than almost any other group in the population. They also are the most easily mobilizable stratum; ideas which arise as a response to a given issue may move readily among them, and may move them more readily, since they have fewer responsibilities in the form of commitments to families and jobs.

Why have the politically oriented students become particularly sensitive to social issues in the 1960's when, particularly in America, relatively few of these students had been actively involved in the two preceding decades? Presumably, the explanation is closely related to the changing international picture. During the 1940's and early 1950's, the Western world was concerned with the expansionist tendencies of totalitarian systems, fascist and communist. These threats put a heavy premium on intellectuals justifying the virtues of the societies in which they lived, and contributed to a decline in ideological controversy within the democratic countries. Serious domestic criticism appeared to contribute to the ideological arsenal of the "enemy." From 1956 on, however, much of the political rationale for domestic consensus based on anti-totalitarianism began to disappear, with the revelation that the post-Stalinist Communist world was itself ridden with dissension.

This change facilitated the rise of domestic criticism by those groups in the West that normally press their societies to live up to their ideals. Students, who tend to accept the basic values of their societies in a more absolute fashion than their elders, were among the first to become involved in this reorientation. Here in the United States, student opposition first arose around the issue of civil rights —the supremely moral problem of American society, one that engages manifest violations of the American egalitarian creed. To the activist young who came to political consciousness in the late 1950's, the gap between their sense of what ought to be and what actually existed seemed enormous. They took for granted the existing structure, *including* the changes that had occurred but a year or two before, and reacted with outrage against continued evidence of Negro deprivation. The resistance by Southern whites including governors, judges, and police to the enforcement of the law helped to persuade the advocates of civil rights that the regular peaceful methods of democracy do not always work. The "confrontation" tactic of civil disobedience, which was introduced by the Southern defenders of segregation, was, in turn, adopted by the student movement and then transferred to other issues, particularly in recent years to the struggle against the Vietnam War.

The spread of opposition to this war has become the dominant political issue affecting student activism in many countries. Here we can see a generation gap operating. To many in the older age groups, Vietnam was but the most recent episode in a two-decade long struggle against Communist expansion. For those students inclined to the left—who knew not Stalin, the Hungarian Revolution, or the Berlin Wall—the Vietnam issue became defined in terms that placed American actions at odds with a basic democratic belief— the right to self-determination of politically weak peoples. The very failure of the powerful United States to defeat its small, poor opponent was taken as evidence of the oppressive character of the war, of its being a war in which a foreign power sought to impose its will by force over another people.

Such, in brief, is the background of the student rebellion. In the foreground, however, there are other factors—sociological and psychological—that are more directly related to the university itself and that have a bearing on the question: who are the activists and why are they that way?

The modern American university has become a place of assembly and major occupational outlet for many of the brightest people who seek to be innovative, who wish to be free of the ideological restrictions and materialistic commitments that they believe are inherent in the corporate and professional worlds. It is an institution where "liberalism" in politics and "modernism" in culture has become an established, if unofficial, *Weltanschauung*. It is not surprising, then, that evidence drawn from a variety of surveys of student attitudes indicates that colleges do have a "liberalizing" effect on young people. Samuel Stouffer pointed out over ten years ago that the conservatives who attack the universities for "corrupting" young people were correct, from their political and moral standpoints. Nor is it only the young students who are so influenced.

Although the recent student protest has been directed against much of the adult world, including the faculty, it is important to note that a significant section of the faculty has been quite sympathetic. Indeed, some have themselves been leading "activists." This is not so paradoxical as it seems.

Changes in the backgrounds and opinions of increasing numbers of college faculty have undoubtedly been as marked as, if less noticed than, those of the students. Before the 1930's, the American professoriate was not known especially for having strong political views, or for engaging in political action. This changed somewhat during the depression, with the identification of the New Deal with reliance on academic expertise. But since the war particularly, various segments of the population with strong liberal views, which hitherto played very little role in university life, finally moved in a massive way onto the campus. This has been most visible in the enormous growth in the number of liberal Jewish faculty, but many of the non-Jews who have been attracted to university life have similar views.

"Intellectual Poujadisme"

The shift to the left in the opinions of faculty, and of other intellectuals as well, is, of course, not simply explained by the changing composition of the stratum. It also reflects a heightened resentment among humanistically-inclined, "general" intellectuals toward the increased emphasis on intellectual technology and expertise, toward the decline of the status of diffuse intellectualism in the social and political arena.

The differentiation of social science knowledge into distinct fields of technical expertise has sharply undermined the role of the educated intellectual who has traditionally claimed the right to comment on, and influence, public policy. Economists now contend that many of the decisions about economic policy require technical knowledge beyond the competence of the informed layman. And as the other social sciences have extended their spheres of competence, and have become more systematically empirical and quantitative, they also question the ability of laymen to understand the factors that affect educational achievement, child-rearing practices, international relations, and the like.

Increasingly, the expert tells the general intellectual that the particular matters under discussion are simply too complicated, too technical, for "humanist" intellectuals to influence them through advocacy of relatively uncomplicated solutions associated with a particular ideological bent. Those who seek to affect society in some specific way find themselves up against arguments supposedly derivative from specialized scholarly knowledge. And a commitment to the increasing function of science and specialization reinforces the ideology of the "end of ideology," i.e., the position that ideologically dictated positions are basically irrelevant where expertise is available, a position that was put most strongly in John F. Kennedy's speech at Yale in spring 1963.

These trends have contributed to the rise among many intellectuals and students, plus those in the more abstract theoretical fields of science, of a kind of left-wing "intellectual *Poujadisme*," of a back-lash opposition to systematic and quantitative social science, to large-scale social research, to the very conception of the utility of efforts at value-free objective scholarship in policy-relevant fields. Many intellectuals react to the emphasis on social science, and the concomitant belief in gradualism, expertise, and planning, with a populist stress on the virtues of direct action against evil institutions and practices. They criticize the involvement of the university in policy matters as inherently corrupting the values of pure scholarship and intellectual freedom. This attack, paradoxically, has meant that many of the same faculty who seemingly defend the old ivory tower conception of the role of the university often encourage students to convert the university into a political arena.

The sources of faculty ambivalence

But if faculty helps to create a climate of opinion that encourages students to move to "the left," it is ironic that some of the sources of student malaise stem from the fact that changes in the role of this very faculty have contributed to making the situation of being a student less attractive than it once was. With increasing size and greater pressures on faculty to do research, publish, and take part in "public service" activities, the faculty, at the leading institutions increasingly gives a larger proportion of its ever more limited teaching time to graduate research students, and pays relatively little attention to undergraduates. So, in an odd way, the emergence of the university as a major liberal institution of our society has *reduced* the informal influence of students within the university, as compared with thirty or forty years ago. This development is not simply or even principally a function of the growth of the university; it reflects even more the increased "professionalization" of the faculty, the extent to which "teaching" as such has declined as the main identification of the role of being a professor.

The changes in the role of the faculty, its increased involvement in a national prestige system (based on evaluations of scholarly achievements or extramural activities), the sharp increase in income (derivative in large part from the fact that many schools are in competition for those who have or promise to attain general reputations), and the concomitant decline in faculty teaching obligations have not necessarily made for a "happier" professoriate. Faculty, like students, are in an increasingly competitive situation, one in which men see themselves being constantly judged as to their positions in national and local pecking orders. While some succeed in becoming nationally recognized figures, most faculty necessarily do not achieve any such elevated scholarly status. With the depreciation of the teaching function as a local source of economic reward and status, many who have lost out in the competition within their own generation—or who, if successful, fear or actually see younger men coming up and securing the status they once had—become deeply dissatisfied and anxious. The universities and colleges, which are increasingly competitive in efforts at stockpiling distinguished scholars, encourage such feelings among both their older and younger faculty by invidiously rewarding, often in a very public fashion, those men who are most valuable in this race for institutional prestige. Such sentiments reinforce faculty propensities to dislike the administrations of their schools, as well as the dominant values and institutions of the larger society.

Hence, many professors find solace in student militancy directed against the forces they hold responsible for their felt sense of status inferiority or insecurity. The same faculty that demands and secures lower teaching loads (ironically, this especially may take place after student revolts that further reduce the "bargaining strength" of the university) often tell their students that they are neglected and misused by the administration and trustees. And although the demand for "student power," for increased influence by students over the decision-making process in the university, tends on the whole to be raised by the left-wing activist groups, the receptivity that this demand secures in wider circles may reflect the heightened sense within the campus community that the university demands more, yet gives less, to both the student and the faculty member. Thus, as in the case of workers and employees in a bureaucratized industry, a sort of student syndicalism would seem to be emerging which seeks to regain symbolically for students as a group the influence which they have lost individually. This syndicalist spirit is all the more powerful in that it evokes, not opposition, but ambivalence among many faculty members.

A youth culture

This ambivalence is enhanced by those components of American values that make adults reluctant, even when they have good cause, to sharply call students or youth to task. Rather they like to encourage youth and students to take independent, new positions. This ties in with the part of the American self-image that assumes that the United States is a progressive country, one that accepts reform and change. And the truism that the youth will inherit the future is linked with the sense that the youth are the bearers of all those "progressive" ideas that will dominate the future.

The tensions within the university system are also increased by the fact that the increasing amount of time required for educational development inherently means the prolongation of adolescence. Although physiologically mature, and often above the age legally defined as adult, students are expected to refrain from full involvement in the adult world. Dependency is, of course, built into the very essence of the university system. The American university, in particular, with its stress on frequent examinations, emphasizes this relationship even more than does that of most other countries. Hence, the student who leaves home to attend the university finds that he remains in a highly controlled situation, even while society is urging him to become independent.

It may also be argued that student activism is the most recent expression of the need of youth to have a separate culture of their own. The student stratum, as such, has always tended to create a whole array of age-group symbols, which set it apart from others in society, and from adults in particular. The changes in the political role of the university increasingly make politics a particularly critical source of self-expression. The institution, itself, may be nonpartisan, but its professors fulfill ever-growing roles as party activists, commentators on events, advisors, consultants, and researchers on policy matters. Many students are thus in centers of great political significance, but have little or no share in the political status of the institution. In addition, although most of the faculty political involvement is generally on the left of the spectrum in the United States, it also occurs within the "establishment." Hence, if it is to express a sense of separate identity, student politics as part of the student culture must be outside of, and in opposition to, the politics of most of the adults.

The powerful 2 per cent

The university campus is an ideal place in which to be a radical activist. Many universities have tens of thousands of students concentrated in a small area. It takes only a small percentage of these massive student bodies to make a large demonstration. Thus, in 1965–1967, although opinion polls indicated that the great majority of American students supported the Vietnam War and that anti-war sentiment within the group was no greater than in the population as a whole, the campus opposition was able to have an inordinately great impact because it could be mobilized. During 1967–1968, as the country as a whole turned increasingly critical of the war, campus opinion—both student and faculty—has moved to a majority anti-war position. This has placed the student anti-war activist groups in a very strong moral position, comparable to the one held earlier by the civil rights organizations; their goals, if not always their means, are approved by the community within which they operate.

It remains true, as Herbert Marcuse pointed out recently, that the majority of the students in all countries are politically quiescent and moderate in their views. According to national surveys of student opinion taken by the Harris Poll in 1965 and the Gallup Poll in 1968, approximately one-fifth of the students have participated in civil rights or political activities (17 per cent in 1964–1965, the year of the Berkeley revolt, and 20 per cent in 1967–1968, the year of the McCarthy and Kennedy campaigns). The radical activist groups generally have tiny memberships. Students for a Democratic Society (SDS) claims a total membership of about 30,000 out of a national student body of 7 million of which about 6,000 pay national dues. A Harris Poll of American students taken in the spring of 1968 estimates that there are about 100,000 radical activists, or somewhere between 1 and 2 per cent of the college population. A Gallup survey also conducted in the spring of 1968 reports that 7 per cent of male students indicate that they will refuse to go, if drafted. Given that the activists are such a small minority, the question must be raised as who are they, and what are the factors that contribute to activist strength?

The influence of parents

The major conclusion to be drawn from a large number of studies in the United States and other countries is that *left-wing students are largely the children of left-wing or liberal parents.* The activists are more radical than their parents; but both parents and children are located on the same side of the spectrum. Conversely, studies of those active in conservative student groupings, such as the Goldwaterite Young Americans for Freedom (YAF), indicate that they are largely from right-wing backgrounds. Students are more "idealistic" and "committed" than their parents—but generally in the same direction. In line with these findings, the available data indicate that the student left in the United States is disproportionately Jewish. This is not surprising, since adult Jews in the United States are overwhelmingly liberal or radical for all sorts of historical and sociological reasons.

Intellectuals, academics, writers, musicians, and so forth in the United States tend as a group to be disproportionately on the left. They are either liberal Democrats or supporters of left-wing minor parties. And studies of student populations suggest that students who are intellectually oriented, who identify themselves as "intellectuals," or who aspire to intellectual pursuits after graduation, are also much more prone to be on the left and favorable to activism.

Among faculty and students, there are clear-cut correlations between academic disciplines and political orientations. *On the whole, those involved in the humanities and softer social sciences, or in the more pure theoretical fields of science, are more likely to be on the left than those in the more practical, applied, or experimental fields. Such variations, however, would appear to be more a product of selective entrance into different disciplines than of the effects of the content of the fields on those pursuing them as students or practitioners.* Thus, studies of entering freshmen — i.e., those who have not yet taken a single lecture — report the same relationships between intended college major and political attitudes as are found among seniors, graduate students, and faculty. Morris Rosenberg, who conducted a panel study (repeat interviews with the same people two years apart) of students, reported that political orientation proved to be a major determinant of shifts in undergraduate major. A large proportion of the minority of conservatives who chose "liberal" (in political terms) majors as freshmen changed to subjects studied by conservatives, whereas many liberals who had selected "conservative" majors tended to shift to fields that were presumably more congenial to their political outlook.

The relationships between academic fields and political sympathies are also linked to the finding that the leftist activists within American universities tend to come from relatively well-to-do backgrounds as compared to the student population generally. A comparison by Braungart and Westby of the delegates to conventions of SDS and YAF also indicated that *the left-wingers come from somewhat more affluent backgrounds than the rightists.* The majority of the latter are the children of conservative businessmen and professionals, but they include a significant proportion (one-fifth to one-third) from working-class origins, a group almost unrepresented among the SDS delegates. In general, studies of the social backgrounds of students in different disciplines suggest that those who major in the liberal arts subjects and have an intellectual or scholarly bent have well-educated parents, whereas first-generation college students of lowly origins tend to be vocationally oriented in a narrow sense, and are more likely to be found among those preparing to become engineers, businessmen, and the like. These latter come disproportionately from that segment of the less privileged that is strongly oriented toward upward mobility. Their strong concentration on professional objectives, plus the need of many of them to hold a job during school term, also results in these students being less available for political activities than those from more privileged families. These findings not only hold up within schools, but may also help to explain why colleges attended by large numbers of less well-to-do students, Negroes apart, are less likely to be strongholds of left-wing groups than those that educate the scions of the upper middle class.

Black students, of course, constitute a major exception to the pattern of political passivity, or conservatism, among students of relatively deprived backgrounds. To them, the gains made before they came of age appear empty. And on the major campuses of the nation, the growing minority of black students have found themselves in a totally white-dominated world, facing few — if any — black faculty, and incorporated into a white student body whose liberal and radical wing turned increasingly, after 1964, from involvement with civil rights to activity directed against the Vietnam War. The concern with Black Power has, consequently, won growing support among black students. They have been among the major forces initiating sit-ins during the 1967–1968 school year at schools as diverse and separated as San Francisco State College, Columbia, Boston, and Northwestern universities, and at many predominantly Negro institutions as well. However, as Charles Hamilton has pointed out, black-student protest differs considerably from that of the more affluent white radicals in that the politics of the former is much more *instrumental,* directed toward realistic, achievable goals, whereas that of the latter is inclined to be *expressive,* more oriented toward showing up the "immorality" of the larger society than to securing attainable reforms.

The radical tradition

The political character of certain schools and the resultant political orientation of their students also may be linked to other sources of selective recruitment. High-level liberal arts colleges with an intellectual aura attract students oriented to becoming intellectuals. This may account for the pattern of student protest at such schools as Reed, Swarthmore, and Antioch. The best state universities, as judged in terms of faculty scholarly prominence — e.g., California, Michigan, and Wisconsin — are also schools which have become the most important centers of "confrontationist" politics. These schools attract a disproportionate number of intellectually oriented students.

The political traditions and images of certain universities also may play an important role in determining the orientations of their students and faculty. In the United States, Madison and Berkeley have maintained a fairly long record as centers of radicalism. The University of Wisconsin image goes back to before World War I, when the strength of Progressive and Socialist politics in the state contributed to the university's political aura. Berkeley is a particularly interesting case in point. The San Francisco Bay area has a history, dating back to the turn of the century, as one of the most liberal-left communities in the nation. A history of student activism during the 1930's by Hal Draper credits Berkeley with one of the largest reported anti-war demonstrations of the time. Various pieces of data pertaining to the Berkeley campus since the end of World War II point up the continuity of that university as a center of leftism. In his *Memoirs,* George Kennan reports his puzzlement, as of 1946, that his West Coast academic lecture audiences, and those at Berkeley especially, tended to be much more sympathetic to the Soviet Union than those at other universities. Berkeley was the only large university in the country to sustain a major faculty revolt against restrictive anti-Communist personnel policies in the form of the loyalty oath of 1949–1950. The data collected by Paul Lazarsfeld, in a national opinion survey of the attitudes of social scientists, conducted in 1954 to evaluate the effect of McCarthyism on universities, indicated that the Berkeley faculty was the most liberal of any of the schools sampled in this study. The first major well-publicized student-manned demonstration of the 1960's was the one directed against the House Committee on Un-American Activities in San Francisco in 1960 ("Operation Abolition"). In 1963–1964, the year before the celebrated Berkeley student revolt, San Francisco Bay area students received national publicity for a series of massive and successful off-campus sit-in demonstrations designed to secure jobs for Negroes at various business firms. Prior to the emergence of the Free Speech Movement (FSM) protest, the Berkeley campus probably had more left-wing and activist groups, with more members, than any other school in the country. The vigor and effectiveness of the FSM must in some part be credited to the prior existence of a well-organized and politically experienced group of activist students. A study of the 600 students who held a police car captive in the first major confrontation of that affair, in October 1964, reported that over half of them had taken part in at least one previous demonstration and that 15 per cent indicated they had taken part in *seven or more!*

In stressing that involvement in leftist student activism is a function of the general political orientation which students bring to the university, it is not being argued that changes in attitude do not occur. Universities clearly do have a liberalizing effect, so that there is a gradual shift to the left. However, if we hold pre-university orientation constant, it obviously will make a difference which university a student attends, what subjects he decides to major in, who his friends are on the campus, what his relations are with his teachers of varying political persuasions, what particular extracurricular activities he happens to get involved in, and the like. There is also a special aspect of university life that enhances the chances that certain groups of students will be more likely to find satisfaction in intense political experience. Various studies suggest that mobility, particularly geographic mobility, where one becomes a stranger in an unfamiliar social context, is conducive to making individuals available for causes that invoke intense commitment. *Thus, new students, or recent transfers, are more likely to be politically active than others.* The various Berkeley studies emphasize this. Local students, or those relatively close to home are less likely to be active than those who are a considerable distance from their home communities. In Berkeley, Madison, and other university centers, the activists have come disproportionately from the ranks of the migrants.

Personality traits and activism

Some of the recent research by psychologists seeks to go beyond the analysis of factors which seem to have a direct impact on political choice. They have also sought to account for political orientation and degrees of involvement by examining personality traits. Thus, they have looked at such factors as variation in the way different groups of students have been reared by their parents, i.e., in a permissive or authoritarian atmosphere, as well as investigating family relationships, student intelligence, sociability, and the like. Such studies have reported interesting and relatively consistent differences between the minority of student activists and the rest of the student population. At the moment, however, these findings are unconvincing, in large part because the extant studies do not hold constant the sociological and politically relevant factors in the backgrounds of the students. For example, they report that leftist activists tend to be the offspring of permissive families as judged by child-rearing practices, and of families characterized by a strong mother who dominates family life and decisions. Conversely, conservative activists tend to come from families with more strict relationships between parents and children, and in which the father plays a dominant controlling role. But to a considerable extent these differences correspond to little more than the variations reported in studies of Jewish and Protestant families. Childhood rearing practices tend to be linked to social-cultural-political outlooks. To prove that such factors play an independent role in determining the political choices of students, it will first be necessary to compare students *within* similar ethnic, religious, and political-cultural environments. This has not yet been done.

But if we cannot conclude that the differences in the family structures of committed leftists and rightists are casually related to the side of the spectrum which they choose, that they have been reared differently should mean that they vary in their personality traits and consequent political styles. David Riesman has pointed out that conservative student activists seem to be afraid of the emotion of pity and compassion, that they find a concern for the "weak" threatening. Conversely, the leftists, more likely to have been raised in female-dominated families, are more prone to be open expressively toward "feminine" concerns.

Similarly, it should be noted that there is a special risk in drawing conclusions about the underlying psychological attitudes and behavior of the minority of deeply-committed activists from their responses to attitude surveys. It is often their ideologies rather than their true sentiments which are dictating the answers. Some years ago, a study by a psychologist of the members of the Italian Parliament found that the Communist deputies expressed more liberal attitudes on free speech and political toleration than did the adherents of the more moderate parties. In effect, the Communists were answering the questionnaire by simply checking off the party line on such matters. In considering the reliability of current research on activists, students or others, it is necessary to consider this possibility, that the attitudes expressed by the deeply-committed are more a function of their ideology than of their personal orientations as expressed in deeds. Those leftists who have demonstrated intolerance and other authoritarian behavior traits in practice may still give voice or pencil to liberal values in principle. Unfortunately, the research so far does not deal with this methodological problem, even though Edward Shils addressed similar queries to the conclusions drawn from the *Authoritarian Personality* studies of two decades ago.

In evaluating the growing body of research on the characteristics of leftist activists by psychologists, it is also important to note whether these activists are being compared with other activists or, as often is done, with data from the bulk of the student population, that is, the passive majority. Leftist activists should properly be compared with conservative activists, and with those involved in nonpolitical forms of campus activity. The limited efforts in these directions indicate that *some of the characteristics which have been identified as those of leftist activists, such as greater intelligence, characterize the involved generally. Both leftist and conservative activists, as well as moderates involved in student government, are drawn from the ranks of the academically talented in the United States.*

The quiet conservatives

Efforts that concentrate primarily on activists, in order to distinguish among the social and psychological traits of students of different political persuasions, also present special analytical problems inherent in the fact that whether students direct their extracurricular energies into politics is itself strongly linked to political orientations. Studies of student bodies in different countries indicate that those on the left generally (and the small group on the extreme right) view politics as an appropriate and even necessary university activity. Committed morally to the need for major social changes, leftists feel that the university should be an agency for social change, that both they and their professors should devote a considerable portion of their activities to politics. Conversely, however, the less leftist students are, the more likely they are to disagree with this view, the more prone they will be to feel that the university should be an apolitical "house of study." *Liberals and leftists, therefore, are much more likely to be politically active than moderates and conservatives.* A relatively strong conservative stance will *not* be reflected in membership or activity in a conservative political club. This means that, on any given campus, or in any country, the visible forms of student politics will suggest that the student population as a whole is more liberal or radical leftist than it actually is. Since conservative academic ideology fosters campus political passivity, one should not expect to find much conservative activity among students, and the absence of such activity need not signify the absence of a conservative temper among some, or perhaps many, students.

4

That "generation gap"

SAMUEL LUBELL

ONE of the more disquieting aspects of the much-advertised "generation gap" is our apparent inability to analyze, diagnose, and understand it.

Few phenomena have received more publicity and even study during the last four years than the new "youth generation." Still, all this attention has brought little public understanding.

The dominant impression left by the term "generation gap" is that of a unified younger generation that is breaking drastically from both its elders and society in almost every conceivable way. Actually, though, my interviewing over the last four years on how young people differ in their thinking from their parents suggests that (1) much more continuity than gap exists between the two generations; (2) parents have not been rendered obsolete but continue to exert an almost inradicable influence on their children; (3) we should have second thoughts about proposals to restructure and reform universities, if their purpose is to pacify student rebels.

Our findings — at the Opinion Reporting Workshop of Columbia's Graduate School of Journalism — indicate that the really important challenge to the universities is coming, not from agitations for "student power," but from pressures originating outside the campus, which may necessitate a new relationship of the universities to our society.

The frame of interviewing we employed was to ask students to compare themselves with their parents (or vice versa), how much they differed, how much alike they were. I had tested this approach in a survey of thirty-six college campuses for six months during fall 1965 and spring 1966. Our second study, undertaken with the aid of a Ford Foundation grant, sought to go further and develop effective techniques for measuring the differences between the generations as a pilot experiment in reporting the process of social change itself.

To most people, headlines of "Youth in Revolt" mean young people rebelling against established rules of authority. But in our interviewing we found both much less authority and much less rebellion than popularly imagined. Here are some of our findings:

Only about one in every ten students interviewed showed drastic changes from their parents.

A third of our sample reported no important differences from their parents, while another third revealed moderate changes.

More than three-fourths would vote for the same political party as their parents. Those shifting from the parties of their fathers do so primarily because of a different sense of self-interest.

In personal living — as with drug use and sexual relations — the new generation does differ markedly. Still, more than half the students interviewed would give their own children much the same upbringing as they themselves received.

A general weakening of religious feeling is underway. Only a fifth of the students reported that their parents were "not religious," but half of these same students said they themselves are "not religious." This suggests that within one generation the proportion of "not religious" may have been doubled, whereas the proportion of "very religious" has been cut in half.

Our interviewing also went into what such labels as "Communism," "patriotism," "liberalism," and "conservatism" meant.

On the meaning of "Communism," the overwhelming majority of students rejected the idea of a monolithic Communist world conspiracy and clearly wanted to differentiate between the Soviet Union and Red China.

Nearly three-fourths of those interviewed favored admitting Red China to the United Nations, whereas almost as many thought that the United States and Russia might become allies in a future war against China.

But on this point it might be emphasized that many adult Americans as well have abandoned the concept of Communism as a monolithic world force. A special study that I did for the Council on Foreign Relations in 1963 showed that 60 per cent of the adults interviewed felt that China was a bigger threat than Russia. Even then, nearly a third of those interviewed foresaw a United States-Russian alliance against Red China. Particularly intriguing were the responses given to questions on how Russia and China differed from

each other. With few exceptions the people interviewed attributed to
Red China all the traits they abhorred, while crediting Russia with
being "a mature, responsible" nation with "too much to lose to risk
war" and even "restrained by Christian ethics."

Lest such comments be ascribed to a lower educational level, I
should note that similar responses were given me last year by college
students. They also pinned onto Red China a chilling assortment of
voodoo traits even while declaring "Russia is getting more capitalis-
tic" or "their ideas are moving fairly close to our own."

The dangers of psychology

These and other findings suggest that in reporting change there is
a vital need for separation techniques, for methods of analysis that
make it possible to isolate one influence from many others. In the
matter of generational change, one must be able to determine when
the thinking of younger and older people really clash and when
both generations may be changing simultaneously, even if at different tempos.

A second need is to be able to distinguish between a break *from*
the past and a projection *of* the past, whether it is discontinuity or
continuity that we are observing.

Another vital need is to establish definable limits on psychological
interpretation. Our society seems to have developed a predilection,
even craze, for reading psychological explanations into anything
and everything that happens, moving as far toward this extreme as
Marxians once did in assigning an economic cause to anything and
everything. Certainly everything that happens to people has some
psychological impact, but this does not mean that every "psychological" explanation that is offered up is accurate or sound. At this
time of Freudian menopause, our society needs desperately to be
able to determine where a specific psychological influence ends and
other influences begin; also to measure and report the interplay of
the psychological with the nonpsychological.

The structure of interviewing and analysis that we employed was
specially designed to enable us to separate one influence from another. By asking young people how they differed from their parents
we had a basis for comparing the present with the past. How and
why one student changed — while others did not — provided a
disciplined means for tracing where one current of change ebbs and
another picks up, student by student, building up our patterns for
the whole sample. We did not seek interviews by the thousands. In
all we reached about 350 white collegians plus more than 100 Negro
students at twenty-eight campuses in fourteen states. The interviews, which ran an hour and more in length, ranged from upbringing, drug use, premarital sex and religious beliefs, to attitudes

toward the draft, the war and patriotism, career choices, political and economic thinking.

Our analysis rested not on computerized tables, but on sorting the interviews into batches, representing streams of feeling around specific items of change. At the close of each interview students were asked their names and addresses, which enabled us to reinterview some youths two and even three times.

Handled in this manner, the processes of social change emerge not as one engulfing flood, but as many streams and rivers, flowing at differing speeds — some sluggish, some rapid — and even in conflicting directions, reflecting the resistances or lack of resistances encountered on the way.

Five streams into the "New Left"

Consider, for example, those students who described themselves as members of "the New Left." From our interviews one could identify at least five distinct streams of feeling that feed into this "New Left."

1. Sizable numbers of "draft protesters."

2. "Career" rebels, who reject money-making pursuits in favor of "working with people and ideas" at universities or in public employment. Often these are the sons and daughters of businessmen.

3. The children of one-time socialists, Communists, and other radicals, perhaps the largest and certainly the most influential single "New Left" element.

4. Drug-using beatniks, relatively few in numbers.

5. "Christian Radicals," those who were strongly religious as children, but broke with their faith and who now project a near-missionary zeal into the belief that government can do what God has failed to do. Not overly numerous, they contribute a special weight of zeal and fervor.

Each of these five streams are carriers of differing social influences.

With the "draft protesters," for example, our interviews reveal little evidence of political radicalism until our involvement in Vietnam. Their base of support then broadens steadily as our Vietnam commitment deepens, and as efforts to reform the draft failed. Many of these draft protesters also talked of being solidified in their opposition to the war by the attitudes of other students.

In contrast, the sense of grievance that agitates the sons and daughters of one-time radicals does not originate in any current performance of society. They project the older attitudes of their parents. Often, while interviewing these self-professed radicals, one wonders whether they are accurately described as "rebels." Certainly they resent society; but most of them get along quite well with their parents. When asked how they would bring up their own children, many of these "radicals" reply, "Much the same way," often adding, "but I wouldn't be as protective as my parents were." Many of these "revolutionaries" may want to rip society apart, but they seem to have been almost model children.

With regard to these offspring of old leftists, one must ask whether any change in the university structure could appease their conditioning to be "agin" things. With the draft insurgents, the necessary reforms lie beyond the reach of the university. There is much justification, in fact, for regarding the "student revolts" as efforts to use the campus as staging areas to organize attacks on the government's war and draft policies — an assault in which the students usually have the sympathetic support of their fathers and mothers.

"Alienation"

Still another obstacle to understanding the "generation gap" is the practice of pinning a label such as "the alienated" upon the younger generation without determining what the label is supposed to mean. To some writers about "the revolt of the youth" the term "alienation" must be almost as satisfying as "Darkest Africa" has been to geographers and tourists, hinting of mysterious "happenings" and rituals that, since they are supposedly incomprehensible, it would do little good to investigate further.

Some perspective on the applicability of the concept of "alienation" may be gained from one part of our study that delved into the dynamics of change within the individual. Specifically, we sought to determine whether change within the individual takes the form of a chain reaction, with one break from parental ways triggering other breaks, or whether each item of change might move along on its own.

From our many questions, ten items were selected, some reflecting differences between the student and parents, others hostility toward more accepted beliefs of society. Instead of combining these ten items into a single index, we decided to group them into three linkages. For a student to be considered an example of chain reaction, his change from his parents or hostility toward society had to be evident in each of the three linkages.

The *first linkage* grouped religious feelings, pot smoking, and family upbringing, since we had found these three items tended to inter-react.

Linkage two covered which political party a student favored compared to the party preferred by his parents and how the student's career choice compared with the father's occupation.

Linkage three consisted of five items, which constituted a scale of intensity of opposition to the Vietnam War:

\# Whether the student supported or opposed the Vietnam War.

\# Is it right for the government to draft young men?

\# Should there be a voluntary army instead of the draft?

\# Should the definition of a conscientious objector be broadened to include exemption for a specific war?

\# Is patriotism important or not important?

In psychological terms, "alienation" implies a deep, pervasive mistrust and *general* divergence of the young person from his parents and society. Roughly 10 per cent of the students interviewed fitted the pattern of a *general* break that extended through all three linkages. An intensive analysis of this batch of interviews, one by one, raised doubts that their sense of "alienation" could be accurately attributed to pressures originating on the campus. In more than half of the cases, these students told of in-family rebellions and psychological difficulties that were quite advanced by the time they were thirteen, fourteen, or fifteen years old.

Most of this group, in short, were predisposed to psychological self-conflict before they reached college. Although the university structure may have aggravated their difficulties, it can hardly be singled out as the generating cause.

Much has been written about college students being "alienated" by a lost sense of identity, reflecting the fact that professors preoccupied with research leave the teaching to youthful assistants, or that students resent being treated as IBM cards instead of warm bodies, or that the sheer size of these institutions shrinks the individual, and so on. These and other practices may well need reforming. But there is little evidence in our interviews that they have been particularly damaging to student psyches, or that they are the cause of student troubles.

More important, our interviews indicate the kind of family upbringing the student brings to college with him or her. In analyzing why some students use drugs whereas others on the same campus do not, one is struck by the fact that almost any restraint that parents implant in their sons or daughters hangs on, affecting their behavior. This is what the students themselves feel and say in their interviews. One also notes significant group differences, with Catholic students displaying more self-discipline, more religious belief, and less drug use than Jewish or Protestant students.

Parents, in other words, do count quite heavily. But a strict childhood upbringing no longer seems the norm among college-going families. Only a fifth of the students interviewed reported having had a strict upbringing. Nearly half described their parents as "not religious" or "not very religious."

In different directions

The diversity of student behavior should not be underestimated; nor does it follow that where a young person is undergoing several changes from parental ways at the same time, that they necessarily move in the identical direction.

For example:

Nearly all of the Catholic students from Democratic families who are turning Republican are also becoming much less religious than their parents were. These students would also give their own children a much freer upbringing than they themselves experienced. Becoming more conservative politically, in other words, does *not* mean a person need become more conservative in other attitudes. Partly this reflects the general weakening of religious feeling that is going on; but we need also to be sensitive to the fact that such labels as "liberal" and "conservative," along with indices built up on the basis of *past* findings, can be rendered invalid by the processes of change. Perhaps it would be wiser to employ less ideological and more neutral labels.

On this score, we can point to at least one dramatic shift that has taken place in only two or three years. In my first survey of college students, completed early in 1966, almost every student who smoked marijuana was "liberal" politically. In our second survey, completed in May 1968, fair numbers of pot-users described themselves as conservative politically, even to being supporters of Barry Goldwater and William Buckley. Nearly a third of the students from Democratic families who were *turning Republican* had smoked or still smoke marijuana. Thus, pot-smoking has acquired a new social acceptability which did not exist even two years ago.

The importance of career choice

But perhaps our most important single finding is the quite high correlation between a student's choice of career and his political identification. In my 1965–1966 survey, I found that, at the same schools, students from Democratic families who were moving into business-oriented careers tended to turn Republican, whereas sons of Republicans who were moving into the public sector of the economy (such as university teaching or federal employment) tended to shift to the Democratic party. Our second survey tested this correlation anew and found again that it applied with predictable consistency.

Within the new generation, this conflict of economic identification between those who look to the public purse and those who look to the private purse seems to be the major political divider.

If this relationship — that choice of career is the carrier of economic interest and identification with the future — held true in the past, as I suspect it did, it could serve as a basis for re-interpreting much of history. The emergence of new careers and new occupations in the past must have generated new social and political conflicts. It would be intriguing to reappraise political history in these terms.

We also would do well to apply the career-carrier concept to the transformation our own society is now undergoing and to analyze more systematically the multiple effects of the abrupt increase during recent years in the sheer numbers of young people reaching high school and college age. It would have been a miracle if places could have been found for all of these millions of youths inside the established occupational structure. As it is, even with the rapid economic growth of recent years, sizable numbers of youngsters remain outside the older occupational structure. *This fact may well be the most critical single factor making for a "generation gap" in American society today.*

We might well ask: can organic unity be restored to American society *before* our occupational structure has been altered to absorb the younger half of our population? The impact of these record numbers of youngsters has been particularly heavy, of course, on Negro slum areas and on our universities.

Among middle-class youths, a combination of influences is generating more career ferment than we have ever experienced, at least in modern times. Only a minority of youths think of following in their fathers' career-steps. Often, as with the sons of farmers, it has become technologically impossible. For many other students, the relative affluence of their parents permits a far wider career choice than would have been possible if the whip of poverty had still to be obeyed. Often the attractions of "working with people" seem more meaningful than "just making money."

The draft

Then, of course, there has been the threat of the draft that has caused so many students to stay on in school, distorting their vocational choices and postponing their entry into the world outside the university sanctuary. The failure to change the draft law has been a truly tragic inaction of the government — one which, as long as it is persisted in, will remain a major disturber of the social peace.

Since 1965, this country has had a surplus of draft-age manpower, far in excess of any military need. As against the million youths who reached the age of eighteen each year during the Korean War, the number of new eighteen-year-olds is now running close to 2 million a year. This manpower surplus will continue well into the 1970's and would become even higher if the Vietnam War is ended.

Under the present draft procedures, these extra millions of youths are kept in needless uncertainty as to their careers from their eighteenth to twenty-sixth birthday. Any of several lottery plans could minimize this needless uncertainty and help narrow the gap between our universities and the rest of society.

University renewal?

In conclusion — I shy from employing the phrase "to sum up," since I am aware of too many significant aspects of the "generation gap" that have not been touched upon in this article — I might make the following point:

First, my own analysis of the many forces involved leads me to feel that the crux of our "generation gap" will be found in the career problems — the drive and lack of drives — of the record numbers of young people. The demand for "student power" is not the really critical issue for restructuring our universities. The pressures that should not be ignored in reforming our universities are those which arise out of the expanding career needs of this numerous generation.

What should be avoided is proposals for university renewal which, as with urban renewal, simply tear down what exists to put up something new without meeting the real human needs of the students and the new relationship that has become necessary between the university and the outside society.

5

Columbia
and
the New Left

DANIEL BELL

THE "siege," "insurrection," "re-
bellion" at Columbia — all these terms are extravagant, yet it is hard
to find one which is apt — has been characterized by the Students
for a Democratic Society (SDS) as a spontaneous protest by the
student body, or a substantial portion of it, against the "complicity"
of the university in the war, and against the "institutional racism" of
the university in the neighborhood; they explain the scope and intensity of the events by the extent to which the university was guilty
of these charges. The administration itself attributes these events
to the organized efforts of a small cadre of the SDS that was able,
successfully, to manipulate a larger body of students who had been
politically disoriented by the war in Vietnam. Some observers, noting
that the events at Columbia were almost simultaneous with student
agitation in Berlin and Paris and Milan, have talked of a "world-wide"
movement of students against "bureaucratic" society.

The first interpretation I regard as an untruth, the second as a
half truth, and the third I regard as possibly true, but too gross an
explanation to account for the particularities. What is striking about
any social situation that is examined in detail is how complex all the
circumstances are, and while one risks losing an over-all configura-
tion in the patient effort to sort out the details, the effort to find
meaning — in sociology as in language — has to begin with the
simplest description of what happened. This is especially true in
the case of Columbia, for if one looks at the background — the years,
say, from 1966 to 1968 — the events which exploded in April and

May are, at first glance, largely inexplicable. It is easy, of course, since history is always written after the fact, to give some apparently plausible account of "the causes" and "the determining factors," and these tend to give an air of inevitability to the sequences. But as I have studied this history, and reflected on my own participation in it, I find the "outbreak," "uprising," "revolution" — none of these words is adequate — extremely puzzling. In this essay, I have attempted an answer, but even now I am not entirely sure it is adequate. I have tried to reconstruct the salient events — and the reader will have to be patient with the many details if he wants to follow "history" — and then to provide a commentary and some personal judgments. Even so, I have restricted myself to a single dimension, the relation between students and the administration, in order to highlight, and necessarily in chiaroscuro, the extraordinary change in moral temper that took place on campus in the seven days at the end of April. To this extent, the account neglects many important secondary factors, particularly in the actions of the faculty and the trustees, in this effort to follow the thread of student behavior. On another occasion, I hope to relate the Columbia events — more specifically the phenomenon of the New Left — to some broader historical and sociological contexts.

Microcosm I — the events

On April 19, 1968, Columbia College — or, at least, the Committee on Instruction, which is the policy-making body of the college — had cause for self-congratulation. The end of the term was little more than three weeks away and seemingly Columbia had escaped the "confrontations" that had wracked so many other schools during the year. The "big issue" of the year at Columbia — each school year had a single major issue — had been campus recruitment by representatives of the Dow Chemical Company and the military, and Columbia had been prudent if not sure-footed on the question. For example, when military recruiters were due to appear on campus at the end of October, the Committee on Instruction had voted to postpone all such activities until a college-wide policy had been worked out by the faculty. A poll was conducted by the *Spectator*, the student newspaper, in which 2,750 students voted; it showed 67.6 per cent in favor of completely open recruitment, 14.3 per cent opposed to all recruitment, and 18.1 per cent selectively opposed, most of them singling out the military as the group to be barred. Finally, a faculty committee headed by Professor Allan Silver wrote a long, thoughtful report that reaffirmed the principle of "institutional neutrality," and called for open recruitment on campus.[1] Yet

---

[1] Anticipating the possibility of student obstruction, despite the faculty recom-

when General Hershey recommended to draft boards that they induct young men obstructing recruitment, the Committee on Instruction voted to postpone all military recruitment visits until this procedure could be clarified; and such visits were duly postponed until White House Assistant Joseph Califano, in response to a letter from President Kirk and several other university presidents, disavowed the Hershey statement.

The demonstrations had gone without incident. Military recruiters arrived on campus, and although they were picketed, and a pie was thrown, not many students had turned out. The Dow Chemical recruiting had come to nothing — only a few students signed up for an interview, then withdrew their names — and the Dow recruiter, though he made one appearance on campus, came and went quietly.

In short, the college was being sensitive to and responsive to possibly inflammatory situations. The year before, again on the initiative of the faculty, the college had voted — it was the first major school in the country to do so — to discontinue both the ranking of students and the release of student grades to draft boards. There were moves to widen student participation in the college and reduce some of the academic pressures on students. On the initiative of David Truman, when he was still dean of the college, two students were invited, for the first time, to sit in as consultative members of the Committee on Instruction. Truman himself had spent considerable time appearing at free-for-all "bull sessions" in the dormitories and had acquired an enormous popularity in the college for his responsiveness to students. A "pass-fail" option had been introduced so that students could take one course a term without a letter grade, thus encouraging them to attend classes that interested them without the risk of receiving a low grade because the subject was far from their major area of competence. During the spring term of this year, a full day was set aside, with the agreement of the college, for seminars and talks by various authorities about the impact of the new draft regulations, and there was a full and honest discussion of the consequences of resistance, and even of exiling oneself to Canada.

There was also the issue of the gymnasium. Columbia University was planning to build an $11 million gymnasium on two acres of Morningside Park, a project first proposed by the city in 1959, but which had been delayed for lack of funds. In the past year some

mendations, the Silver Committee stated: "We have, as a practical matter, inquired into administrative arrangements at the University in connection with the prospect of obstruction, disorder or violence among students in these contexts. Your committee believes these arrangements to be eminently sensible, reasonable and prudent. They call for the invoking of disciplinary sanctions — such as warning, probation and suspension—in the case of students who deliberately obstruct University activities or who physically attack other students. We recognize that penalties such as these are not trivial. . . . We agree, however, that in view of the gravity of these offenses, such sanctions are appropriate and should be applied."

people had expressed doubts about unilateral control of the gymnasium by Columbia, and there had been negotiations in an attempt to widen the area of community facilities in the gym. But the public — and the college — remained apathetic. A poll of the neighborhood by the Columbia *Spectator* on November 21, 1967, revealed that almost half of "the community" bordering the eastern part of Morningside Park (i.e., in Harlem) had not even heard about the gym, and among those who had, 56 per cent favored its construction. At a faculty meeting, a motion to discuss the gymnasium aroused so little interest that it was not even seconded, and a report in the spring by a faculty committee on civil rights, which had raised some questions about the propriety of the gymnasium, received scant attention. The Columbia faculty, by and large, was little concerned with neighborhood issues, except for those living on Morningside Drive facing Morningside Park. This group felt a strong apprehension, often discussed in the meeting of the Committee on Instruction, about the fact that muggings and thefts, largely unreported, increased alarmingly when the gates of the park were opened to Harlem, after being closed for years. It was hoped that the presence of the new gymnasium, with many students moving back and forth, would reduce crime in the area. When the first construction cranes appeared on the park site in March 1967, some Harlem groups called for sit-downs and the blocking of construction. Yet only one or two demonstrations materialized, and only a handful of opponents of the gymnasium turned up.

In sum, the situation at Columbia had *not* been going from bad to worse, and it is this record of seeming progress which makes the subsequent events of April and May all the more incomprehensible.

Enter Mark Rudd

Toward the end of term, one new factor did appear. Traditionally, about three-quarters of the way through the spring term, student organizations elect new officers for the coming year. The *Spectator* had changed editors. The student radio station, WKCR, had changed officers. So had the Students for a Democratic Society. In the SDS elections, the old administration of Ted Kaptchuk had been attacked violently by a group of young Turks — or, rather, young Maos and young Ché Guevaras — for having conducted only peaceful demonstrations and for having limited its activity to "building a base" on campus. What was now needed, the group opposing Kaptchuk claimed, was the thrust of guerrilla fighters who would see to it that the campus seethed with continual confrontations. On this platform, in early April, the SDS elected a hitherto unknown student, Mark Rudd, as president.

Mark Rudd, a junior, is a tall, hulking, slack-faced young man with a prognathic jaw and blue-gray eyes so translucent that his gaze seems hypnotic. Rudd's father, born Rudnitzky, had mild left-wing sympathies before World War II, then joined the army, found it a place for a congenial career, served long enough to become a lieutenant colonel and to retire on a pension, and subsequently became a real-estate agent in New Jersey. The first stirrings of radicalism in Mark Rudd himself, according to his mother, occurred during his boyhood visits to his grandmother's candy store in the Newark slums. His high-school record was good, and he applied to Harvard, which rejected him. Columbia, which accepted him, was his second choice. At Columbia he was virtually unknown on campus until he was elected president of SDS and, at about the same time, published a series of articles in the student newspaper entitled "The Cuba I Saw," reporting on a youth convention he attended in Havana earlier that term. In the articles Rudd acclaimed the progress he had observed in Cuba; as an example of the new spirit under Castro, he quoted an aging bellboy at his hotel who told Rudd that he felt he "owned" the hotel. What bellboy in an American hotel, Rudd wrote, would ever make such a remark? As part of his platform for election, Rudd wrote a "Position Paper on Strategy for the Rest of the School Year — Complicity," in which he said that the goals of SDS now had to be: "The radicalization of students . . . showing them how our lives really are unfree in this society and at Columbia, getting them to act . . . and striking a blow at the Federal Government's war effort." He concluded: "Let us clearly state that our goal is to end the university complicity with the war."

On Monday, April 22, SDS called for a demonstration the next day at the sundial, which is at the center of the university campus, on the issues of the universities' ties with the Institute of Defense Analysis (IDA) and the suspension of six students who had conducted an indoor demonstration on March 27 in Low Library, the administration building, in violation of a published university rule. That same day, SDS issued an eight-page newspaper, as a rallying call for the demonstration, called *Up Against the Wall,* and the dateline read: "April 22, 1968 — The Year of the Heroic Guerrilla." One entire page was devoted to two woodcuts of Ché Guevara speaking at mass meetings, with the caption: "The Duty of Every Revolutionary Is to Make the Revolution." The lead article was an open letter to President Kirk from Rudd, headlined "Reply to Uncle Grayson." It was a reply to a speech Kirk made in Charlottesville, Virginia, on April 12, 1968, in which Kirk expressed concern about the "turbulent and inchoate nihilism whose sole objectives are destruction," which had seized young people "in disturbing number." (In this same speech, though SDS did not mention it, Kirk said he wanted to reduce the American involvement in Vietnam.) Rudd threw down the gauntlet to "Uncle Grayson": "Your cry of nihilism represents your inability to understand our positive values," and Rudd concluded: "There is only one thing left to say. It may sound nihilistic to you, since it is the opening shot in a war of liberation. I'll use the words of Leroi Jones, whom I'm sure you don't like a whole lot: 'Up Against the Wall, motherfucker, this is a stick-up.' Yours for freedom, Mark."

Two issues and their background

In all eight pages of the SDS newspaper there was not a word about the gymnasium. The agitational cry was "Protest the IDA and University Repression," and those two issues alone, being quite complicated, seemed to offer little promise for rousing the students; certainly they did not seem to carry the emotional appeal of Dow Chemical. Nor were these new issues. Behind each of them there was a long, involved history of discussion on campus.

On September 27, 1967, at the beginning of the fall term, President Kirk had unilaterally issued a policy statement forbidding demonstrations within any university building. The reason for the ban was not ideological but utilitarian. In the previous year, members of SDS had clashed with athletes and other students during a demonstration inside a student hall, and it was pure luck that there had been no injuries. The university placement office is on the sixth floor of Dodge Hall, which has narrow corridors, and the administration was afraid that any picketing or demonstration against outside recruiters using those offices would lead to violence. Hence the ban. On three occasions during the year, SDS groups had nevertheless held small demonstrations inside some buildings, mostly against recruiting; but the administration prudently chose to ignore them. On March 27, Rudd, as the new head of SDS, announced that an indoor demonstration would be held in Low Library to present a petition to the administration against the university's affiliation with IDA. Using bullhorns, which had also been forbidden, Rudd and about a hundred SDS members rampaged through the corridors, but both President Kirk and Vice President Truman refused to meet with them.[2]

Some weeks after this demonstration, five students in the college were asked to report to the dean's office on April 22 on the charge of

---

[2] A characteristic distortion of the incident was presented by *Ramparts,* whose account was widely distributed on the campus: "Grayson Kirk's ban on student demonstrations inside campus buildings was so sweeping that it prevented candidates for student office from collecting signatures in their dormitories. It was assumed that the rule, hastily enacted a few months ago, would only be used to outlaw unruly demonstrations. Therefore, Columbia students were amazed when Kirk employed the ban to put on probation six students out of a group of 200 who showed up at his office one day with a petition bearing the names of ten percent of the student body."

violating the ban on indoor demonstrating; they were told that they could request a formal hearing or respond in any other way. All five chose not to respond at all, and they were placed on disciplinary probation for the remainder of the spring term. (The sixth student was a graduate student.) Instead, the SDS called for a demonstration in Low Library for April 23 to protest these suspensions. Why the administration waited so long to take this action is unclear. Most likely it hoped that the issue could in some way be avoided. On April 12, for example, Dean Platt, the dean of students, proposed a meeting of three SDS leaders with President Kirk to discuss the ban on demonstrations and the IDA connection. The SDS leaders flatly refused to meet with President Kirk. Later, student groups accused the administration of "entrapment" by not acting on the earlier infractions and thus giving the students the illusion that any violation of the ban would go unpunished. In actual fact, the administration had been indecisive and unwilling to be punitive. This was the extent of "university repression."

The IDA

The Institute of Defense Analysis had been picked by SDS, at its national convention, as a symbol of the universities' complicity in the Vietnam War, and a national campaign had been underway all year. IDA was formed in 1955 as an effort of the Defense Department's Weapons System Evaluating Group, to enlist the help of scientists in weapons evaluation. Like many government agencies, defense had been unable to build an adequate "in-house" staff because of the reluctance of independent-minded scientists to work either in uniform or in government laboratories. The RAND Corporation, which was set up originally by the Air Force, was a successful demonstration of the possibility of recruiting top-flight brains for work on defense projects, under appropriate conditions. IDA was a similar effort on the part of the Pentagon's research arm to set up a nonprofit corporation. At first five, and subsequently twelve, universities were invited to become members of the consortium to administer IDA, as a means of guaranteeing academic independence for researchers. Columbia was an institutional affiliate, along with MIT, Chicago, Princeton, Stanford, Berkeley, Case, and others. Grayson Kirk, as president of Columbia, and William Burden, a trustee, sat on the board.

At Columbia, the ties with IDA had stirred no interest on campus. Nor was there any significant participation by the university in IDA projects. Yet the SDS sought to imply otherwise. A year earlier, a number of students and faculty met with Ralph Halford, then the dean of the graduate faculties, to question him about the university's contract obligations to defense agencies. The meeting, a public one, was held in the rotunda of Low Library. Halford stated that the university had no contract obligations with IDA. He was asked about Kirk's status on the board of IDA, and he answered that Kirk was present as an individual but that Columbia had no institutional affiliation with IDA. Halford had in mind his own status as a trustee of Associated Universities, Inc. (the Atomic Energy Commission laboratory at Brookhaven), and he assumed that Kirk's status at IDA was the same. When he learned that this was not so, he soon corrected himself. But the following year SDS repeatedly asserted that "University officials had lied" to the students about the university's tie with IDA.

There was also the Electronics Research Laboratory that had conducted defense research. This unit was set up by Professor Lawrence O'Neill, of the Engineering School; under contract with the Defense Department, it had expanded considerably. The ERL conducted research for the Advanced Projects Research Agency of the Defense Department on classified radar design, not weapons, called "Project Defender." But the university had become unhappy about the scope of ERL. In the previous decade and a half, much of the nation's defense systems planning had been tied into university research laboratories, such as the Jet Propulsion Lab at Cal Tech, or the Lincoln Lab and MITRE (MIT Research and Engineering). Increasingly, too, universities were discovering that the administration of laboratories not connected with basic research was becoming more of a liability than a help to a campus. (For one thing, researchers at these labs often demanded faculty status, and this created conflicts with established departments.) As a consequence, MIT had divested itself of MITRE, which had then been set up as an independent nonprofit corporation. For the same reason, Columbia in 1967–1968 decided to divest itself of the Electronics Research Lab, which was reorganized as the Riverside Research Institute, an independent nonprofit corporation. Because IDA also did some research work on "Project Defender," SDS tried to tie the Electronics Research Lab to the symbol it had created of IDA.

As for IDA itself, a number of individual faculty members — principally four physicists, Henry Foley, Leon Lederman, I. I. Rabi, and adjunct professor Richard Garwin — maintained membership in the IDA's "Jason Division," an effort by IDA to acquaint the nation's outstanding physicists with advanced research problems in order to solicit their advice. The university was originally affiliated institutionally, but after the issue was raised by the students, Columbia, as a corporation, severed its ties with IDA. Kirk and Burden retained their seats on the IDA board as individuals — a move later attacked by SDS as a sneaky device. In a sense it was: since the institutional affiliation of Columbia was largely symbolic, Kirk's membership retained something of the symbolism. But a different change was in the offing. In its report on military recruitment and university policy, the Silver Committee had proposed that the university set up a committee to investigate all institutional ties of the university with the defense agencies. President Kirk then named Louis Henkin, Hamilton Fish Professor of Constitutional Law and a respected faculty member, to head such a committee, which would formulate university policy on all such affiliations, including IDA.

To this extent the university, in its slow and lumbering way, was beginning to scrutinize all these issues. But this fact was almost entirely ignored by the SDS, which repeatedly demanded that the university "end" its ties with IDA. And this became the chief substantive issue of the demonstration which erupted into the Columbia insurrection.

Storming "The Bastille"

The Students for a Democratic Society had called a rally at the sundial for noon on Tuesday, April 23. There had been a desultory meeting the night before, attended by about 100 students, in which the main theme had to do with breaking the ban on indoor demonstrations by going into Low Library. It was also announced that the question of the gymnasium, even though construction had already begun, was being added to the list of grievances in order to indict Columbia's policy of "institutional racism."

At noon, on Tuesday, the rally began. Various speakers denounced the university for "complicity" in the war. They demanded the reinstatement of the six students who had been put on probation. To the delight of the crowd, a representative of the Students' Afro-American Society mounted the sundial and denounced the university for proceeding with the construction of the gym against the wishes of the "Harlem community." At this point a letter from Vice President Truman was read to the crowd, which by now numbered about 500 demonstrators and listeners. In the letter, Truman declared that, since it was the intention of SDS to conduct a demonstration inside Low Library, and a large crowd of students would constitute a hazard, Low Library was being locked. He offered to meet with the students "immediately" in the McMillin theater on campus, if they wished to do so. The *Spectator* reported the ensuing events thus:

> At first, SDS and SAS leaders were divided over how they should respond to Dr. Truman's offer. However, after an extended debate behind the sundial, Rudd informed Dean Platt that he would agree to move the demonstration into McMillin only if Dr. Truman would allow the protestors to set the ground rules of the meeting.
>
> Rudd asked that Dr. Truman permit a student to chair the meeting and to allow the student audience to decide the case of the six disciplined students as a "popular tribunal."

Dean Platt stated that he could not commit Dr. Truman to any ground rules prior to the meeting, but the dean suggested to Rudd that he ask Dr. Truman to allow the students to set down certain conditions once the demonstrators are inside McMillin.

"Dr. Truman gives us this alternative because he is a very liberal man," Rudd told the crowd. "After we've gone up to the son-of-a-bitch a million times before with our demands, he has refused to discuss them, and now he decided to meet with us," Rudd added.

At this, the crowd howled down the invitation and began marching up the steps of Low Library. At Low, a group of about 100 counterdemonstrators were massed to block entry. After a slight scuffle, the crowd tried to storm a side entrance that was maintained by security guards, and they were again repulsed. The SDS crowd marched back to the sundial and, after some debate among the leaders, marched off to hold a demonstration at the gym site on Morningside Drive and 112th Street, about a quarter of a mile away. At the gym, a chain fence was torn down, some policemen were assaulted, and finally the crowd fell back, though one of the protestors was seized by the police and arrested. Back at the dial — it was now two and a half hours after the start of the demonstration — the crowd again milled around, and various suggestions were shouted. Clearly, neither Rudd nor any of the SDS leaders had a specific tactical plan; at that point the demonstration could just as easily have dispersed as gone forward. At that moment, someone in the crowd shouted that since the original intention was to hold a demonstration *inside* a building, the crowd ought to go inside Hamilton Hall, the college building. Someone else shouted that since the police had seized one of the students, the crowd itself ought to take a hostage. They surged toward Hamilton Hall. Within a few minutes, the acting dean of the college, Henry Coleman, who had just entered the building, was pinioned by some students and told that he could not leave until the administration met their demands. Coleman said that he would not negotiate under coercion, and walked into his office. The students sat down and the siege was underway.

At that point, and well into the evening, the students' aim was simply to sit in. Classes had not been disturbed. Professors went to their offices. The building was still open. In the early hours of the morning, the first fateful steps that transformed the demonstration from a sit-in to a siege and from a siege to an insurrection were taken — not by the SDS, but by the blacks.

Enter the blacks

During the early evening, a prolonged debate about their next tactical moves had taken place among the demonstrators. Some students wanted to barricade the building, others felt that such tactics would merely alienate the rest of the student body. A vote was taken, and the barricade resolution lost. At that point, the black caucus stepped in. Only about half of these blacks were connected with Columbia. Some came from other colleges, quite a few were from the Harlem branch of CORE, and others came from SNCC and from Charles Kenyatta's "Mau Mau" group. They stated that they were going to barricade Hamilton Hall and keep it that way until construction of the gym was halted. If the white students wanted to stay they could, but only by accepting the leadership of the blacks. Many of the white students were outraged. Rudd himself was shocked and open-mouthed. Again there was a debate, this time involving Tom Hayden, one of the founders of SDS, who had come to Hamilton Hall in the early part of the evening and was acting as a "counselor" to SDS. Hayden advised them to accept the leadership of the blacks. But now the black caucus had made its own ultimatum: The whites would have to get out. One black leader was quoted as saying: "The whites would vacillate and panic, and we felt they could not be depended upon."

The action by the blacks was the *first turning point* of the Columbia insurrection, and its effect was threefold. First, it made the gymnasium — and the cry of "institutional racism" — the central issue on campus. Now the issue of the gym was "legitimate." As one of the black student leaders remarked afterward:

> We didn't care if the majority of Harlem wanted the gym; they were wrong. We have to build a sense of black community and we didn't want Columbia crossing the line, even if it was providing some facilities for the community. Harlem has to control its own actions.

Second, the black stand on the gym embarrassed the administration. For the past two years, Columbia had energetically sought to attract black students to the university. A black man had been named assistant director of admissions. The college itself now had about eighty black students, as against five only a few years ago. A large number of them were on scholarship and special aid. Now, in their first organized political action, they were separating themselves, symbolically and literally, from Columbia, and declaring themselves to be, primarily, the representatives of the "community" *to* Columbia. And, in addition, there was the ominous threat, whose magnitude nobody knew, that if any police action were taken against the blacks in Hamilton, "Harlem" might march onto the campus and, as the idea was repeatedly expressed, "burn it down."

Third, there was the tangible fact that by their determination and discipline the blacks had provided a model of action for the white students, many of whom were still playing in the doll's house of revolution. ("Some of those black guys were willing to die," one white boy said. "That really frightened me. It made me wonder how far I'd go. They certainly have more guts than we do.") The fact that the blacks were uninterested in the larger political issues underlying the original SDS demands, and more importantly (as became clear only later) that they differed sharply with SDS about their attitudes to Columbia ("The SDS seized a building in order to wreck the university," a black leader remarked later. "We retained a building in order to gain some power in the university"), did not become apparent at the start. What mattered at the time was that the blacks had "acted." Given the touchiness, fear, sensitivity, and guilt about the blacks that is so predominant in liberal society, their action provided a guise of legitimacy for the extreme tactic of uncivil disobedience.[3]

Into Kirk's office

The white students were now perplexed. "They got out and congregated around the sundial, waiting for somebody to decide what to do," Jon Shils recalled to an interviewer from *The Washington Post*.

> "I remember telling Mark that if he didn't pick the demonstration up somewhere else, he was through at Columbia. . . . Somebody suggested that we go around pulling fire alarms; somebody else said we should take Low Library. Somebody got a bullhorn, so they went up to Low Library, broke through the door, rushed the security people and went into Kirk's office. There must have been 130 people.

The students entered the outer rooms of the President's four-room suite early Wednesday morning. One of the participants, writing in *New York* magazine under the pseudonym Simon James, recreated the subsequent events thus:

> "We expect the cops to come any moment. . . At about 8:30 A.M. we heard that the cops are coming. One hundred and seventy-three people jump out of the window. . . . That leaves 27 of us sitting on the floor, waiting to be arrested. In stroll an inspector and two cops. We link arms and grit our teeth. After about five minutes of gritting our teeth it dawns on us that the cops aren't doing anything. . . . they tell us they have neither the desire nor the orders to arrest us.

The police entered Grayson Kirk's inner office to remove a Rembrandt, valued at $450,000 and a television set.

Even then the students did not have a long occupation in mind. As Simon James tells it:

[3] An added factor, revealed initially by SDS students who had been in Hamilton, was the rumor that a number of the blacks had guns and were prepared to use them.

> Enter Mark Rudd, through the window. He says that 27 people cannot exert any pressure, and the best thing we could do is leave and join a big sit-in in front of Hamilton. We say no, we're not leaving. . . . Rudd goes out and comes back again and asks us to leave again, and we say no again. He leaves to get reinforcements.

Buoyed up by the decision to stay, a number of students decided to search Kirk's files for material about IDA and on the gymnasium. As an account in *Ramparts* tells it:

> They knew that the fourth room, Kirk's personal office, was likely to harbor documents elucidating these matters. And after some debate, a small group — which called itself "the radical caucus" and did not put its action to a vote — broke into it. They did indeed find evidence. . . .

All day Wednesday, the campus seethed with rumors of impending police action and of Harlem militants marching onto the campus. In a special session of the college faculty early that afternoon, the right to protest was overwhelmingly endorsed, but the use of coercion was condemned. The faculty also voted against giving amnesty to the protestors, proposed the creation of a tripartite faculty-student-administration body to deal with disciplinary affairs, and recommended immediate suspension of work at the gymnasium site. It also declared that "we believe that any differences have to be settled peacefully and we trust that police action will not be used to clear university buildings." The purpose of that resolution was to begin negotiation and to encourage the students to leave the buildings.[4]

Because of the fear of outside intervention — by Harlem residents and by radical groups in the city who were mobilizing that week for a city-wide peace march — the university called on the police to seal off the campus and thus close all the buildings. Early Wednesday evening, students of the School of Architecture refused to leave their building, Avery Hall, and later that night fifty graduate students decided to occupy Fayerweather, the social-science graduate building. When a large group of counterdemonstrators tried to oust them, they set up barricades at the two front doors. Thursday morning, a group from Low Library, largely Maoist in their political stand, decided to seize a building for their very own and moved over to Mathematics, where, according to the ubiquitous Simon James, "We are joined by 20 radicals who couldn't stand establishment liberal Fayerweather any longer. We get inside and immediately pile up around 2000 pounds of furniture at the front door."

Thus, within three days, in a series of unplanned and often accidental events, five buildings were occupied and Columbia was on the

---

[4] The writer of this article was the author of the faculty resolution.

historical map of student revolutions. The significance of all this
was not in the number of demonstrators involved — in the first three
days there were not more than 250 people in the buildings, about
50 of whom were outsiders — but in the *double* nature of the
actions: tactically, the student actions had "leaped" five years, by
adopting the latest methods of the civil-rights and peace movement,
which had passed, in "five hot summers," from protest to confrontation to resistance and to outright obstruction; even more startling,
the university as a general institution, itself, was now regarded as
the enemy, the target for disruption.

This attitude was all the more paradoxical in that, over the past
eight years, universities provided an arena for radical action, and in
some instances even a sanctuary. The universities in the previous
five years had been the initiating center for the peace movement:
the teach-ins had begun in the universities, most of the antiwar
pressure had come from the universities (at Columbia, Vice President Truman was one of a small group of distinguished professors
who, for more than a year, had tried to influence the White House
against the escalation of the war and to halt the bombings), and
most of the draft resistance found its source in the university. But
now the radical students sought to identify the university as the
"intersect" of the corporate and military worlds; to ignore all other
aspects of university life, particularly scholarship and learning; in
fact, to tear it down. However accidentally the events occurred, the
intentions to disrupt and the continual efforts to exploit situations
that would lead to extreme action, were there. If not in April 1968
at Columbia, it might have happened the following year; if not at
Columbia, then at some other university. The point is that little in
the Columbia situation per se provided the basis for the "rebellion."
The decisive fact lay in the changed character of left-wing student
intentions and tactics, and in the responsiveness in the substantial
minority they were able to influence.[5]

---

[5] At this point it is useful to cite the testimony given to the Cox Committee,
which has been inquiring into the events at Columbia, by Christopher Friedrichs, editor of the *Spectator* from March 1967 to March 1968 and one of the
most thoughtful observers on campus. In his testimony, Mr. Friedrichs stated
that prior to April 23, the Columbia campus was *not* on the brink of revolution; large numbers of students, although they had grievances, were essentially satisfied with the existing institution (or satisfied to the extent that they
never would have contemplated becoming involved in the extreme disruptions
that occurred). Mr. Friedrichs argued that the events that occurred between
the afternoon of Tuesday, April 23, and Wednesday, April 24, were the
critical elements that turned the situation into a full-scale crisis. He further
argued that had decisive action been taken by the administration any time
in this period, the entire crisis would have been averted. In his view, the administration's failure to call the police was crucial. He stressed his belief
that police action, at least against students in Kirk's office, would have been
widely viewed as "appropriate, if not inevitable," and that the Hamilton Hall
situation could have been dealt with separately because it was, in fact, a

A moment suspended in time

For the next five days, the world shrank to the dimensions of Columbia. Time seemed suspended, and for the students inside the buildings, cut off from the campus and living in a siege atmosphere, "reality" took on an intensity they had never known before. There was the shared sense of danger as rumors about police action spread, and each demonstrator wondered whether he would be man enough to "take it" when the time came. Emancipated from many of the psychological restraints and taboos of customary life, the students began to poke around freely within previously closed-off premises.[6] There was the intense, frenetic discussion of ideas, strategies, and tactics, in which words become all-important, for the right words would magically transform the situation into victory. Negotiations with famous professors were conducted on the level of equality and, in some cases, of triumphant insult (as when Mark Rudd told an audience of two hundred faculty members that their conciliatory efforts were just "bull shit"). Emotions were lifted high by songfests and films from Cuba and Vietnam. Red flags were raised from the roofs of two buildings. As national and international attention mounted, famous journalists and poets thrilled to the adventure of being hauled up onto ledges and entering the barricaded buildings through the window, to be told by the embattled students about the inequities of Columbia. (Neither the journalists nor the poets bothered to go to the administration later to find out if these stories were true.) It is little wonder that, for most of the students, those five defiant days were a transfigured moment which made them feel that the prosaic routine of study and classes was empty and hollow.

The single problem, of course, was how the defiance would end. Ever-present was the threat of the police — though as the days

---

totally different situation in which no actual criminal actions had been committed.

When the administration failed to call the police immediately, it lent a sense of "legitimacy" to the actions of the students. This factor, he felt, led other students to occupy buildings because it was "acceptable" and resulted in their later anger that the university did not live up to this theory of its sentiments and intentions.

[6] An account in *The Village Voice*, entitled "The Groovy Revolution," stated: "Don't underestimate the relationship between litter and liberty at Columbia. Until last Tuesday, April 23, the university was a clean dorm, where students paid rent, kept house rules, and took exams. Then the rebels arrived, in an uneasy coalition of hip, black and leftist militants. They wanted to make Columbia more like home. So they ransacked files, shoved furniture around, plastered walls with paint and placards. They scrawled on blackboards and doodled on desks. They raided the administration's offices (the psychological equivalent of robbing your mother's purse) and they claim to have found cigars, sherry, and a dirty book (the psychological equivalent of finding condoms in your father's wallet)."

passed and the police still did not come, many students began to
have a deceptively safe feeling that they never would. When they
were warned later by faculty emissaries that the danger was acute
and the consequences might be savage, they half refused to believe
it would ever happen. As the days moved on, the substantive issues
too began to recede. It became clear early on that the gymnasium
was stymied and would have to be reconsidered; IDA itself was being
studied, but in fact it had always been a vague and ambiguous issue
to most of the students, few of whom ever knew what IDA actually
did. The primary issue now was the students' demand for "amnesty."

The meaning of the demand was singularly clear to the SDS. As
one student put it, quite precisely, in the *West Side News,* a local
community newspaper, just before the police action:

> SDS members are holding out for total amnesty because less than that
> would put them in the position of admitting the administration's right
> to punish them. Such an admission would be tantamount to repudiat-
> ing their guerrilla tactics and agreeing with the logic of the administra-
> tion, which is: we don't dispute your right to criticize, but we disagree
> with your tactics — i.e., subverting our authority. For this reason
> SDS members cannot settle for less than total amnesty. *The fact is
> their tactics are their ends* — that is, to show that the students could
> take over the university and bring that consciousness to the whole
> student body. . . . The unspoken politics of the battle are that the
> student rebels are afraid that they will lose popular support by asking
> what they really want, which is student control of the university, and
> the administration, consciously or unconsciously aware of this, can
> avoid the heart of the matter by pretending to take the rebels' de-
> mands at face value. (Italics added.)

In actual fact, there was a double complication. While SDS was
basically uninterested in the specific demands being made — they
were simply tactical maneuvers — a large number of students who
followed them, including many in the buildings, were sincere about
the limited aims. They were uneasy about the morality of such
extreme tactics for specific ends, and they sought to justify these
tactics on the ground that the administration would not listen and
that there was "no other way." On the other hand, the administration,
well aware of the true aims of SDS, refused to take the demands at
face value, and was waiting for a propitious moment to call in the
police to clear the buildings. What tied the hands of the administration was the attitude of an active group of faculty.

A third force?

On Wednesday morning, April 24, the day after Hamilton was
taken over, a group of college faculty, dispossessed from their offices,
met informally in the lounge of Philosophy Hall in order to establish
a central place for faculty information and to discuss some mediating

role.[7] Out of these discussions grew the idea of a tripartite commission to handle disciplinary matters. This proposal, presented to the full college-faculty meeting that afternoon, was quickly accepted by the administration. As the threat of violence on campus grew, especially when a group of counterdemonstrators surrounded Low Library and tried to prevent people and food from getting inside, the faculty meeting in Philosophy Hall transformed itself into an ad hoc committee in an effort to become a "third force" between the protesting students and the administration. This committee had three aims: to prevent violence among students; to prevent police from coming onto the campus; and to negotiate the specific demands being made, principally the gymnasium. The ad hoc faculty group had no clear constituency. The meetings were held almost around the clock in the Philosophy lounge, and as crises developed, votes were taken among those present. While many of those present were junior faculty, the heart of the body was a fifteen-man steering committee, made up principally of individuals who were politically liberal in orientation, who had studied radical movements, and who had some experience in the study of "comparative politics."[8] Few of them had any illusions about SDS, but they were united in two convictions: (1) if the police were brought in, the student body would be "radicalized," thus giving SDS the victory it wanted; and (2) there was a majority of protestors who were not of SDS, but had joined the action because of the issues, and these students might be convinced to leave the buildings peacefully if the administration would negotiate. About 200 faculty members signed a statement proposing a halt in the construction of the gymnasium and the transfer of discipline to a tripartite body. They also promised that if the students evacuated the buildings, they would not hold classes until these proposals were accepted.

On Thursday, at midnight, Vice President Truman appeared before the Ad Hoc Faculty Committee and stated, rather abruptly, that because of mounting tension on campus and fights between

[7] The initiative in this matter was taken by the writer of this essay and Professor Eugene Galanter. For a detailed account of all the actions, and the various factions, both student and the faculty, see the informative article by Dankwart A. Rustow in *The New Leader*, May 20, 1968.

[8] The members of the steering committee were: Alan Westin (government), chairman; Alex Dallin (government), Dankwart Rustow (government), Immanuel Wallerstein (sociology), Terence Hopkins (sociology), Allan Silver (sociology), James Shenton (history), David Rothman (history), Robert Fogelson (history), Walter Metzger (history), Robert Cumming (philosophy), Sidney Morgenbesser (philosophy), Robert Belknap (Russian literature), Seymour Melman (industrial engineering). The writer was out of town when the Ad Hoc Committee was formally created, but when he returned on Saturday, he was "co-opted" to membership. All except one of the committee were tenured professors; nine were full professors.

demonstrators and nondemonstrators, the administration was asking the police to clear the buildings. The response was a storm of boos and cries of "shame," and the faculty present voted unanimously to interpose themselves between the police and the students in the buildings. Taken aback by this reception, Truman reconsidered and called off the police. He told the Ad Hoc Committee, in effect, that finding a way out of the situation was now up to them.

For the next few days, the Ad Hoc Committee suggested a variety of formulas to mediate the dispute. A considerable body of sentiment on campus swung behind the committee.[9] Yet the faculty group encountered intransigence on both sides. Although construction on the gym had by now halted, the university insisted that it could not make any further statements because of legal complications. More important, while the administration agreed to the creation of a Joint Disciplinary Committee, President Kirk refused to surrender to it "ultimate disciplinary powers." The students in the buildings, fearful of what this might mean, held fast to the demand for amnesty.

The failure of mediation

By Sunday, it was clear that the mediation efforts of the Ad Hoc Committee had failed. Spurred by information from the mayor's office that unless a break in the dispute came by the next day the administration would probably call in the police — and the committee members were given a vivid account of how brutal such police actions might be — the Ad Hoc Committee decided to "impose" a solution on both sides. It drew up a settlement that, it stated, would be a "bitter pill" for the administration and the students, but that represented a "just" arbitration. It called for continuing the suspension of work on the gymnasium, with no further action to be taken unless reviewed by community groups; it proposed that final disciplinary power be lodged in a tripartite judicial body; it rejected amnesty but stated that in light of the fact that the students had acted collectively, there would not be individually different punishments — thus making sure that strike leaders would not be singled

---

[9] While student sentiment during a changing and explosive situation is difficult to determine, a referendum organized by the student services societies gives some indication. While the organizers of the poll stated at the time that it had been impossible to conduct it on a sampling or organized-referendum basis, the tally compares in all respects with the results of a poll taken six days after the police action by the Bureau of Applied Social Research at Columbia. According to the account in the *Spectator* of Monday, April 29, of 5,500 ballots the following responded thus: (1) In favor of amnesty for all students involved in the demonstration of the last three days: Yes, 2,054; No, 3,466. (2) To end the construction of the gym: Yes, 4,093; No, 1,433. (3) To end the university's ties with IDA: Yes, 3,572; No, 1,855. (4) In favor of the demonstration tactics used by the SDS and SAS thus far: Yes, 1,325; No, 4,124.

out for heavier punishments — but uniform penalties would be applied to all. Again, since it was unlikely that all the demonstrators would be suspended, in effect this meant that all the students would be placed on probation.

A massive effort was made all day Monday to mobilize support for the Ad Hoc Committee position. Within a few hours, 2,500 students including almost all the established student leaders on campus, had endorsed the proposals. Prominent figures in New York's political and community life sent in statements of support. Faculty emissaries met with the administration and with the Student Strike Coordinating Committee to persuade both sides to accept. The students were warned, as forcefully as possible, that police action was imminent. The administration was told that if the students accepted the faculty proposals and the administration rejected them, the faculty would stand before the buildings if the police came.

All these efforts also came to nothing. The administration did make a conciliatory gesture in which it warmly endorsed the action of the Ad Hoc Committee, but it refused to accept community review of any future decision on the gymnasium, nor would the President give up his final disciplinary powers.[10] The Strike Steering Committee rejected the Ad Hoc Committee proposal out of hand; at the end, in a typical gesture, they even refused the faculty negotiating committee the courtesy of a written statement. Instead, they insisted that they be allowed to read their own statement before the faculty body. Despite the unanimity of the Strike Steering Committee, however, it was later revealed that the Ad Hoc Committee proposal had been accepted, in part, by the students at Fayerweather, who in a "counterproposal" dropped the demand for amnesty and suggested that the issue of discipline be submitted to a "bipartite" faculty-student committee. The leaflet listing these counterproposals stated: "The above rough proposal was voted by the majority of strikers in Fayerweather Hall to be forwarded by the Strike Steering Committee for consideration by the rest of the liberated community." As it

---

[10] To illustrate the legalism which ensnared many of the administration's actions, in his testimony before the Cox Committee, Vice President Truman noted that a serious question had arisen about what disciplinary powers could be delegated by the president or the trustees under the university's charter. He pointed out that Columbia was operating under the original colonial charter, which antedates the establishment of the New York State Board of Regents. Thus Columbia is the only university in the state that does not come under the jurisdiction of the regents. Truman said that efforts to revise the charter in one detail might have opened the way to revision of other portions of the charter, and the university wanted to avoid this.

On reflection, I would say, too, that the tone of the ad hoc document was peremptory, and given the need to extend the time, and to reduce tension, the imposition of a deadline was a mistake. By firing up both sides in this way, the committee's effort probably served to sharpen the confrontation. I shared in this mistake.

turned out the Strike Steering Committee, dominated as it was by SDS, did not circulate the Fayerweather proposals. Nor did the SDS leaders pass along to a number of the buildings the full import of the faculty warnings.[11] The SDS leadership certainly wanted the police to come. As one of them said later: "The eyes of Berlin were upon us and we wanted the police to come in and drag us out." They did.

The bust

The irony is that the more extremist of the demonstrators, politically and rhetorically, escaped the main brunt of the police savagery, but the moderates did not. There is little doubt that after a while the police action did indeed turn brutal, and as many bystanders as participants were hurt. The police command had assured the administration that a "minimum" amount of violence would be used. Everyone, particularly the mayor's representatives who were on hand, was mindful of the blacks in Hamilton. In fact, it was only after the mayor's representatives could be sure, after a check throughout the community, that Harlem would take no action, that the signal to bring in the police had been given at all.

The administration had made many efforts before April 30 to negotiate with the black students in Hamilton. Percy Sutton, the black Borough President of Manhattan, went into Hamilton at Kirk's request, but departed without telling the administration what he had learned — an action that led some administration people to believe Sutton had advised the students to stay. Kenneth Clark, the black psychologist at the City University, and a member of the New York State Board of Regents, entered Hamilton with Theodore Kheel, the labor mediator, on Monday afternoon. While the black students in Hamilton decided to stay, it was made clear that they would put up no resistance. When the police came, including by protocol a black patrol, the students in Hamilton walked out quietly, through the tunnels in the building, to the waiting police vans. In Mathematics Hall which was dominated by the Maoists, kooks, and hippies, there was little resistance and few students were hurt. The same scene was repeated at Low, where the SDS leadership had congregated. Ironically, the worst incidents of brutality happened in Avery and Fayerweather, in which the moderate students predominated. Having wavered before, the students in these buildings

---

[11] Equally relevant was the students' intense suspiciousness of the "outside world," which their self-exile under siege conditions generated among them. When Professors Peter Kenen and Seymour Melman tried to enter Fayerweather, Melman, who has been active in SANE and left-wing causes and who had spoken at SDS rallies at the sundial, thought the students would listen to him. But he and Kenen were met, as they put it, with "naked distrust and paranoia."

now seemed intent on "proving their manhood," and they resisted
bitterly. As the police were forced to clear them out of barricaded
room after barricaded room, they became more savage. But one part
of the police action that had nothing to do with the clearing of the
buildings was largely responsible for the intensity of campus reaction
the following day.

Except for Hamilton, all the buildings being cleared were on the
north side of College Walk. On the south side, almost a thousand students had congregated to watch the action, many of them inevitably
jeering and taunting the police. Once all the buildings were emptied,
the police were assembled in a line on College Walk, facing the
students. They were then suddenly ordered to clear the field. Without warning, the police — enraged by the jeers and taunts they had
been hearing — charged the students in front of them, flailing away
with their nightsticks, running after the students fleeing across the
field, and clubbing those who failed to move swiftly enough. In all,
about a hundred students were hurt. But it was not the violence itself
that was so horrible — despite the many pictures in the papers of
bleeding students, not one required hospitalization. It was the capri-
ciousness of that final action. The police simply ran wild. Those who
tried to say they were innocent bystanders or faculty were given
the same flailing treatment as the students. For most of the students,
it was their first encounter with brutality and blood, and they
responded in fear and anger. The next day, almost the entire campus
responded to a call for a student strike. In a few hours, thanks to the
New York City Police Department, a large part of the Columbia
campus had become "radicalized."[12]

A new idea: "restructuring"

The day after the police action, the joint faculties on Morningside
Heights met for the second time in the history of the university.[13]

---

[12] In all, 705 persons were arrested; exactly how many were arrested in the
buildings, and how many on South Field after the police charge, it would be
hard to say. Of the total arrested, 181, or 26 per cent, were not connected
with Columbia. Of the 524 identified as registered Columbia students, 400
(or 77 per cent) were undergraduates. Of these, 239 were from Columbia College, and 111 from Barnard, the remainder from General Studies. In effect, almost 10 per cent of the college student body was arrested.

[13] Columbia University is a strange congeries of institutions, as a result of
its long history and growth. Barnard College and Teachers College students
receive Columbia University degrees, but the two institutions, though on Morningside Heights, are not part of the Columbia Corporation and each has its
own trustees. The medical faculty, the School of Public Health, the dental
faculty, and the School of Social Work are members of the Columbia Corporation but are not on Morningside Heights. This makes it difficult to be exact
about the total number of faculty and students of "Columbia University." The
faculties on Morningside Heights comprise the college; the graduate schools,
divided into three faculties of science, philosophy (including the humanities),

On the Sunday before the buildings were cleared, the joint faculties
had met and overwhelmingly adopted a formal vote of confidence in
the administration. Now, two days later, the mood of the senior
faculty had changed. Although a motion expressing support for the
administration was introduced, a substitute motion, introduced by a
group from the Law Faculty, took precedence and carried the meeting. It called for the creation of an executive committee that would
be empowered to take "needed steps to return the university to its
educational task." It was clear that the faculties no longer had complete confidence in the administration, and wanted their own means
of expression.

Not only had the faculty mood changed, but that of the students
as well. The new Executive Committee met that evening and the
next day with about forty student leaders. Few of them had been
in the buildings and few had supported SDS. But now all of them
supported the strike, and a new, overriding issue was raised which
had not been heard before: the need to "restructure" the university
— "to structure" has become an acceptable, in fact a highly favored
sociological verb, these days. SDS had been making political demands, and few of these student leaders were interested in them.
But they now felt that the archaic organizational arrangements of
the university, and the exclusion of students and faculty from the
decision-making processes, even in consultative capacities, had now
to be changed.

The question of purpose was soon to divide the students. At the
start, SDS sought to capture the strike movement. The Strike Committee — a carryover from the committees in the occupied buildings
— announced that "any" group of seventy students could send a
representative to the enlarged strike committee. It was a shrewd
move, consonant with the idea of smashing "bourgeois student"
power, since many of the established student leaders (e.g., the board
of managers of Ferris Booth Hall, the Student Union) had no specific
"constituency." It also meant that a student could often vote several
times, in different capacities (in the dormitories, as a member of a
club, or as a member of a departmental student group), in electing
a representative to the Strike Committee. Within a week, about sixty
students had been elected to the Strike Committee, and while some
double counting was inevitable, the total represented — presumably
4,000 — was still impressive.

It is the very nature of any extremist movement to keep things
churning. It must maintain activity and excitement in order to main-

---

and political science (including the social sciences); and the professional
schools: law, business, engineering (which includes an undergraduate college), architecture, journalism, and the school of arts (writing and the per-
forming arts). In addition there is a College of Pharmacy, which is neither
on Morningside Heights nor a member of the Columbia Corporation.

tain a zealous morale. But the police "bust" had been an exhausting emotional experience for everyone on the campus, and shortly afterward some of the tension began to ebb as the questions of how to "restructure" the university came to the fore. The executive committee of the faculty had been instrumental in setting up a Fact Finding Commission, under the chairmanship of Archibald Cox of the Harvard Law School, to hold hearings on the causes of the recent events. It had persuaded the Board of Trustees to set up a panel to inquire into the organization of the university. It had begun to create a large-scale summer study program to evaluate different plans of university organization. To SDS all such activity was a threat, because it raised questions requiring research and answers, it asked for various student programs and proposals, it raised the vexing issue of "complexities." As the faculty statements pointed out, an institution as complicated as Columbia could not be overhauled in a day or by the flick of a rhetorical phrase.

SDS responded to all this, on May 17, by uniting with some local tenant groups to seize a Columbia-owned apartment building on West 114th Street. It charged the university with "colonialism," and with creating a "white ghetto" on Morningside Heights by "deliberately forcing the removal of almost every black, Puerto Rican and Oriental" from the neighborhood. A black flag was raised over the building, and the students demanded that the building, more than half-vacant since it would before long be torn down and the site used for a new school of social work, be used for community housing. Within a few hours the police cleared the building and area without violence.

The effort by SDS to keep things churning inevitably created tensions within the Strike Steering Committee. At least half of the committee was not interested in the political aims propounded by SDS. Their concern was, genuinely, with the reorganization of the university. When Mark Rudd began making appearances at Brooklyn College, and calling upon Columbia students to demonstrate there, and when SDS issued proposals for support of other direct-action measures, a split developed within the Strike Coordinating Committee, and one group, representing about half the total, left to form The Students for a Restructured University.

Hamilton II

It was at this point that the administration decided to assert its authority by suspending four of the leaders of SDS. The move was technically in accordance with the procedures set up by the new Joint Disciplinary Committee, which had been created after the first police action. The timing of the suspension, however, was ill-considered. Its result was Hamilton II.

On May 23, four weeks to the day after the first sit-in, about 250 students took over Hamilton Hall. This time the demonstrators were white. The Students for a Restructured University, which now claimed to represent 3,000 students, declared that it would not participate. A majority of those who did sit in chose to do so for the symbolic reason of making a protest. But once the building had been taken, the SDS leaders began to argue that it was necessary to stay and force the police to throw them out again. At first only 25 students wanted to stay and 150 to leave. But the SDS leadership refused to accept that vote and after several hours of debate, the majority of those inside Hamilton were shamed into staying.

After ten hours, the police moved in at 2:30 in the morning and quietly cleared the building. The action was peaceful, but the students, having been brought to a fever pitch, needed some cathartic release. The entry of the police on campus triggered an emotional reaction among hundreds of students who, in the pre-dawn hour, roamed the campus, hurling bricks at the police, smashing windows, and lighting fires in several university buildings. President Kirk gave an order for the police to clear the campus. A larger force of police was called in to contain the students. Savagery on both sides erupted. About 68 persons were injured, this time including 17 policemen; 174 persons were arrested.[14]

The action of the police again brought a surge of sympathy for SDS — though this sympathy was somewhat tempered by disapproval of the vandalism of a number of "kooks" and by the vengeful burning of a history professor's notes. The Students for a Restructured University attacked the administration for "provoking" the disturbance by starting the disciplinary action, but refrained from commenting on the fact that such action was not final and still subject to review by the Joint Disciplinary Committee, was responded to so violently by the SDS. A *schadenfreude* judgment was made by a writer for the "underground" newspaper, *The New York Free Press*, who, chortling over the fact that the administration had "played into the hands of SDS," wrote:

> It is part of the philosophy of the radical left that the "Liberal Establishment" when confronted with ideological political force "cannot act reasonably even for its own ends . . . and when pressured will make mistake after mistake after mistake." Fortunately for the radicals at Columbia, this prophecy turned out to be especially true in the case of Grayson Kirk.[15]

---

[14] Of those arrested, 46, the single largest group, were outsiders; of the remainder, 45 were from Columbia College, 23 from the Graduate Faculties, 17 from Barnard, 15 from General Studies, and a total of 23 from all other units of the university. Five faculty were also arrested.

[15] That writer continues: "At about 4:30 A.M. hundreds of tired students gathered around the Sundial where Dean Platt 'regretfully' announced that

Life imitates art

After Hamilton II, the violent passions began to subside. Examinations were suspended, and in the college any student who wanted it could obtain a simple pass grade if he notified his instructor. On the grass, in the spring sun, the Strike Education Committee now devoted itself to "counter-classes" as part of a new Liberation School. The rules were simple:

> The question of expertise of the leader(s) of a counter-class is to be determined by the (relevant) community of faculty, students and others together. This implies that anyone (including undergraduates and custodians) will be allowed to run a counter-class as long as the community of students, faculty and others in his alleged area of expertise recognize him.

Anyone who wanted to, could give a class. The teacher was not to stand in front of the class and each person, including the teacher, was supposed to take no more than his proportion of the time, so that if there were twenty persons present, each person, including the teacher, would take only one-twentieth of the time. Leaders of Trotskyite sects flocked to the campus to hold courses on the "History of the Russian (and other) Revolutions." Professors *manqués* analyzed the contradictions of capitalism; and lay psychoanalysts and lecturers, whose usual audience is "Over 28, Singles Only" clubs, spoke on "Intimacy games, their meaning, the individual and society." Others did their "thing," which had one Phyllis Deutsch giving a course in Arabic Belly Dancing ("dress to move freely") and Howard Press lecturing on "Culture and Constraint Dimensions of Freedom in Marx, Freud, Marcuse, Reich." And amidst all the din, one student gave a course on "A Slightly-less-liberated Talmud," in front of Earl Hall, the religious counselors' building; why not, for as he explained to Professor Sidney Morgenbesser, it was a commandment and a blessing to teach Talmud anywhere.

It was, we were told, 1848 all over again, the revolution of the students. But if it was 1848, then history had begun to imitate art rather than itself. The model had been laid down by Flaubert in *A Sentimental Education,* his novel about 1848. In the Rue Saint-

---

President Kirk had given the order for the police to move in and clear the campus.

"Exhausted students who had been dragging themselves from place to place suddenly woke up with the announcement. One girl who had been just about to leave for her apartment said, 'That makes me feel as if I'd just gotten a shot of adrenalin.'

"Students immediately rushed to the barricades to prepare themselves for the coming struggle. Had Kirk at this point stationed five uniformed policemen in each of the academic buildings and not provoked the students with a confrontation, a Strike leader privately commented, 'the whole thing would have broken up and everybody would have gone to bed.'"

Jacques, the Club de l'Intélligence, whose chairman is the incor-
ruptible pedagogue Sénécal, is debating the aims of the revolution:

> The audience showed great respect for their chairman. He had been
> among those who had on the 25th of February demanded the im-
> mediate. organization of labour; the next day, at the Prado, he had
> urged an attack on the Hôtel de Ville; and since it was the custom
> for figures of that period to model themselves after a pattern — some
> imitating Saint-Just, others Danton, others Marat — Sénécal tried to
> resemble Blanqui, who was a follower of Robespierre. . . .
> "My turn!" cried Delmar.
> He leapt on to the platform, pushed everyone aside, and took up
> his usual pose. Declaring that he despised such mean accusations
> [against actors] he dilated on the actor's civilizing mission. Since the
> theatre was the centre of national education, he was in favour of re-
> forming it. First of all, there should be no more managers and no
> more privileges.
> "That's right! No more privileges at all!"
> The actor's performance inflamed the crowd, and the air was thick
> with revolutionary proposals.
> "Down with academics. Down with the Institut!"
> "No more missions!"
> "No more matriculation!"
> "Down with university degrees!"
> "No," said Sénécal, "let us preserve them; but let them be con-
> ferred by universal franchise, by the people, the only true judge."

Microcosm II — a commentary

The Columbia "student rebellion" is now passing into the mythos
of revolutionary history. It is being linked, in temperament and
impulse, with the outbursts against authority that marked working-
class action in early nineteenth-century England (the Luddites),
the violent opposition to industrial discipline in Victorian England
(the Chartists), and the anarchist plots of the early 1900's. Along
with the Sorbonne and Berlin, Columbia will serve for historians as
a notch in the recurrent cycles of radical social movements. And
there can be no doubt that the Columbia disorders reflect a reaction
to some deep-running structural changes in our society. But the more
difficult question is why the imp of the *Zeitgeist* happened to land at
this time, in this place.

As I have indicated earlier, what happened was unexpected, even
by the instigators, and accidental. There was no long history of
angry, unresolved conflicts that had been boiling for some time and
had to explode. The administration had not been repressive; if anything, it had been, in disciplinary matters, at first lenient and then
wayward. The manifest issues had impinged little on the consciousness of the students. Those issues that were raised did not seem

salient: the IDA was already being studied by a university committee as a result of previous protests; the gymnasium, while a nagging
thorn to the black militants of Harlem, had not aroused much
attention on the Heights. There were latent grievances and dis-
contents, as are present in most institutions; and there were serious
shortcomings in the administrative and decision-making procedures
of the university that arose out of its sprawling and uncoordinated
structure. But students, and even most faculty, were not really aware
of these.

In short, before April 23, few people assumed the issues to be
important, and even fewer would have justified the extreme tactics
which, as means, were so disproportionate to the ends allegedly
being sought. But during the events and since, history has been
quickly rewritten in order to make it seem that the university was
repressive and unresponsive, so as to give a cast of desperation to
the action of the students, as though no other course was open, or
because the issues were so crucial.

Events make history, but how does one explain the trajectory of
events? How is it that, on one campus at least, the politics of confrontation and the tactics of extreme disruption were able to evoke
so large a student response as to make once marginal issues become
so immediate and burning, and questions of ends and means, once
so central to a liberal philosophy, be waved away as irrelevant? How
could an administration, tolerant to a fault and even avuncular in
its responsiveness to students, albeit in a fumbling way, become,
after a series of fitful indecisions, so punitive as to make a fortuitous
conflict with the police seem to be the culminating event in a chain
of purposeful confrontations?

What this suggests — in answer to the first question — is that a
considerable portion of the student body, in the course of becoming
"radicalized," underwent a "conversion experience" so intense and
embracing as to blot out all qualifying and self-critical thoughts
about the nature of their challenge to the university, and — in
answer to the second — that the administration experienced a reaction so traumatic as to make the reassertion of formal authority
the sole criterion of its policy. Locked into this double confrontation,
the only resolution for both sides was force. How and why this
happened I am not sure can be made clear; I can only try.

Liberalism in crisis

The ethos of an institution embodies its legitimations, and the
ethos of Columbia is liberalism. There is complete academic freedom. A teacher, even assistants and preceptors, teaches his own
courses without any interference, and gives a staff course in his own
way without supervision. To my knowledge, no administrator or

departmental chairman has ever dropped into a man's course to "observe" his teaching. Most of the faculty is, politically, liberal. The men who give Columbia its reputation — Lionel Trilling, Meyer Schapiro, Ernest Nagel, Richard Hofstadter — have been in the forefront of liberal causes for more than thirty years. A number of Columbia's leading political scientists and law professors — Roger Hilsman, Zbigniew Brezinski, Richard Gardner, Charles Frankel, William Cary, Wallace Sayre — have served in recent Democratic administrations. In the year-and-a-half before April 23, 1968, a group of ten leading professors, led by Fritz Stern, the historian, and including Vice President Truman, had worked actively to reverse the nations' Vietnam policy. In the college and the graduate faculties, a Republican is a rarity. A poll revealed that 70 per cent of the faculty favored withdrawal from Vietnam before President Johnson's statement.

The student body itself, cosmopolitan and coming from parents in the professional class, is largely liberal. More than 900 students work in the Citizenship Council, an extracurricular activity that has devoted itself in recent years largely to service—tutoring and community organization — with the poor and in Harlem. Several hundred students were in contact with pacifist organizations such as the War Resisters League, the Fellowship of Reconciliation, and the Resistance — the more so since, under the new draft regulations that went into effect in June 1968, graduate students no longer received deferments, and college students were likely to be drafted right after graduation. This had heightened apprehensions on campus.

But in the last two years liberalism itself, particularly in the student movement, had come under severe attack. The Vietnam War, it was argued, had grown out of "liberal anti-Communism." The restlessness and militancy of the blacks was taken as a portent that peaceful social change is ineffective. The Great Society was mocked for the inadequacy of its domestic programs.

That political liberalism was in crisis was quite true, but perhaps not for the reasons given by the student Left — in fact, for reasons that would not be to its liking. For if there is a single source for the crisis of liberalism — apart from the Vietnam War — it is owing to the complexity of our social problems, to the linked nature of change and a lack of knowledge or adequate research about where and how one can effectively "cut into the system" in order to direct social change. The old simplicities about "more" schools and "more" housing, or even "better" schools or "better" housing, have not proved very useful in breaking the cycle of poverty or in dealing with Negro family structure. For those given to moralisms or "sophisticated" chatter about "power," such talk about complexities is irritating. Either they regard it as an evasion of the "real"

problems, or they retreat from any analysis by simply insisting that
more money will solve any problem, or, in the case of the New Left,
they insist that the entire society is sick and corrupt and that "the
system" must be overturned in one fell swoop.

The Students for a Democratic Society was itself in a great quan-
dary. During the previous five years it had become steadily more
"left," yet it felt itself to be increasingly frustrated. SDS had its
first flowering in the civil-rights movement, but that movement had
now become exhausted. SDS then turned its attention to "community organizing" and sought to build interracial "unions" of the
poor in a dozen cities; but these efforts had been fruitless. It had
its own "identity crisis" in not knowing whether the students were
a "class," or how they stood in relation to the "means of production."
(Some SDS members, more theoretically minded, latched on, interestingly, to the idea propounded originally in France by André
Gorz and Serge Mallet of a "new" working class, made up of technicians and professionals — a left-wing version, so to speak, of the
post-industrial society.) But for most of them, there was simply the
tension and rancor fed by the war, and the attraction of the propositions, distilled second-hand from Régis Debray, that it was sufficiently revolutionary to act without any program, to act simply
for the sake of the revolution. In this spirit, they conceived themselves to be guerrillas in the urban society, and for their field of
action they chose the university.

The university as microcosm

SDS sees the university as the microcosm of our society. If the
society is sick and corrupt, so is the university. Having made this
assertive leap, SDS sought to document this charge with "evidence"
of the university's "complicity" in the war. The moralizing of belief leads to the vulgarization of politics, for if politics is seen as a
case of *either/or*, one needs rhetoric that is simplified and does
not admit of complication or compromise. SDS found its rhetoric
in a primitivized and stilted Marxism, rooted in a conspiracy theory
of "hidden networks of power," in which all motives are economic
and all actions are sinister.[16]

---

[16] In an extraordinary brochure entitled "Who Rules Columbia?," published
by the self-styled North American Congress on Latin America, but distributed
widely by SDS, the effort is made to show the "nexus" between Columbia
and the "military-industrial complex." Thus in one section we read: "It was
General Dwight D. Eisenhower and Grayson Kirk who brought Columbia
University's financial support for defense or defense related projects from less
than 1% (in 1945) to about 48% in 1968." The statement typically confuses the
total of *all* of Columbia's contracts with the federal government with "defense
or defense-related" contracts. Of some $55 million in Federal government
contracts, comprising about 48 per cent of Columbia's operating budget as of

What SDS could not do to the larger society it could attempt against the university: to wreck it. A university, after all, is essentially a defenseless place. It commands no force of its own, other than the reluctant power of expulsion, and commands its loyalty through the moral authority growing out of the idea that the university is a special institution in our society, drawing its grace from the most "sacred" source of rights in a free society — the commitment to open inquiry and truth. Even so, the SDS militancy was largely verbal — until the barricading of Hamilton Hall by the blacks — an open defiance of the university by individuals who had no regard for its intellectual and scholarly role, but saw it only as a secular power on the Heights overlooking Harlem. The occupation of the buildings by SDS had a largely different consequence, for here, directly and for the first time, the moral authority of the university, qua university, was being denigrated. Talk had now passed. The tear in the social fabric had now been made. The SDS had taken the first step in becoming guerrillas.

First deeds, then words

What of the other students, the four hundred or so who did not belong to SDS but who, in the five days, followed SDS into the buildings and stayed until the police got them out? This is a group that shares the underlying vague, inchoate, diffuse dissatisfaction with our society and its liberal culture, the more so because of the Vietnam War. Many of them disdained the SDS and its self-inflated posture of revolution. But they were restive — the undergraduates because of their new status in the draft, the graduate students because of their subordinate positions in the departments — and, in the demonstration of the inadequacies of liberalism in a liberal institution, they were receptive to protest actions against the administration. But few of them, before the events, ever would have conceived of themselves as occupying buildings and justifying such means that were so disproportionate to the manifest ends. It was their unexpected action — and the failure of the administration to differentiate them from the SDS — that gave a very different coloring to the events. Why did they act as they did?

Freud once remarked that you commit yourself first in words and then in deeds. This is a curiously rationalistic description of the way people change their views. The revolutionary psychology is

March 31, 1968, $22.9 million was from the U.S. Public Health Service, and went almost entirely to the Medical School. The total from the Defense Department was about $12 million—of which $9 million was from the Navy for the maintenance of two laboratories concerned with oceanographic research, one of which is devoted to basic or "pure" research concerned with mapping the ocean's bottom, and one of which, whose scope is being reduced, was devoted to classified research.

more subtle: first you commit yourself in deeds, and then you find the words to justify the action. But the first leap has to be a big one, a tearing down of a major taboo. In this case, the very audacity of seizing a building by the blacks was the bold act that preempted many doubts, for the implicit meaning was communicated: if such drastic steps are being taken, something must be wrong. The way then is open for others. In the contagion of excitement, there is a stampede to action; in the call of one's friends there is involvement with a group; in the polarization of antagonists there is the tension of impending conflict which keeps one firm no matter what the silent or wavering doubts.

The deed having been done — the acting out of forbidden impulses — the words came next. Along with the occupation of the buildings there was an extraordinary barrage of propaganda — sustained, concentrated, intensive, repetitive, simplified — all of it making one or two reiterated points: Columbia was the "intersect" of a corporate-military-CIA nexus to advance American imperialism, and Columbia was guilty of "institutional racism" in its neighborhood policy. All of this was "documented" with the corporate affiliations of the university's trustees and the connection with IDA, and with the charge that Columbia in its "expropriation" of the neighborhood had expelled seven, eight, or ten thousand families from Morningside Heights, all of them black or Puerto Rican. These were the themes of numerous leaflets and of a half dozen or so newspapers sympathetic to the New Left which were widely distributed on the Columbia campus.

In this hothouse atmosphere of frenetic excitement, in which the world had shrunk to the dimensions of a single campus, and students felt themselves to be actors in a great historical drama ("Columbia is at the beginning stages of the revolution" was the intoxicating refrain), there was a massive shift in the frames of reference of hundreds of students. Most of us, implicitly or otherwise, work from some basic premises about a society, the values which make some actions seem right or wrong. When such premises are codified, given a moral content and often an antagonistic stance, it becomes an ideology, a formula that allows an individual, without further doubts about his premises, to make a whole series of related judgments about new circumstances. Ideology, thus, is a cognitive map with a built-in set of emotional judgments and rationalizations. What happened to hundreds of students during those last five days of April — the imprint of the conversion experience as a result of their impulsive commitment to action — was this shift in social perceptions, a shift given greater vividness by the *éclaircissement* of Columbia as a malevolent institution, by the dramatic revelation of hidden "secrets," the tearing down of old beliefs and the substitution of a new, stark "reality." In short, what we had here was a classic illustration of the contagion phenomenon of a mass that Gustav Le Bon described so graphically in *Psychologie des Foules* in 1895.

Any new set of beliefs requires some confirmation of its validity by some "significant others," or by a testing of reality. At Columbia, one legitimation was quickly supplied by members of the New York literary "establishment," who were ecstatic at having a real revolution on their doorstep. Norman Mailer threw a large fund-raising party.[17] Dwight Macdonald wrote a "begging" letter to his friends for money in support of SDS. Moreover, the fact that the French students at Nanterre had begun occupying their university buildings, in an action that spread quickly to the Sorbonne, gave the Columbia students the heady sense of participating in an international movement of historic scope, and this identification strongly reinforced their belief that their actions were legitimate.

But the acquisition of new beliefs or judgments also requires confirmation at the cognitive level, some real test of the intellectual validity of the new conception. This can — in more neutral areas and in quieter times — take the form of intellectual debate about the consistency of the argument, the quality of evidence, the congruity with other beliefs, its place within a larger theoretical or intellectual structure, and so on; reality testing also takes the form of prediction, and the falsification of such judgments becomes the basis for the beginning of disbelief. Where emotions are deeply involved, such testing is never wholly persuasive, of course, but it is still necessary, if only to rationalize earlier action when a glimmer of disbelief or disillusionment has set in.[18]

---

[17] Radical history has the unfortunate habit of repeating itself in pop form. In 1913, Wild Bill Haywood of Wobbly fame had a party thrown for him, during the Paterson strike, by John Reed at Mabel Dodge Luhan's house, an event that went down as one of the "glories" of Greenwich Village history. More than fifty years later the scene was replayed in Brooklyn Hights.

[18] Most conversion experiences are superficial or temporary, and if the surrounding social environment is powerful enough, or retains its legitimacy, or if the new converts become repelled by discordant elements of the new belief, or disillusioned in the character of the new prophets or leaders, or feel they have been manipulated, there is a quick erosion of the new belief, and the converts feel betrayed or angered. Where conversion involves a "leap of faith" to a sharply different set of counterbeliefs, religious and political movements protect themselves from reality testing by "encapsulating" themselves from the hostile environment. In the nineteenth century this often took the form of utopian colonies physically separated from the dominant social environment. In the twentieth century this has taken the form of adopting a sharp "combat posture"—it is no accident that the extreme right and the extreme left glorify combat (one directly in the form of war, the other in the form of revolution) as the highest virtue.

At Columbia the "hothouse" nature of the events and the experience of danger reinforced the sense of solidarity and encapsulation which engulfed those in the buildings. The use of the word "commune" and the shared way of life that prevailed created a *Gemeinschaft*, intense and personal, which made it difficult for doubters to leave—particularly in the face of an impending "bust"--and made it easier for the leaders to manipulate those in the buildings.

The accusations — and beliefs — of the students were never challenged by the administration: in part out of bewilderment with their whirlwind appearance and their patently intellectual simplifications, which the administration thought few would believe; in part because the administration was enraged at the tactics used — holding a dean hostage, rifling the president's files, raising of red flags, barricading of buildings, and refusing, initially, even to meet with the vice president and discuss the issues. Thus, there was no intellectual debate, and the "reality testing" was provided by the police. The "bust" confirmed the students' new beliefs. Whatever psychological guilt or unease was felt about the demonstrators' coercive and disruptive tactics was dissolved in the payment of broken heads and spilled blood. As the students saw it, the administration resorted to force because it could not answer them. With the police action, the administration lost a large part of its legitimacy — its moral authority — which had previously commanded the loyalty of students and faculty.

The university as a community

In a hard and brilliant piece in *The New Republic* of June 1, 1968, entitled "Revolution and Counterrevolution, (But Not Necessarily about Columbia!)," a rather Machiavellian essay written from the balcony, Zbigniew Brzezinski coldly analyzed the mistakes of the Columbia administration and faculty. It is worth quoting him at length, though I shall take issue with his analysis:

A revolutionary situation typically arises when values of a society are undergoing a profound change. . . .
The crisis of values has several political consequences of relevance to revolutionary processes. First of all, it prompts ambivalent concessions by the authorities in power. The authorities do not fully comprehend the nature of the changes they are facing, but they are no longer sufficiently certain of their values to react in assertive fashion — concessionism thus becomes the prevailing pattern of their behavior. Secondly, increasingly self-assertive revolutionary forces begin an intensive search for appealing issues. The purpose is to further radicalize and revolutionize the masses and to mobilize them against the *status quo*. . . .
The critical phase occurs when a weak spot has been identified, appealing issues articulated, and the probe becomes a confrontation. At this stage the purpose of revolutionary activity is to legitimize violence. If the initial act of violence is suppressed quickly by estab-

---

In such an atmosphere, the one who is most "left" or "radical" has a psychological advantage over any others who may raise questions of compromise or doubts. Many students who were only vaguely "left" or "liberal" came under the psychological pressure of having to prove their political *bona fides* by suppressing their doubts and giving assent to the actions.

lished authorities, the chances are that the revolutionary act itself will gain social approbrium; society generally tends to be conservative, even in a situation of crisis of values. Thus a revolutionary act is likely to be condemned by most, provided it is rapidly suppressed. If the revolutionary act endures, then automatically it gains legitimacy with the passage of time. Enduring violence thus becomes a symbol of the authorities' disintegration and collapse, and it prompts in turn further escalation of support for the revolutionary act. . . .

An important role in this revolutionary process is played by legitimist reformers and intellectuals. Intellectuals by their very nature are unwilling to pick sides, since they are better at identifying gray than siding with black and white. In a revolutionary situation, they are particularly concerned with not being stamped as counterrevolutionary conservatives. . . . Accustomed generally to dealing with established authorities, they are more experienced in coping with the authorities than with the revolutionary forces. Thus, in the process of interposing themselves, they are inclined to apply most of their pressure against the established authority, with which they have many links, than equally against established authorities and the revolutionary forces on behalf of reformist appeals. In effect, irrespective of their subjective interests, the legitimist reformers and intellectuals in a revolutionary situation objectively become the tools of the revolutionary forces, thus contributing to further aggravation of the revolutionary situation and radicalizing the overall condition.

When faced with a revolutionary situation, the established authorities typically commit several errors. . . . They display an incapacity for immediate effective response. Their traditional legalism works against them. Faced with a revolutionary situation, instead of striking immediately and effectively, they tend to procrastinate, seeking refuge in legalistic responses. . . . An early confrontation would work to the advantage of the authorities, since mass support begins to shift to the revolutionaries only after the situation has been radicalized. . . . When finally force is employed, the authorities rarely think ahead to post-use-of-force consequences, concentrating instead on the application of force to the specific challenge at hand. They thus neglect the important consideration that the use of force must be designed not only to eliminate surface revolutionary challenge, but to make certain that the revolutionary forces cannot later rally again under the same leadership. If that leadership cannot be physically liquidated, it can at least be expelled from the country (or area) in which revolution is taking place. Emigrants rarely can maintain themselves as effective revolutionaries. The denial of the opportunity for the revolutionary leadership to re-rally should be an important ingredient of the strategy of force, even if it is belatedly used. . . . Finally, established authorities often fail to follow up effective violence with immediate reforms. Such reforms ought to be designed to absorb the energies of the more moderate revolutionaries, who can then claim that though their revolution had failed, their objectives were achieved. This is very important in attracting the more moderate elements to the side of the authorities.

Now, there is much that is true here: an authority which is unsure of itself is bound to hesitate and lose its effectiveness. The democratic regimes of Europe in the 1930's did succumb in part because of their failure to control private violence by the Fascists and Communists. If the university were a microcosm of society, his points would be well-taken. *But the university is not the microcosm of the society; it is an academic community,* with a historic exemption from full integration into the society, and having an autonomous position in order to be able to fulfill its own responsibility, which is to conduct untrammeled inquiry into all questions. If the university is a community, asking for special loyalty from its members, how can it sanction the clubbing of its students?

It was SDS which initiated the violence at Columbia by insisting that the university was the microcosm of the society, and challenging its authority. After some confusion, the administration, in its actions, accepted this definition and sought to impose its authority on the campus by resorting to force. But in a community one cannot regain authority simply by asserting it, or by using force to suppress dissidents. Authority in this case is like respect. One can only *earn* the authority — the loyalty of one's students — by going in and arguing with them, by engaging in full debate and, when the merits of proposed change are recognized, taking the necessary steps quickly enough to be convincing.

The true difficulty is that the Columbia administration, both in its experience and in its conceptions of politics, was ill-equipped for either the Machiavellianism of Brzezinski or the politics of persuasion that, I think, would have served the university far better. The administration leaders, though they are reputable political scientists, were familiar only with the American political system, in which one operates either legalistically or by "making deals." Neither Kirk nor Truman had any "feel" for the volatility of social movements, or for the politics of ideology. The administration above all failed to understand the *dynamics* of the student protest: that whatever reason there may have been for early police action, when the buildings were seized by the hard-core SDS members, the subsequent surge of political support on the part of 500 other students — most of them liberal, moderate, pacifist, and not members of SDS — effectively changed the *political* character of the situation. The failure to make the necessary distinction between these students and SDS, and thus to understand that these students were not wreckers but were now trying to express their inchoate grievances against the university, permitted SDS to call the tune — which, in the five crucial days of the occupation of the buildings, it did.

This led to the second turning point — the first was the seizure of Hamilton by the blacks — the calling in of the police. Thus the SDS was able to prove the truth of an old revolutionary adage that no demonstration is successful unless it compels a repression. For the strategical intention (as Howard Hubbard showed in "Five Long Hot Summers and How They Grew," *The Public Interest*, 12, Summer 1968), even when the tactic is nonviolence, is to provoke brutality on the part of the opponent, and thus win the moral — and psychological — case. The lesson of Berkeley four years ago, and of Wisconsin earlier in the academic year (when the police were called in to clear an occupied building and ran wild) is that such repressive force is self-defeating. The Columbia administrators may have known about Berkeley and Wisconsin, but they did not show it.

What might have been

What would have happened had the police had not been called in — if, for example, the adminstration had simply shut down the university while trying to meet with the students and discuss the questions they had raised? In all likelihood — a view admittedly strengthened by hindsight — the students would have split badly among themselves: in part because of the deep differences among them; in part because of the manipulativeness of the SDS leadership which, as it became increasingly dominated by a Maoist faction, was lying to, and thus alienating, its own supporters. The nature of an emotional "conversion experience" is that the new converts, anxious to prove themselves, insist on purity of motive and selfless zeal on the part of their leaders. Disillusionment in such circumstances can be as quick as conversion. SDS had no real interest in any specific program, or in reconstructing the university. But actual reform had motivated many of the students in Avery and Fayerweather, and when they began to discuss these issues, or to question the insistence on "amnesty" by the "revolutionary leadership," many were shocked at the savagery of the response against them. A sensitive graduate student who was a member of the Strike Coordinating Committee, David Osher, has written about this state of affairs in the pacifist publication *WIN*, for July 1968. Radicalization, he writes,

> in effect attitudinal change, is a delicate and fragile process. It can be reversed, and depends on the good faith and sympathy of the individual. The distrust engendered by the unresponsiveness and lack of candor of the [strike] leaders and the overemphasis on amnesty (which whether or not it was a proper demand, was unsellable even to many of the strikers) worked against radicalization. . . . People and buildings changed their positions at different times and responded in various ways. Some caucused, some passed resolutions, some people were upset and quietly left. Ultimately people inside as well as outside the buildings were polarized, and a number of intimate observers

felt that if the cops had not come Monday night an internal rebellion would have developed inside the buildings during the next few days.[19]

After the first police action there was an immense storm of support for the dissident students, and a general strike effectively cancelled most of the classes in the college and the graduate school. But the tensions that had been latent within the Strike Committee became evident as well. SDS had no program, only "tactical issues," and could only try to whip up other incidents. The students who had been angered by the police action began talking of the need to "restructure" the university and explore the role that they, as students, could play in the university. The Faculty Executive Committee began to take an active role in initiating studies on the ways in which the university could be reorganized.[20] In a leaflet distributed to the students, the Faculty Committee said that the tactics of provocation must give way to the politics of reconstruction, and that students had a large role to play within the university. Credibility had begun to revive among the students. The Strike Committee itself was

---

[19] In his account, Oscher describes the tensions within the strike movement:

"Although all the buildings held meetings, had steering committees, and had representatives on a central strike steering committee, power within the strike did not lie in the buildings. Power lay in two bodies, Strike Central, the bureaucracy which resided in Ferris Booth Hall (the unliberated student activities building), and the Central Steering Committee. Both of these groups appeared to be dominated by Progressive Labor-oriented [i.e. Maoist] Columbia SDS leadership. . . . Once they had gained a position of power, the monopolizing of information by those meeting and working in Ferris Booth Hall facilitated their keeping it.

"Strikers in each building depended on the Central Steering Committee for news concerning the positions of allies in other buildings. No one wanted to fink out on the other building, but few knew how the other building felt. At times this was the normal product (and problem) of occupying separate buildings, but in other cases, as in Low Library, leaders censored incoming and outgoing information. While that case may be extreme, buildings were played off against each other. ('Do you want to cop out on your brothers in Hamilton?')"

[20] A news analysis in the Columbia *Spectator* during this period called attention to the change. In the article Paul Starr wrote: "As the Strike Committee moves aimlessly in the midst of its own bureaucracy, making little progress toward achieving its demands, conducting a successful but paradoxically ineffectual strike, and staging confrontation on peripheral issues to keep its troops together, the executive faculty committee has begun to cast itself as the productive and positive force driving at significant change.

"In a sense the faculty committee is trying to reverse roles with SDS. During the occupation of the buildings, the strikers were the only group with a substantial program. Their opponents all seemed defenders of the status quo, and the most conspicuous part of their opposition was a faction that seemed to have no understanding whatsoever of the problems facing the University. SDS held the initiative and clearly controlled the issues that were before the students, if it did not control opinions students held on those issues.

"That, however, is now changing. The strikers are no longer presenting the issues that are being debated. They are no longer the only group with a program for change. Instead, they are now in a position where they, not their opponents, appear obstructionist and negative. The executive faculty committee instead of SDS is proclaiming itself the vanguard."

divided and finally did split on this question, and the majority left the SDS-controlled strike to form the Students for a Restructured University. The SDS itself seemed close to becoming a shambles.[21] At this point the administration, without consulting the Executive Committee of the Faculty, suspended four strike leaders, and out of this confrontation arose Hamilton II, the second uncontrolled police action, and a renewed attack on the administration by the moderate students. Whatever chance the administration had had of winning over the moderate students who wanted the restructuring of the university was lost in this headlong effort to suspend the strike leaders.

In initiating the suspension the administration was — belatedly, by Brzezinski's standards — seeking to assert its authority. It was, to be fair about its own dilemmas, under enormous pressure from a "constituency" of its own — alumni, other universities, and some trustees — to take "action" and demonstrate its "decisiveness." But even in these circumstances — in part because it still did not completely recognize the need to engage students in debate; in part simply for the lack of an adequate apparatus — the administration's public relations were singularly inept. The university never presented its own case for the gymnasium: how it had sought to enlist some Harlem participation but had foundered, partly because it could not deal effectively with a community that itself had no coherent structure or leadership. When the gymnasium plans were completed, the ministers of five of the largest churches in Harlem, as well as Dr. Mamie Phipps Clark, the wife of Dr. Kenneth Clark, and the director of the Northside Center for Child Development, had publicly endorsed the project. But few students in the university knew this. Nor did the university make its case — a legitimate one — for its own needs in the neighborhood. The university itself, as a provider of jobs and as a great intellectual resource, was finding itself choked for space; students wanted more faculty, and wanted the faculty to be available for more sustained contact — yet little faculty housing was available. Any urban environment is necessarily subject to change, and tenants do not have "absolute" rights to apartments, especially slum apartments; the balance of rights should be determined by appropriate planning for the area and the city as a whole.[22]

---

[21] This view is confirmed by a review of strike tactics by the SDS leadership in *New Left Notes,* the national SDS weekly, for June 16, 1968.

[22] The question of how many persons have actually been dispossessed has become a numbers game. In an article in *The New Republic* for May 18, 1968, entitled "Columbia's Real Estate Ventures," James Ridgeway wrote that "*Since World War II,* Columbia and the *other* [institutions on Morningside Heights] methodically pushed out 7,500 residents, most of them poorly off . . . many of them black or Puerto Ricans." In the *Ramparts* account of "The Siege of Columbia," this became: "The population displacement wrought by *Columbia's* institutional programs in Morningside Heights amounted to almost 10,000 people *in the last decade. . . .*" (italics added)

But the major lapse of the administration was its failure to respond to the evident desire for structural change which became
manifest so rapidly once the buildings were seized. There was probably no one at Columbia University with a surer sense of this need
than David Truman. In his report as dean of the college, in June
1967, before the sudden shuffle in which he became vice-president
and provost, Truman had quietly pointed out the defects of the
existing arrangements, and had proposed a new integrative structure which would have brought together the liberal-arts portions
of the university — primarily the college and the three graduate
faculties — and given them an effective voice and leadership in the
university as against the professional schools, which had set the
pace of expansion in the previous decade. In his year as vice-president and provost, Truman had begun to rebuild some weak departments and to revamp the central administration. But Truman worked
cautiously, cards close to the chest, and consulting only a few senior
persons, instead of involving the faculty and even the student body
in broad discussions. And given the sensibilities of Grayson Kirk,
who was close to retirement, and the exigencies of the first large-
scale centralized fund drive in the history of the university, it is
evident that Truman was constrained in effecting the changes that
he wanted to bring about. The consequence was a lack of boldness
in leadership when, psychologically, it was needed more than ever.

The romantic spasm

The New Left, as a social movement, is passing through a phase
ranging from protest to resistance to desperation. Over the past few
years it has modeled itself on the Black Militants, just as the young
middle-class rebels of the 1930's aped the Revolutionary Proletariat.
But the Blacks themselves are in a bind: no matter how much the
leaders rant against The System, a huge "constituency" wants "in,"
and the effectiveness of any continuing black leadership is the degree to which such gains can be achieved. The rhetoric and the
threats are levers for bargaining. Black Power, if it has any meaning,
is a device for the redistribution of privilege and power, not for
total revolution.

The New Left in contrast, wants "total" change in the society.

According to Morningside Heights, Inc., a group of ten institutions including
Columbia, Union Theological Seminary, and St. Luke's Hospital, as of June 1,
1957 the ten institutions owned 151 parcels of land, containing 3,561 apartments at the time of purchase which, after renovation or removal for new
buildings, contained 3,072, or a loss of 489 apartments. Of the 107 buildings
which Columbia itself owned, there was *a net loss of 166 apartments*. These
would be apartments in which individuals were evicted for new institutional
building. In the retained buildings, Columbia and the other institutions gives
preference, when apartments become free, to its own personnel.

But is hoist on the dilemma that it has no effective vision of a "counter society," other than the ephemeral "participatory democracy" — which, in hothouse revolutionary situations such as Columbia, quickly gave way to cadre organization and manipulation — and as a "total" movement it does not want to bargain. Worse, being a tiny minority it has no lever for change other than disruption. Disruption in the society at large is at present impossible; hence The New Left has been forced to retreat more and more into the university and to resort to more grandiose dreams and more megalomaniacal visions. The title of an article by Tom Hayden in *Ramparts* is entitled "Two, Three, Many Columbias"; he does not explain the title, but the allusion is clear to those in the know: Ché Guevera's call to create "Two, Three, Many Vietnams" in Latin America. It is a call for guerrilla action. In that curious merger of apocalyptic language and practical instruction that forms the catechism of the revolutionary, whether Nechayev or Debray, Hayden writes:

> Columbia opened a new tactical stage in the resistance movement which began last fall: from overnight occupation of buildings to permanent occupation; from mill-ins to the creation of revolutionary committees; from symbolic civil disobedience to barricades resistance. Not only are these tactics already being duplicated on other campuses, but they are sure to be surpassed by even more militant tactics. In the future it is conceivable that students will threaten destruction of buildings as a last deterrent to police attacks. Many of the tactics learned can also be applied in smaller hit-and-run operations between strikes: raids on the offices of professors doing weapons research could win substantial support among students while making the university more blatantly repressive.

Such desperado tactics are never the mark of a coherent social movement, but the guttering last gasps of a romanticism soured by rancor and impotence. The SDS will be destroyed by its style. It lives on turbulence, but is incapable of transforming its chaotic impulses into a systematic, responsible behavior that is necessary to effect broad societal change. In fact, its very style denies the desirability of such conduct, for like many chiliastic sects its ideological antinomianism carries over into a similar psychological temper, or rather distemper. It is impelled not to innovation, but to destruction.

But the questions it raises—the challenges to hierarchical decision-making and the desires for broadened participation in the institutions that affect their lives — are real ones. They reflect the more generalized sources of student unrest which themselves arise out of world-wide structural changes in advanced industrial societies — the imposition of "organized harnesses" in a technological society, just as, more than a hundred years ago, a "machine-paced harness" was imposed on a rurally transformed industrial working class. In both instances the reactions have been familiar: an anarcho-syndicalist mood of rebellion, which today is psychologically joined to the rebellion of the color-shaded agrarian *tiers monde* against the world's cities. In the post-industrial societies of tomorrow — in which the university is, I would claim, *the* paramount institution — the problems of decentralization, of the balance between technical and political decision-making and of greater participation, will be pressing ones. I shall discuss these broader questions in another article. But in the world of the university, as the experience of Columbia demonstrates, these problems have already come to the fore, and are now on the agenda.

The issue of disruption and of the character of the university are one. The authority of a university is not a civil authority but a moral one. It can deal with disruptions — or its threats — not by invoking civil force but by rallying an entire community to establish common rules of common procedure. Disruptive students can only be contained by a faculty and by other students, not by the police. The nature of a university, as a moral community rather than as a political society is its openness to all points of view within the primary values of the search for truth and the maintenance of open procedures. Hence confrontation politics — as a means of imposing a particular political point of view, and particularly through coercion — is inadmissible. But all this is only possible when a university makes the fullest commitment to being a participatory institution, to an extent consonant with its full responsibilities. This means, of course, neither student power nor faculty power nor any such shibboleths, but the definition of areas of rights and powers and responsibilities appropriate to the division of function and place in the university itself. Unless it takes those steps, convincingly, to enlarge that participation, the university — and Columbia — may be forced to the wall by those who, in the words of Fidel Castro that the New Left has adopted, are "guerrillas in the field of culture."

6

The case
of
the Columbia
gym

ROGER STARR

IN the days when every eastern preparatory school for boys staged an annual Gilbert and Sullivan operetta, it was not uncommon for three prominent faculty members to appear together in a curtain raiser: *Box and Cox*. Messrs. Box and Cox were two Victorian gentlemen who, unknown to each other, rented the same room from the same landlady, an economic feat made possible by the fact that Mr. Cox worked during the day while Mr. Box worked at night. The arrangement remained hidden to both tenants until Mr. Cox was let off early one day by his employer, and returned to discover his room occupied by an apparent interloper. The farce reached a stirring climax — a scene in which the landlady, frequently played by the headmaster in a stringy red wig, at length pacified her two part-time tenants, who indeed are discovered to be long-lost brothers.

Box and Cox come to mind in connection with the now notorious episode of the Columbia gymnasium in Morningside Park, not only because the gymnasium would have involved a similar stratagem of mutually exclusive utilization of the same area by two occupants, but because the stratagem itself, like the operatic curtain raiser, may suffer from obsolescence. Then again, it may not. One's judgment of the feasibility of the stratagem involves an inquiry into the current state of relations between the two occupants — the urban university, on the one hand, and that squirming human conglomerate called "the community," on the other. The state of their relations is also necessarily affected by a third party — the headmaster-landlady, or municipal government.

The geography of Morningside Heights

Some of the present tension between Columbia University and those who reside in its environs derives from simple geography. Columbia University's main plant is located on Morningside Heights, a section of Manhattan Island that lies between 110th Street and 125th Street on the West Side, between Morningside Park on the east and the Hudson River on the west. This high ground falls sharply toward 125th Street on the north, as much as 100 feet below Low Library, the administrative heart of the university. To the east, the land similarly drops away rapidly across narrow Morningside Park. Frederick Law Olmsted and Calvert Vaux, who were engaged as landscape architects to prepare the plan for the use of this park, described its terrain in their official 1873 report in these words: "The only surfaces within it not sharply inclined, are two small patches lying widely apart, against the northeast and southeast corners respectively; most of the remainder being precipitous hillside, formed by the rounded face of a ledge of gneiss, difficult, unsafe, and in parts, impracticable to travel over."

At the bottom of Morningside Park, on the flats below the Heights on which Columbia perches, Harlem begins and spreads east and north. The topography expresses itself symbolically — the spires of learning on the sunny heights; the teeming black slums at their feet; Morningside Park, the sterile separator.

Columbia's presence on the Heights and the insulation of this plateau from the hurly-burly of New York, attracted a number of so-called "sister" institutions to the area. These now number sixteen, including among others the Union Theological Seminary, the Jewish Theological Seminary, St. Luke's Hospital, the Woman's Hospital, the Cathedral of St. John the Divine, International House, and The Riverside Church, whose neo-Gothic structure was endowed by John D. Rockefeller, Sr. That gentleman's interest in the church probably accounts for a continuing involvement in the Morningside Heights area by his descendants, none of whom attended Columbia, but who have endowed the institutions and contributed to Morningside Heights, Inc., an institutionally sponsored land development company.

The impressive institutional aura, added to the naturally desirable topography, sustained a residential rental demand for apartments on Morningside Heights in the years before World War II, even when much of the rest of the West Side sagged badly. Faculty members installed themselves in stately turn-of-the-century apartments on nearby Riverside Drive, Claremont Avenue, and on some of the cross streets. The strength of market demand can be measured crudely by the fact that no Negro families could be found on the "better" blocks on the Heights before World War II (few enough are to be found there today). This contrasts markedly with the situation below the Heights, across Morningside Park. Solid, middle-class apartment houses, similar to those on the Heights, were originally built on Morningside Avenue, the wide, handsome street that forms the eastern boundary of the Park. White families occupied them as late as the early 1930's; but by the end of that decade, they had been entirely taken over by Negroes, a fact that testifies not to the generous human impulses of their owners and residents, but rather to the lack of attraction of the avenue for white tenants.

Although the Heights in general retained much of their dignity, deterioration began in certain specific areas, usually following the elevated transit lines, which surge out of the ground at 120th Street. In the shadow of the "El," LaSalle Street became a notorious slum. Market weakness for standard apartments on the side streets and less attractive avenues stimulated the growth of so-called Single Room Occupancy buildings, in which the old apartments were cut up to take care of individual lodgers, each with a locked bedroom, but sharing common baths. These developments may have originally catered to students. Ultimately, many were taken over by poor households, by elderly individuals with tiny incomes and serious health problems, or by problem-ridden vagrants, alcoholics, prostitutes, and petty criminals.

This spotty deterioration aside, there was no significant problem of adjustment between the neighboring residents and the institutions in the depression decade before the war. Columbia lacked the funds or a motive for expansion. Even if the university had wished to expand, the large number of residential vacancies would have mitigated the potential threat. After the end of World War II, these situations changed drastically. Higher education emerged as one of the major urban growth industries: many Morningside institutions began to expand their plants to take care of the greatly expanded demand for their services. Simultaneously, the supply of available apartments in New York City disappeared, and the fear of losing irreplaceably one's rent-controlled home to the land appetite of a large university overshadowed the comfort and prestige of living in its environs.

Columbia expands

For its part, Columbia's expansion involved several different objectives. First, the university required land to meet its burgeoning

graduate programs — a new law school, a new business school,
and other specialized academic buildings, all advocated strenuously
by the deans of the several faculties involved. The university had
other needs as well — sensed and perceived needs — aside from
those connected with the rise in the number of students. Thus,
Columbia, like many other urban universities, sought to maintain
its attractiveness for students and staff by cleaning up crime and
personal danger in its environs. Columbia tried to accomplish this
by purchasing properties that were notoriously deteriorated, removing the occupants, and — sometimes after substantial reconstruction — finding a new tenancy. Morningside Heights, Inc. sponsored one of the first completed Title I redevelopments in New York
City, a total clearance and redevelopment project called Morningside Gardens, which replaced badly deteriorated slums with a
racially integrated cooperative for middle-class families. The scheme
included facilities to be shared jointly by the middle-class families
of Morningside and the low-income tenants of the federally subsidized public housing project — General Grant Houses — which
had been built next door. Currently, such a calculated juxtaposition
of middle-class and low-income families attracts enthusiastic en-
comia such as "imaginative planning," and "innovative social de-
signs," but no one seems to remember that this was first accomplished
ten and more years ago on Morningside Heights under the combined auspices of the Rockefeller family and Mr. Robert Moses.

From the point of view of Columbia and the other institutions,
purchasing buildings for rehabilitation simply to get rid of "unde-
sirables" has not been a profitable activity; at least its profits have
not included a noticeable improvement in local good-will toward
the institution. Even though the process is directed toward a goal
— less crime, less sluminess — which respectable neighbors treas-
ure, it simultaneously emphasizes the determination of the institutions to shape the neighborhood to suit their own needs, even if
they must displace people in the process. The implications of such
a program are clear to the neighbors of the displacees, especially
if they are aware that, since 1957, Columbia has acquired properties
on the Heights with an assessed valuation of nearly $12 million.
The number of apartments in these buildings has been reduced by
approximately 12 per cent (2,957 to 2,582); the number of single
room units by approximately 70 per cent (466 to 146). On Morningside Heights, the local political clubs and other civic organizations
have denounced Columbia's tactics in emptying buildings in order
to erase pockets of decay and disorderliness. In response, Columbia
has, in one Single Room Occupancy building, mounted a program
in collaboration with St. Luke's Hospital dedicated to relieving the
"social pathology" of the tenants without physically removing them.
In the current jargon, this is "upgrading people rather than build-

ings," and is greatly commended by the residents' organizations who perhaps sense that it is so difficult, complicated, expensive, slow, and ultimately dubious in its effectiveness that it represents no danger to the status quo.

The need for recreational space

Finally, Columbia has special land needs that derive from the fact that its full-time undergraduate college is located on Morningside Heights and that Columbia classes itself among the Ivy League colleges. All of the rest of these have ample recreational facilities for their male undergraduates. Dartmouth, for one, has a Field House designed by the noted Italian engineer, Nervi, in which standard baseball games may be played indoors. City-bound Harvard enjoys forty acres of playing fields primarily for intermural sports. Even the completion of the new gymnasium, that provoked such a furor, would leave Columbia College outclassed by its peers, and at a disadvantage in the competition for students.

The existence of such competition is hidden from the public and the parents of young men who wish to go to Ivy League colleges. These innocents are led to believe that these famous institutions are inundated with prospective students in a market so grossly favorable to the deans of admission that it cries for federal redress. The colleges, however, and especially those with special disadvantages — such as Columbia, are fighting with one another — politely, of course — in an effort to attract the greatest number of those future undergraduates who reveal the highest promise. Why should an institution subject itself to the pressures of this competition? Columbia College's insistence on being an Ivy League college may reflect the pride of senior faculty, the affiliations of the board of trustees, the wishes of alumni (who are, of course, also financial contributors) or the value system — perhaps not even articulated — of the university's high administration. But whatever the reasons for Columbia's Ivy League orientation, so long as it continues, adequate recreational space — approaching Ivy League standards — must be provided for its male undergraduates. The search for recreation space brings Columbia into contact with Harlem below Morningside Park and to the east of it; the other demands for space involved only the neighbors living on the Heights.

A shortage of outdoor play space, particularly for the organized athletics of young men, has caused thoughtful New Yorkers to deprecate Manhattan as a place in which to raise their children. Olmsted noted, in his 1873 report on Morningside Park, that "New York . . . has no ground for the athletic exercises of young men, the open spaces of Central Park not being suitable for the purpose. . . ." Since 1873, Manhattan has become vastly more crowded, while public acceptance of the need for physical exercise and games in schools has become much more intense. The play-space standards of Manhattan schools — both public and private — appall educational planners who have established the standards generally accepted elsewhere in the United States. New York public school playgrounds can accommodate only desultory play after school, or on holidays. Only one Manhattan high school has a field adequate for football or soccer. As a result, organized outdoor athletics can be held only on parkland.

The Department of Parks has sought to schedule athletic activities in its public facilities so that organized teams can make the best use of them. Thus, Randall's Island, a park developed on an island physically separate from — but politically attached to — Manhattan, provides a number of baseball diamonds and soccer fields, where use is scheduled for private and public school students by the parks department. In the past two years, however, private school headmasters have noted that the growing racial tension in New York City has undermined the arrangements for sharing such facilities. There have been too many "incidents," some of them serious.

Predecessors of the gym

Columbia's own post-war efforts to provide informal outdoor recreation space for its college undergraduates involved a similar joint use of public facilities. While public and private schools use public park facilities without having constructed them, Columbia paid for the construction of facilities on parkland which would then be open to its students and to non-Columbia people on a prearranged schedule. For its part, the park department pays to maintain the facilities constructed by Columbia. Under such an arrangement, ratified by the city, Columbia constructed two softball baseball diamonds in Morningside Park, in the southeast end of the park on what Olmsted had noted to be one of its two flat areas. The university installed a fence around the diamonds, which, with outfields and other open space, took some five acres of land. The university also constructed a locker room and office. (Hulan Jack, the first Negro Borough President of Manhattan, was in office when the Columbia-Community Athletic field was approved.) The agreement between Columbia and the city provided, and still provides, that the Columbia-Community Morningside field will be reserved for Columbia use on all weekdays between September 30 and June 1, except during college vacations. On all other days the field is reserved for non-Columbia users. Coincidentally, the softball fields have almost precisely the same dimensions as regulation little league baseball diamonds, and the field is used for regular teenage and sub-teenage baseball during the summer months. These are unquestionably the best public baseball facilities in Harlem. Columbia provides a coaching staff which has no responsibility other than that of supervising the athletics. In the fall months, football is played on the field; a board track is installed during the winter.[1]

The Columbia-Community Athletic Field has been widely praised by Harlem politicians, clergymen, social workers, and parents. The teams are sponsored by local block associations, settlement houses and community centers, merchants, housing project tenants' organizations, and such political action groups as the Urban League. Few criticisms of the Field are heard; explosive events on the Columbia campus had no discernible effect on the Field or its program. Yet it would be a mistake to believe that the program is universally acknowledged a success, with no offsetting costs. Some local groups, including particularly those with a special interest in parkland, feel that any appropriation of parkland to a special use is questionable. The Columbia-Community Athletic Field is off-limits to everyone who does not actively participate in its programs. The programs, furthermore, are open only to those boys and young men who either belong to a team, or are stable enough to join one and remain with it, after presenting themselves for a tryout. The players, though most of them come from poor or nearly poor families, are not the delinquent or pre-delinquent children of Harlem; they are, rather, its future middle-class citizens. One alumnus of the Columbia-Community Field program later developed into one of the outstanding athletes to play baseball and football for Hofstra; others have done well at other high schools and colleges in the metropolitan area.

For those who feel that social welfare programs should accord absolute priority to the most disturbed and badly used groups in the population, the Columbia-Community Field Program may seem a trivial contribution to the psychological prosperity of Harlem. The dedication of five acres of the thirty-one in Morningside Park to organized sports may offend those who believe that parkland should be open to all, at all times and places, but the Box and Cox sharing of the Columbia-Community Field works smoothly. As noted, Columbia undergraduates have exclusive use of these five acres on weekdays when the university is in session. It is precisely at

[1] At the present time, Columbia reports that forty-five baseball and softball teams, playing in five permanent leagues, use the field on a scheduled basis. There are forty other teams using the facilities regularly, but not in league competition. The leagues are arranged by age, and include boys from ten to seventeen years. All games are umpired by umpires who are paid by Columbia; this community program costs Columbia $25,000 per year, without including the interest on the approximately $250,000 that was spent on erecting the structures. To run the program, Columbia picked a Negro social worker with an M.A. in sociology; by all accounts, his work has been excellent. The field is used by approximately 2,500 boys each year.

these times that the community users are themselves in school. Columbia's student use terminates in the spring, just when longer daylight and school vacations make the field more usable by the young community team players. Any effort to abolish the Field would surely engender disappointment and opposition by the great majority of those who use Morningside Park or are likely to use it. The park department may terminate the arrangement on one-month notice; it has, of course, chosen not to do so.

The gym is envisioned

The absence of serious friction over the use of the Columbia-Community Field led to the construction by Columbia of tennis courts in Riverside Park. These are shared by university and non-university users on a time-schedule similar to that established for the athletic field. The success led also to the development of plans for a gymnasium in Morningside Park.

In 1958 — according to Harold McGuire, vice chairman of the Columbia board of trustees — President Grayson Kirk of Columbia approached the then Commissioner of Parks of the City of New York, Robert Moses, to explore the possibility that Columbia might construct a community gymnasium adjacent to the joint playing field, reserving for itself the air rights over this building on which to build a gymnasium for the use of the university. On the surface, the plan made sense. The city would get a gymnasium free, while Columbia would have for its own use a gymnasium building near to the playing field, without having to purchase new land and without the necessity of demolishing approximately two-thirds of a block of residential buildings on the Heights.

To explore the matter, President Kirk appointed a gymnasium committee of university administrators, faculty, and alumni. The committee initially turned the proposal down on the grounds that it would leave the university's investment in a gymnasium resting precariously on the roof of a building which, in turn, would rest on land to which the university would lack clear tenure. The gymnasium committee urged the president to ask Mr. Moses if he would sell enough parkland to erect a gymnasium on, perhaps with the proviso that an equal amount of good land would be added to the park in exchange. Mr. Moses declined to advocate the sale of parkland. Ultimately, the committee reconsidered its position to the extent that it agreed to the construction of a gymnasium on parkland, provided that the parkland site was approved by the State Legislature, the Governor, the City Council of New York, and the Board of Estimate of the City of New York, which is the city's eight-man governing body. This stipulation was somewhat super-fluous. All of these steps would have had to be taken in any case, because in New York State the city is deemed to hold parkland only as an instrument of state government. Under New York City's Home Rule powers, the state government will consent to the sale or lease of parkland only on the city's official request.

The basic agreement, as negotiated by the park department and Columbia University in 1960, provided that the university would lease 2.1 acres of land in the park, adjacent to the playing field and notched into the difficult ledge of gneiss, of which Olmsted wrote. On this site the university would, with its own funds, erect a community gymnasium containing the facilities that the park department specified, including primarily basketball courts and locker rooms; this would be leased by the university to the Department of Parks, which would pay no cash rent. Above the community gymnasium and extending to the receding rock ledge, the university could build its own gymnasium. No limit was placed on the size of the gymnasium that the university would construct for itself, but the university was asked by its neighbors on the Heights to limit as much as possible the elevation of the building's roof above the level of Morningside Drive. The roof parapet of the gymnasium was therefore to be only twenty-nine feet above the street level.

The initial period of the land lease to Columbia, together with the sublease of the community gymnasium to the park department, was fifty years. The land lease provided that Columbia would pay a rent of $3,000 per year for the land. This figure, arrived at by the city's real estate department, after the city and Columbia had presented independent appraisals, reflected in theory the rental value of the land itself, less the rental value of the facility that Columbia was building for exclusive use by the park department. The rental figure did not, however, include any offset to Columbia for the cost of coaching and other athletic services provided in connection with the joint field and the indoor space, a cost then estimated at $50,000 per year, including the $25,000 already being spent on the outdoor program. The net land rental figure was subject to re-negotiation at the end of each of the terms of the lease, but in no case to be lower than its original figure. At the expiration of the last possible renewal — 100 years from the opening of the building — the entire building, including both gymnasiums, would become city property.

The gym is discussed

On February 2, 1960, State Senator James L. Watson, a Negro who represented the Morningside-West Harlem area in the upper house of the State Legislature, introduced a bill authorizing the city to enter into a lease of specified parkland in Morningside Park to Columbia University. A companion bill was introduced by the late John Brook, a Republican, in the State Assembly. The City Council's Committee on State Legislation held a public hearing on March 1, 1960, to determine whether or not the city should send a Home Rule message to the State Legislature, asking for passage of the Gymnasium Bill. The committee, with the enthusiastic endorsement of Minority Leader Stanley M. Isaacs, unanimously recommended the sending of such a message; the council accepted this recommendation. The mayor signed the Home Rule message, and the gymnasium bill passed the Assembly and Senate on March 21 and 22 without a negative vote. The law was signed by Governor Rockefeller on April 14, 1960. This permitted the city government and Columbia to negotiate the terms of the lease which the legislation authorized. The negotiations took fifteen months. Finally, on July 27, 1961, the Board of Estimate, on due notice, held a hearing on the proposed lease.

Although it has been charged that the gymnasium matter received little attention at the time, and was sneaked through stealthily much as the landlady sneaked Mr. Box into Cox's room, a number of citizens appeared at the public hearing at the Board of Estimate. The Citizens Union opposed the lease primarily on the grounds that it was opposed in principle to construction of such a structure within a public park. Harmon Goldstone, then representing the Municipal Art Society, opposed the structure for much the same reason. St. Luke's Hospital and the Cathedral of St. John the Divine also opposed the development.

All of the local organizations from Morningside Heights *and* West Harlem that appeared at the hearing testified in favor of the gymnasium proposal. These were the Adult-Youth Association, which had tried to develop an athletic program in the park before the development of the Columbia-Community Field; the Grant-Morningside Neighborhood Group, an organization developed by some of the tenants in Grant House and the tenant cooperators of the adjacent Morningside Gardens. James Murphy, Chairman of the Morningside Citizens Committee, spoke in favor of the lease on behalf of his organization.

At the conclusion of the hearing, Borough President Edward Dudley, successor to Hulan Jack and similarly a Harlem resident, moved approval of the lease. The motion carried unanimously. On August 3, 1961, a *New York Times* editorial praised the gymnasium arrangement as a worthwhile exception to the *Times'* general principle that parkland should not be invaded for "nonpark purposes."

A contract is signed

At the end of the month, the commissioner of parks, then Newbold Morris, and Columbia University signed the agreement of lease, which then became a binding and enforceable obligation on both parties. Simultaneously, the two parties executed a supplemental agreement that spelled out the coaching services and equipment that the university would provide both within the community gymnasium and on the joint playing field. The city, however, had full and exclusive rights to the use of the community gymnasium, and was not restricted to the use of Columbia staff, or to the hours when the Columbia staff was obligated by the agreement to be present.

The lease included preliminary plans for the building containing the two gymnasiums. Under it, Columbia was obligated to prepare within nine months a second set of plans, called "intermediate plans," which could not deviate significantly from the preliminary plans, except with the approval of the city. After receiving these intermediate plans, the city had a six-month period in which to take exception to them. Following approval of the intermediate plans, Columbia was required to provide final working drawings; these had to be presented to the city no later than five and one-half years after the execution of the lease. (The reason for this long lead time turned out to be crucial to the whole project.) Columbia was given the option of cancelling the lease at any time within five years after its execution if the university was unable to raise enough funds to see the construction through. If the lease was not so cancelled, Columbia had to begin construction of the gymnasium within six years of the signing of the lease, or by August 29, 1967. If it started the construction, the university was further required to complete the building of the gymnasium within five years after the initial ground-breaking.

Columbia's wish for extended time to commence construction was based on the fund-raising theory that people will give money to a building more readily before it is completed than later, when they are already sitting in it. The applicability of this theory to the gymnasium issue is, in the bright light of today, highly questionable. Columbia surely had the funds to proceed with the construction, which, at the beginning of the project, was estimated to cost $6 million. By the time ground was actually broken, the university had spent three-fourths of a million dollars on architects and fund-raisers, while the prospective cost had risen to more than $13 million. This increase reflects changed specifications and initial over-optimism, as well as the inflation in costs through the passage of time. While recognizing that the comparison is not entirely valid, one cannot help but compare the $5.2 million raised in contributions and pledges during the years between 1961 and 1966 with the escalation of $7 million in the cost of the building in the same period. The delay does not appear, in retrospect, to have been economically profitable. Politically, it was disastrous.

1961–1966: conditions change

Between 1961 and 1966, the world changed — most particularly the urban world. The question was raised whether municipal decisions taken in 1961 were still valid in 1966, especially if they had not yet been rendered into steel and stone. Current critics of the gymnasium project have urged its cancellation on these grounds, without appearing to recognize the implications of this view: If contractual relationships between governments and private parties cannot be extended longer than the favor of the public, who will enter into contracts with the government? And if governments can reshape contracts retrospectively, to win public favor, why should they remain hampered by a Constitutional restriction against reshaping laws retrospectively, to make unpopular persons guilty of offenses for acts that were not illegal when committed? The issue at stake may be "merely" legal; but it is not trivial.

That adapting governmental process to social change is difficult, however, by no means denies the reality of social change. Between 1961 and 1966, in New York City, a new political administration had come into office, following one election in which the Democrats retained power only by dismembering their own party. In the resulting scramble, each municipal office-holder felt himself justified in disclaiming loyalty to the acts of his predecessors, and the sense of party continuity had all but vanished from local political life. Meanwhile, momentous changes in the fervor with which Black Americans articulated their grievances changed the political implications of every urban decision in which people of different races were involved. Widespread suspicion of local government, based primarily on its inability to devise programs to meet the most serious urban needs, made inevitable a growing belief that the local community must join in the formulation of programs. This belief was not accompanied by any clear suggestion as to what the local community is or who can speak for it.

In Morningside Heights, these issues have had particular impact, and, in combination, they produced the gymnasium crisis. Most probably, however, they would not have interacted so strongly, had they not been triggered by a longstanding urban political question: the question of parkland use.

Enter Mr. Hoving

Park lovers are among the most obstinate of urban citizens. The tireless emotions of park lovers kept the mere signing of a legal contract between the City of New York and Columbia University from extinguishing the conviction in their breasts that the use of parkland for an alien building is *never* pardonable. Note that this axiom is a universal; if parkland is not suited for a gymnasium, the size of the gymnasium neither aggravates nor mitigates its unsuitability. Nor do the nature of ownership of the building or its accessibility to the general public change matters for park purists, of whom, one supposes, Mayor Lindsay's first Park Commissioner, Thomas P. F. Hoving, is an example. Mr. Hoving frequently stated that a permanent building in a park is unacceptable; in the pursuit of this principle, he prevailed upon Mr. Huntington Hartford to withdraw the proferred gift of a cafeteria restaurant to the city. The cafe would have been open to the public, but it would have been fixed to the terrain of Central Park, smothering parkland below it. Similarly, Mr. Hoving had taken the position that permanent kiosks for the sale of refreshments are unsuitable in Central Park, but that movable and demountable kiosks are all right.

One may or may not be persuaded by the principle that parkland must remain forever green, but even those who disagree with it can scarcely attack it on logical grounds. As a result, this objection to the Columbia gymnasium — its intrinsic unsuitability in a park — is unassailable. Unfortunately for many of those who base their opposition to the Columbia Community gymnasium on this axiom, it, like so many other universals, is weakened, not strengthened, by the addition of particularities. To add to one's opposition that the Columbia Community gymnasium does not properly belong in Morningside Park because it is *big* or *open in large part to undergraduates only,* raises new arguments which at least inferentially suggest that a smaller gymnasium or one open to everybody would be acceptable and that, therefore, in certain cases parkland can be used properly for buildings. Moreover, the absolutist argument that no parkland is ever suitable for permanent building raises difficulties in practice; even Mr. Hoving himself approved the construction of a police stable in Central Park, perhaps because he proposed to construct a polo field on the roof. When the Board of Estimate cancelled out the polo field, Mr. Hoving nevertheless continued to press for the construction of the stables; on one festive occasion he appeared in public with a sign purporting to reproduce a fictitious endorsement by "C. Vaux and F. Olmsted" of the stable-cum-polo-field project. The laws of New York State, incidentally, favor the flexible Hoving as against the absolutist Hoving, because, as we have seen, they establish conditions under which parkland may not only be built on but alienated.

In testimony before the Cox Commission (named not for Mr. Box's co-tenant, but for Archibald Cox, former Solicitor General of the United States, its chairman), which the executive committee of the faculty of Columbia University established to investigate the spring disturbances of 1968, Harold F. McGuire, testifying as chairman of the university's gymnasium committee, said that in Mr. Hoving's opposition to the gymnasium project "you have the germs, and all the ideas, that we have heard a great deal of in recent weeks here that you have been asked to investigate." That Mr. Hoving played a large role in the final turn of events is clear. That this role was particularly disturbing to the university officials concerned in the gymnasium is also clear, because they saw Mr. Hoving as a double agent — a city official sworn to uphold his government's laws and to execute its responsibilities, yet who was quoted as having said he would defeat, *by extra-legal means if necessary,* a contract entered into by that same city government. But it is not quite accurate to believe that he originated all opposition: he rather gave focus and official concentration to what seems to have been generally inchoate and disorganized opposition among residents of the Heights and local groups.

The opposition spreads

Simply viewed, normal self-interest should have inclined the organizations of Morningside Heights to favor the use of parkland for the gymnasium. After all, this land was unoccupied and unoccupiable, and to build a gymnasium in the park reduced the pressure to build it somewhere else on Morningside Heights. Nevertheless, major political and community groups on the Heights adopted resolutions of opposition to the gymnasium after Mr. Hoving's accession to office. The Riverside Democrats, a local political club, had long been in opposition because, in the words of one leader, "the park gymnasium represented more piecemeal planning." The criticism is an interesting one, because it reflects the shapelessness of the fear of displacement that hangs over the residents on the Heights. From their point of view, the university's failure to define precisely the long-term nature of its expansion works a special hardship of uncertainty. The university, pursuing its policy of land acquisition without announcing the purpose for which it is acquiring each parcel, resisted any effort to make it disclose in detail its long-range plans — merely consenting to the designation of certain gross areas of the Heights for possible future institutional expansion. One is left to theorize about the reasons for the silence. Foremost, one supposes, has been the unwillingness of the present university administration to place limits on future land use that the future will later reveal to be inadequate. Whatever plan is revealed, the university administration may be afraid that the plan itself will engender conflict that might precede by years the actual preparation for relocation and demolition: why, one imagines the administrators asking themselves, provoke a quarrel now about something that may not happen for fifteen years? The university administrators may also be chary about announcing long range plans because of the uncertain nature of

their cash flow: the prediction of the future financial capacity of a
university is a hazardous venture, depending on the forecast of
fund-raising efforts and possible future government assistance. These
may indeed be good reasons, convincing to the administrators, but
even if they were articulated, they could scarcely convince local residents to submit quietly to years of mysterious but undefined menace.
In this atmosphere, the gymnasium issue became a weapon with
which to attack the menace.

In March 1966, shortly after Mr. Hoving took office, the Morningside Renewal Council, a semi-official group representing "the
Morningside community," adopted a resolution opposing the gymnasium project because "it involves the use of parkland for non-
public and non-park purposes." The council asked the city to rescind
its agreements with Columbia covering both the gymnasium project
and the outdoor Columbia-Community Athletic Field. Within two
months of the meeting at which this resolution was adopted, Mr.
Hoving spoke at an outdoor rally of the Ad Hoc Committee for
Morningside Park, and was quoted by the *West Side News and
Morningsider*, April 28, 1966, as saying: "I am dead set against this
gymnasium and I will fight as hard as I can to stop it." A long list
of organizations and individuals were identified by the newspaper
as having affiliated themselves with the Ad Hoc Committee, including Amalia Batanzos, then a Democratic District co-leader, and State
Senator Basil Paterson, who was the first prominent Negro legislator
to come out in opposition to the gymnasium. Mr. Paterson was quoted
by the newspaper as saying that "Columbia shall not build a gym
in this park. Let the first bulldozers come here and you'll know what
we mean." In the State Legislature he, together with Percy Sutton,
later to become Borough President of Manhattan, sponsored a bill
that would have rescinded the city's power to grant the lease on
the gymnasium site; the bill failed to pass and would, in any case,
have been of doubtful constitutionality.

The activities of Mr. Hoving and the legislators almost certainly
would have fallen short of stopping the gymnasium by themselves.
The city was, inescapably, bound by a contract leasing the land to
Columbia University, and so long as Columbia executed its part of
the agreement, only a suit successfully challenging the legality of the
basic lease itself could have annulled its obligations. However, the
administration of Columbia and high officials of the city began meeting in February and March 1967 to see whether any terms of the
lease might be amended in an effort to meet Hoving's criticism that
the community facilities were too small. He was quoted by the press
as having said that the toilets were inadequate and that since the
"community" had provided all of the land, the community should get
a majority of the benefits. On this last proposition, Columbia's view
had been that it was constructing what the park department had

wanted. Whether the facilities needed by its own students were larger or smaller than what the park department said it wanted for the public was therefore irrelevant.

As a result of the meetings of 1967, it was agreed that the lease should be modified to extend the time of execution, and to provide that a swimming pool be included in the community part of the structure. The amendments to the lease were approved by the Board of Estimate in October 1967, on a somewhat reluctant motion by Borough President Percy Sutton, the same man who, one and a half years earlier, had sought to introduce legislation rescinding the entire lease. When these amendments were passed by the Board of Estimate — bringing the total community gymnasium cost to Columbia to $3 million (including the capital needed to provide income for coaching services and maintenance) — all parties appear to have breathed a symbolic sigh of satisfaction. Columbia thought it would get its gymnasium; the city administration had got a "better deal" for the community than its predecessors; the "new" Negro legislators and officials could claim part of the credit for the same achievements. Mr. Hoving himself had left the administration, to be replaced by August Heckscher whose view of the uses of parkland and recreation was at least flexible enough to permit himself to be quoted in July 1967 in favor of the Columbia-Community Gymnasium.

Enter Black Power

But all of these cheerful expectations were curdled by the rapid development of the theories of Black Power. Local exponents of Black Power mobilized in two years (from early 1966 to early 1968) so much intellectual energy in opposition to the gymnasium that they ignited a formidable protest among university undergraduates, and caused Borough President Sutton to announce on numerous occasions that the gymnasium was being imposed on the black community against its will.

In place of Mr. Hoving, who had fought the gymnasium with all his power because it was a "bad deal" for "the community" — meaning, one supposes, the city's people taken collectively — Columbia found itself confronted by a new municipal opponent, Chairman William H. Booth of the city's Human Rights Commission. Mr. Booth, a Negro, opposed the gymnasium because he said that it would segregate New Yorkers into two different areas, one for the community — black — one for the university — white. (The existence of black students at Columbia was ignored.) He also criticized the fact that entrance to the gymnasium was to be had by two different doors; one, on the top of Morningside Park, would admit matriculated students into the Columbia section of the building; the other door, at the foot of the hill, would admit all others into the community section of the building. The building, therefore, became, in the words of a number of speakers, "Gym Crow."

Active protests began with the actual start of construction, in February 1968; by April, when the Columbia campus erupted, the dissident students made the cessation of gymnasium construction one of their principal demands. The park, some of them said, should be preserved intact, not because it was parkland, but because it had been taken from the black community to which, they claimed, it "belonged." In the midst of this turmoil, the faculty of the school of architecture adopted a resolution condemning the gymnasium project, and urging that construction be discontinued. This, seven years after the issue had been joined, was the first position taken by the architectural faculty.

The vehemence of the protest persuaded Mayor Lindsay to request that Columbia cease work on the gymnasium, a request to which the university acceded, without prejudice to its right to recommence. On the same day, the Fire Department cancelled its explosives permit, apparently in fear of further, more serious disturbance. At the time the work was suspended, rock drilling had proceeded along the entire face of the escarpment, which has been partially squared off to accept the new building. Even if the gymnasium is never completed, one wonders how the park can be left in its present condition. The university had contracted with the George A. Fuller Company to construct the building; presumably it will be liable for costs sustained by that company, in the event that the building does not proceed. This and all other questions of liability remain open and incomplete, like the excavation itself.

Although the present opponents of the gymnasium stress the alleged outrage committed against the black community by the segregated gymnasium, it cannot be said fairly that this state of mind is shared by all or even a majority of Harlem residents. The Citizens Care Committee, an active group in the area, continues to support the gymnasium. A number of Negro political and community figures, including Assemblyman Lloyd Dickens, Assemblyman Hulan Jack, Arthur Reed (Executive Director, Morningside Community Center), have frequently spoken in favor of the community gymnasium, although they have been critical of Columbia's dealings with local people. A public opinion poll published in July in *New York Magazine*, indicated that nearly one-half of the Harlem residents had no opinion on the gymnasium issue. Of the others, those who favored the gymnasium numbered 50 per cent more than those who opposed it. It has been said that the leaders of the black militant undergraduates at Columbia claimed to have made an issue of the gymnasium precisely because Negro New Yorkers had no opinion on it. They were demonstrating to *create* a sense of public grievance, rather than to express one.

The contribution of ARCH

Any attribution of effect to cause in such a social crisis is intrinsically guesswork. One cannot ascribe the intellectual ferment in black nationalist circles, therefore, to any one cause with sublime confidence that one has found the prime mover. Certainly, however, the Architects Renewal Committee for Harlem (ARCH) has worked hard enough on the gymnasium issue to deserve credit for inflaming it. ARCH was originally funded, late in 1965, by foundations; more recently it has attracted federal support. Its first office was on Lenox Avenue at 125th Street; originally staffed professionally by whites, ARCH's primary purpose was to establish itself as professional planning consultants to the Harlem community, to become advocates-in-planning for the local residents, most particularly, the poor local residents. To achieve its purpose, ARCH first undertook the job of client development; in a sense, the job of client creation. To accomplish this work, the Columbia gymnasium was an ideal vehicle. From early 1966 until 1968, ARCH has, in its own newspaper, its own press releases, and the speeches of its principal staff (now black), sought to rally Harlem against the "colonial" invasion that it detected in the plans for building the gymnasium in Morningside Park.

For the purposes of such community mobilization, the gymnasium was an instrument so well suited that it might have been deliberately designed. By the nature of topography, it symbolized the superior status of the white or university community as against the black or resident community. By virtue of the separation in the two gymnasiums — community and university — it lent credence to the allegation of deliberate racial segregation. Because it was to be built on public land, it lent credence to the supposition that government itself was in league with the university to create a structure intended to keep blacks in their place. Its offsetting virtues — that it would provide basketball courts for teams of young people organized for the purpose and a swimming pool for similar groups — were so limited in their appeal, and so unescapably middle-class in their connotation, that they could be conveniently disregarded by militants. The gymnasium could be threatened with bombing, if necessary, without imperiling the life of a single sleeping resident; and the explanation of its division of space (that squash courts, indoor rowing machines, and fencing rooms are of little or no interest to adolescents; that the cost of coaching these sports would be prohibitive; that a championship basketball court with a seating capacity of several thousand can be profitably used only for university games, etc.) are so complicated as to be unconvincing. As an issue, it possessed the added virtue of being incapable of compromise, and of not requiring positive action on anyone's part to make it effective; on the contrary, the continued uproar over the possible construction of the gym makes unnecessary the development of a positive program for improving conditions in Harlem.

The Harlem News (published by ARCH), I, No. 6 (June 1968), devotes its first page to an article entitled "Why?" The article consists of thirty-seven questions, beginning "1. Why is Columbia University (private enterprise) attempting to expand its lily white campus into Morningside Park?" As one finds his way down the list — e.g., "17. Is Columbia University being used as a tool to reclaim Harlem for the white power structure so that middle class and rich white people can have the best area of the city in which to live?" to "24. Do you want the bulldozer knocking down your apartment?" and "31. Will the barbers know how to cut your hair?" — the impression gains that nothing indeed need be done to improve Harlem, because it is already a thoroughly satisfactory environment. Yet, behind this calculated distortion for the purposes of community mobilization, lies a perception of some considerable importance, certainly to the future of the urban university in cities in which the percentage of the black population continues to grow.

What is Columbia's future?

Talking to the ARCH principals, and to other militants, and passing beyond the propagandistic utterances which are, in a sense, only a public face, one ultimately comes to the word: "relevant." The question asked of the Columbia gymnasium by the most potent of its adversaries is whether a gymnasium incorporating the standards of Ivy League sport and physical training is *relevant* to the needs of the people who live nearest it. And if the gymnasium is not, as they put it, "relevant," can the institution itself be relevant? When Columbia faculty and administrators are asked why there are so few (reportedly, six) Negro faculty members, the answer comes back that it is hard to find qualified faculty. The militants then pose the question as to whether the qualifications should not be adjusted to the human candidates, not merely by lowering the standards for acceptance, but by changing the taught subject matter, changing the curriculum, changing the student body, changing — perhaps entirely — the value system of the university. Perhaps, in the atmosphere of the new cities, a university must become an educational institution with wholly different aims: to teach race pride, applied sociology, pedagogic reform, small business techniques, revolutionary strategy. *But what, then, is the future of our great universities that are located in urban environments? What, specifically, is the future of Columbia? Can it remain "Ivy League" or must it become, at best, a superior city university?*

Certainly anyone who believes that the urban university can make peace with its encircling militants by clever public relations, by putting a few dark faces on the board of trustees without changing the essential role of the institution, would appear to be deluding himself. Nor does the university's involvement in community good works provide a bridge of understanding, as the optimists among us would have one believe. Columbia, responding to the plea for "community involvement," has taken Harlem Hospital under its wing; with astute public relations, it has managed to increase the number of Negro department heads over the number in the hospital previous to the affiliation. Unfortunately, in the process the heads of some of the more important departments, the truly senior black men have, presumably for good reasons, been replaced. Or so Harlemites have been told. Perhaps the majority of Harlem residents would prefer a slightly better chance to live at the hands of a more broadly experienced and better trained white surgeon, to their chances of survival at black hands. But a significant minority — the vocal and intellectual minority — are now asking themselves whether more important values are not to be achieved in submitting oneself to black hands, whatever the putative hazard.

Does Columbia have to change radically or might the demands of the urban blacks be more fleeting than they now appear? Perhaps the black urban citizen is making a more rapid adjustment than we realize to the university standards that already prevail; perhaps he, himself, will fight most vigorously against a major change in the value system under which he has painfully won acceptance. Perhaps — and perhaps not. Perhaps a forthright decision to proceed with the gymnasium will mobilize the support of those whose children will use its facilities.

The ability to choose wisely between these hypotheses separates the brilliant educational administrator and creative urban statesman from the rest of us, who merely write about his problems. While the choice hovers unresolved, the unfinished excavation for the Columbia-Community gymnasium building will continue to scar Morningside Park, and a reconciliation, or even a *modus vivendi* between Box and Cox — those long-lost brothers — will be impossible.

7

Four
crucial years
at
Cornell

NATHAN TARCOV

Cornell did not have a revolution last year. Although public interest has been captured by the dramatic events at Columbia, which certainly deserve attention, it may also be useful to examine one of the many American campuses that have not been paralyzed by violence but on which many of the same difficulties and dilemmas can be found as at the more notoriously troubled institutions. I have recently been graduated from Cornell's College of Arts and Sciences and my impressions of the not untypical changes that have taken place at my *alma mater* over my four years there suggest to me that riots are not the only signal of trouble, and that success in avoiding the riots can pose other problems.

When, in 1964, as a high-school civil rights, anti-war, and socialist activist, I considered going to Cornell, the warnings of my comrades that Cornell was an "unpolitical" school, notable more for the dominance of its fraternities than for any kind of politics, made me hesitate. If one was interested in activism, then New York's City College, Chicago, Wisconsin, Berkeley, and Antioch were places to go, not Cornell. Friends in Cornell's minuscule Young Socialist League told me that there was a massive but inert body of "progressive" political opinion, cynical about free enterprise and hostile to U.S. foreign policy, as well as a crude right wing, almost as inert and more attached to the fraternities, ROTC, and athletics than to debating with young radicals, although perhaps not averse to rougher kinds of conflict.

But having decided that Cornell might have compensating advantages, I appeared in the fall and discovered that my comrades were right: there was a notable lack of radical or revolutionary activity. Furthermore, in that fall of 1964, the specter of Barry Goldwater's finger on the button both made liberals self-confident when cautioning their more militant friends not to rock the boat and elect the bogeyman, and put radicals on the defensive. Even within the SDS chapter, the radicals were diffident; the compromise of holding debates on whether or not to support Johnson came to nothing. The only issue that mustered much support was the abolition of junior women's curfews, but even that was half-hearted and the administration beat SDS to the punch anyway. I hardly suspected that Cornell might become an activist center or that Lyndon Johnson's conduct of a far from hypothetical war might entirely reverse matters, giving radicals an aggressive and invincible moral posture and leaving liberals with nothing but a bad conscience with which to face a new left.

Although Cornellians were passive by the standards of radical activists, they could still point with pride to a riot of a few years back, inspired by the enforcement of sexual regulations and reinforced by high spirits, and to the "pot bust" of the previous year. Many arts college students felt a dissatisfaction with the university or with their lives as students.[1] Impersonal mass instruction, unreasonable requirements, the necessity of an often arbitrary specialization even before one became an upperclassman, and the diminution or even elimination of leisure by the demands of course work — all these were targets of complaint. Academic work was often criticized as irrelevant to "real life" and "the real world." It meant reading books instead of being concerned with people, studying instead of doing things, contemplating the status quo rather than changing it, and examining the past instead of the present. Scholarship seemed dull and dry, and academic life an easy rut, a baited trap, or even a vicious circle of scholars training scholars to train scholars, for no visible purpose beyond self-perpetuation. Objects of dissatisfaction included not only the education the university offered, but also its claims to act in other realms of students' lives. The university's role *in loco parentis* seemed to have neither substantial justification nor any relation to the instruction presented.

But dissatisfaction, nonetheless acute for being vague, was rarely

---

[1] I confine my observations to the arts college for two reasons. Like that of most Cornell students, my experience was startlingly limited to my own college. Furthermore, like Robert Nisbet (see *The Public Interest*, 10 [Winter 1968]), I think the current crisis of the university is actually one of the liberal arts college, for reasons I hope to make clear.

expressed by public activity; and even then it manifested itself not within the university but in the South, the Peace Corps, or Cornell's own projects abroad. Such activity was not revolution but "doing good" — and even "doing good" was less common than dropping out, the latter being possible either inside or outside school, either with or without turning on.

Berkeley shows the way

That same fall, events began to occur at Berkeley that transformed the Cornell community, inspired its most important movement — Students for Education — and provided slogans and tactics, if not clear goals, for a new generation of activists. Berkeley began with the questions of free speech and the relation of the university to off-campus political activity, particularly illegal activity (mass picketing is not illegal). It went on to raise the banner of rejection of the Multiversity, as well as to import into campus activity concerned with university affairs the spirit and methods of political activism, especially those of the Negro civil rights movement. Berkeley revealed to many Cornellians that all their grievances could be seen as aspects of a system, the Multiversity, which could be actively and collectively struggled against. A would-be political activist no longer had to go outside the university, only to return reluctantly to an unchanged Cornell. Now it appeared possible to incorporate activism fully into one's life at Cornell. Struggle and confrontation didn't have to be merely means for righting specific wrongs, such as compulsory ROTC or fraternity discrimination; they could in themselves supply what was lacking in the university, the qualities of "real life" and "the real world."

Following the example set by Berkeley, the Cornell students took as their model, not merely the general phenomenon of political struggle against a system, but the particular one of the civil rights movement, a choice that seemed to assume that the grievances of students stemmed from a position similar to that of Negroes, and that the university administration could be fruitfully confronted like a Southern sheriff or a bigoted proprietor. It implied not only that disobedience and disruption were necessary within the university, but that even the provocation of repressive violence could be useful. It is clear, however, that the choice of the civil rights struggle as a model was not made with an awareness of all the possible implications. That movement was chosen because it was heroic, morally unquestionable (at least for Northern liberals), effective (at least it was considered so then), and familiar, rather than because it was perceived to be truly analogous.

The appeal to students of the model of the civil rights worker as heroic and morally absolute can be comprehended as part of a more general argument or sentiment that has become clear since then. Accepting the rules of the democratic game, whether by obeying federal laws or following university procedures, seems to imply that one's opponents are decent and act in good faith, at least that they are not the most dangerous villains, and that the issues at stake are not of absolute moral import. Such a position seems necessarily unheroic and far inferior to that of a man who must resort to disobedience because of the character of his oppressors or the crucial nature of the issues involved. Later, the position of a man who must resort to violence — the partisan or the guerilla — would appear to some to imply an even greater evil in one's enemies and a greater worth in one's own cause.

An accidental symbol of Berkeley's impact is that when the fall term president of Cornell's SDS returned to campus briefly, in the spring, as a member of the Steering Committee of Berkeley's Free Speech Movement, she attracted more people to a public lecture than had attended Cornell's own SDS meetings — even though left-wing students already had enough to do that week with Herbert Marcuse and Leroi Jones speaking on campus. The most obvious reaction to Berkeley was the sudden appearance of Students for Education, a full-blown reform movement. SFE protested the notoriously bad bookstore, large lecture classes, lack of faculty-student contact in general, the grading system, and the frequent absences of President James Perkins. It ran itself on principles that later came to be known as participatory democracy: regular open mass meetings and voluntary subcommittees. There was considerable talk of such methods, not as temporary expedients, but as permanent features of the university, which would make it a more responsive and truly democratic community. The tactics of confrontation were also employed, though chiefly only as threats. A demonstration greeted the president on one of his returns to Ithaca, a picket line and boycott against the bookstore were threatened, and sit-ins were discussed.

Where Cornell differed

But Cornell was only a pale imitation and not a repetition of Berkeley. In the first place, SFE was an artificial movement created with the sponsorship of the student establishment — Student Government, and the *Cornell Daily Sun* included — rather than an expression of immediate and spontaneous outrage over local incidents. A meeting organized from above (even the dean of students' office helped), held in the freshman dorms to search for grievances, found a bunch of fidgety freshmen who were vehement only over the cost of cleaning shirts at the laundry serving the dorms and the cost and quality of the food in the frosh cafeteria.

Secondly, Cornell's administration, more than Berkeley's, tried to be responsive, undoubtedly from fear of large-scale disruption and consequent adverse publicity as well as from genuine sensitivity to student feelings and concern with improvement (not that there is anything intrinsically wrong with such fear). Expansion and improvement of the bookstore were promised (it actually followed; surely one of the swiftest, most unambiguously beneficial, and least distorted responses to student agitation that I know of). Other responses turned out to be less direct, though still effective in avoiding immediate confrontations and even conducive to some distinct educational improvements. A demand which had surfaced for a 15 per cent across-the-board increase of the faculty, effective the next fall, met with agreement in principle, a recitation of efforts already made in that direction, and an explanation of the practical exigencies of budgetary problems and hiring procedures. In the meantime, a commission was appointed to study the problems of undergraduate education, and individual departments were encouraged to consider ways of providing smaller classes. The grading system would be revised, and it was even rumored that the president would try to spend more time in Ithaca, instead of traveling about cultivating alumni, foundations, and the government (but where then was the money for improvement going to come from?).

The criticism of the grading system had been that it encouraged conformity and competition instead of individuality and learning for its own sake, and that it was deceptively precise. Oddly, the revision enacted consisted of replacing the old 50 to 100 system of ten grades with a new F to A+ scale of thirteen grades. The real reason for this revision had more to do with putting the transcripts of Cornellians on a par with those of competing colleges than with meeting the demands of SFE, although the latter were reflected in the establishment of a limited Satisfactory/Unsatisfactory option. It is difficult, however, to fault the administration for using the promise of revision to calm the campus. Similarly, the motivation for the abolition of Freshman English (and its replacement by required Freshman Humanities Seminars, retaining the aim of teaching composition but refreshingly diverse and often precociously esoteric) sprang more from a desire to relieve the English Department of the burden of teaching all the freshmen of every college of the university than from any concern with students' complaints about their education.

An ageless balm for student unrest is the vacation, and an expert administration such as Cornell's knew how to postpone final response to key demands until after spring vacation, or, ideally, the summer. SFE was cured in precisely this fashion. By the end of the spring term its mass meetings had become steadily less massive (they had never involved more than a small percentage of the student body anyway), and it had degenerated into little groups, each doing its own thing, from pressing for legal pot to urging the abolition of all grades, demands which the university could now safely ignore.

That year there was also activity related to outside issues. Lecturing on foreign policy, Ambassador Averell Harriman was interrupted, insulted, and deprived of the microphone as a defender of imperialism. At the time it was generally considered an impolite aberration, at odds with a tradition of free speech, but even then one could hear such actions defended precisely as expressing the right of free speech or, what was considered its equivalent, the necessity of making oneself heard. That year there were almost as many right-wingers with "Bomb Hanoi" signs forcibly blocking buses going to protest the war as there were protestors inside. This crude confrontation demonstrated pretty well that the benefits of the new interpretation of free speech (later "participatory democracy") could not very easily extend to everyone at the same time. If a radical's "right to be heard" could include shutting up a spokesman for the Establishment, then yet another party might claim, and exercise, the "right" to interfere with the radical's "right." Somehow, Proctor Lowell George managed to talk the right-wingers into going away after they had made their point and gotten their pictures taken, and the buses rolled on. An even more dangerous confrontation occurred when a sit-in was held to disrupt the annual presidential review of ROTC. This time the right wing, challenged on its own ground, far outnumbered the left and, according to report, stones, brass knuckles, and other crude weapons were seen. President Perkins impressed the campus by personally protecting the protestors and preventing violence. However, in a display of the even-handedness and concern for order which in at least a formal way has continued to characterize the administration's responses, the demonstrators received not only protection but also penalties for their disruption of a university activity.

Reforming undergraduate education

My sophomore year, 1965–1966, found that Berkeley and the possibility of more Berkeleys had given the Multiversity a guilty conscience over impersonalized education, the computerization of undergraduates, and putting the servicing of society before paying attention to students. From now on, in discussions of university affairs, undergraduate education was never forgotten. The form and content of the curriculum were debated in the *Sun* and the Interfraternity Council's new magazine, *The Walk*, edited largely by independents. One commission reported on the quality of undergraduate education; another was formed to coordinate reforms.

Each college held meetings to discuss reform of its own undergraduate education, and the various academic departments attempted to implement the recommendations.

As a result of this ferment, many changes were actually made. The academic requirements of the arts college began to disappear. Required minors and much of the foreign language requirement eventually joined Freshman English on the junk heap of history. To the general survey lectures, required both for majors and for satisfaction of the Arts College's distribution requirements, many departments added seminar versions covering similar material, with faculty as well as graduate assistants participating. The History Department established, in addition to its required History of Western Civilization, a new introduction to American history, with lectures by four or five faculty members, who also joined the graduate assistants' discussion sections. The Government department established an additional program of seminars for all of its majors (comprising a large fraction of upperclass arts college men). By drawing on the resources of several departments, the new Freshmen Humanities Seminars were supposed to involve more faculty members in teaching small groups of freshmen. The advisor system was rearranged and co-ordinated with the various seminar programs to provide more student-faculty contact and more useful guidance for underclassmen.

Although many of these changes represented improvements, there was nevertheless a radical disproportion between the students' dissatisfactions and the program of reforms which was carried out. Smaller classes and larger, earlier, and more frequent doses of "contact" with members of the faculty did not speak to the demands for "relevance." Many students wanted the arts college to offer more in the way of education than just a choice of trainings in the techniques of a variety of professions, many of which appeared to consist of nothing more than the teaching of those techniques to others. The problem with survey courses was, not simply their size, but that they usually presented only the first facts to be learned in a discipline rather than its goals, its relation to other disciplines, or its place within the education of someone not intending to make his living by it. Of course, few Cornell students could articulate what they meant by "relevance,"[2] or perceive that smaller classes would not by themselves do the trick. Only revolutionaries and alarmists were convinced that the university's attempts to appease student discontent and ward off the threat of insurrection would not be enough.

---

[2] It has become customary for this word (along with its new synonyms, "meaning" and "significance") to be used without further elaboration. One does not demand, for instance, that a course have relevance to some specific other concern, or that it mean or signify something particular — only that it have relevance, meaning, or significance.

At a public meeting held to discuss reform of the arts college, a student who argued that the college's liberal education must be more than professional training — that it must address itself to the questions students bring with them as to how to lead their lives and how their society should be ordered — was told by the dean of the college not to worry, as a coffee house was to be opened in a few months: this would bring the faculty face to face with the students in a situation conducive to more comprehensive discourse. The student retorted, with some exaggeration, that such responses found their logical conclusion in a college consisting only of library facilities, draft deferments, and a coffee house.

Vietnam

The years 1965–1966 also saw serious escalation of our part in the Vietnam War, a development that inspired within the arts college almost universal distrust and dislike of an administration that had first entered the national arena under the mantle of the martyred New Frontier, and had gone on to pass historic civil rights legislation, initiate the War on Poverty, sign the Test Ban Treaty, and slay the dragon of Goldwaterism. Students became anxious about what was going on outside, and began to suspect that it made everything inside the university comparatively unimportant. By the next year the spring Anti-War Mobilization in New York was able to draw more than a thousand Cornellians, undoubtedly including a major fraction of the arts college. Counterdemonstraters seemed to have lost their nerve as well as most of their numbers. In ordinary conversation, most arts college students assumed opposition to Johnson and the war. The *Sun* turned sharply toward the New Left and its rhetoric permeated campus thought.

The most serious incident of the year stemmed from the national draft-card burning movement organized from Cornell. A fine example of "symbolic speech," draft-card burning stirred intense feelings on all sides, probably more than any words could. SDS, no longer a conglomeration of liberals and radicals, but the focal point of the New Left, tried to solicit draft card burning pledges at a desk at Willard Straight Hall, Cornell's student union. The Board of Managers of the Straight refused to permit the solicitation, as its regulations forbade illegal activity; whereupon the solicitors decided to persevere, and continued to occupy the Straight's main lobby every day despite the confirmation of the Board's refusal by the Scheduling Coordination and Review Board (the supreme student body for regulating other student bodies). The proctor attempted to take the ID cards of the solicitors in order to cite them before the Undergraduate Judiciary Board, but was forcibly prevented. Amid surprise and controversy, he was granted special emergency power (which no one, except the Faculty Committee on Student Conduct, had known he could have) to suspend students on the spot. Meanwhile the Straight had taken on the appearance of a two-ring circus: the lobby was completely packed, partly to prevent outside interference, by a crowd listening to constant anti-war harangues, while the adjacent Memorial Room was filled by students come to hear a series of faculty discussions on the use of civil disobedience, sponsored by the Executive Board of Student Government. Emotions ran high; when one professor participating in the discussions argued against the use of civil disobedience and cautioned against a fascist note in the New Left, without discussing the war, a student ran up to show him photographs of napalmed babies and urged him to feel rather than to reason coolly. Despite the proctor's new power, further confrontation was avoided; vacation intervened, the forty or so pledges that could be gotten had been gathered, and the issue subsided along with the danger of violence.

The Straight seizure displayed the attitude of the New Left, an attitude which affected the other political groups on campus and transformed the atmosphere of the university. The New Left had become so confident of itself, so convinced of the immorality of the war and its perpetrators, that it had come to have contempt for any other considerations such as legality, the procedures of liberal democracy, university procedures, the proper atmosphere for education, or simple politeness. The catchword of the day was "technicalities," describing, it seemed, any matters other than the war brought up in criticism of New Left actions. Such "technicalities" provoked not only contempt but hostility, and they were dismissed with relish, rather than with scruple or regret. The search for an evil enough enemy and a great enough moral issue had gone a step further. The condemnation of the war was itself often made in a similar way. Advancing any consideration other than *the* moral one — as defined by SDS — was a sign of gullibility or moral insensitivity.

Liberals, especially those of a previous generation among the faculty and in the administration, generally seemed to feel obliged to defer to the "moral conviction," "courage," and "sincerity" of the members of the New Left, at the expense of their own opinions. Even many of those who voiced criticisms did so diffidently, and had to preface them with acknowledgments of their admiration of the New Left's forcefulness.

"Free speech"

The defense of free speech assumed, in a way, that the university was not only a political community, but indeed an unjustly oppressive one. Free speech in its extreme form of the right to advocacy of *any* action, and even to self-expression through any action that might be construed as protest, implied a denial of any understanding of the university that claimed that education was necessarily prior to action, that an atmosphere of certain kinds of actions (such as passionate and partisan ones) was detrimental to education, or even simply that students had to be quiet and listen or think. There are general problems concerning free speech which apply with particular force to the university setting. Everyone cannot speak at once, at least not in the same place and certainly not if they want one another to listen (this is one of the reasons why disobedience and other symbolic *acts* appear to have become almost necessary in order for one to be *heard* in a libertarian, speech-soaked society). In a university classroom particularly, simple free speech cannot be the rule; there is reason to think that the purposes of education are sometimes better served by having one individual, a professor, speak while the others listen, or by having that one individual regulate the speech of the others. Indeed, alarmists claimed at the time of the Straight seizure that professors' rights to freely conduct their classes were threatened by the tactics of the New Left, combined with the deferential attitude of many liberals.

One other tendency exemplified by the Straight seizure is the snowballing of "free speech" issues. If a certain number of people in a university are willing to advance a particular view or to participate in a particular action, ten times that number will be found willing to defend the "rights" of the first group to speak and act, and ten times *that* number will defend the "rights" of the second group. Consequently, if mass participation is wanted, it is useful to fight one's battles on the grounds of one's *right* to do such-and-such, rather than on the merits of such-and-such. This method is nearly always bound to further the original purpose, if only because the press will fail to distinguish between the first cause and later ones. And when part of the purpose actually is to involve large numbers of students in a confrontation with the university administration, or with some other organ of "the Establishment," thereby helping to achieve "participatory democracy" here and now, this tactic is perfect. The results of its employment can be seen dramatically in the riots at Berkeley and Columbia, in the spread of revolt from Nanterre's six activists to millions of Frenchmen, as well as in the increase of numbers from the signers of the card-burning pledge, to the crowd at the Straight, and finally to those dismayed at the proctor and the FCSC.

Cornell's administration, however, did not join in the escalation of tactics and rhetoric. It was not going to play "Bull" Connor or Gestapo with clubs, hoses, and mass arrests. This may have been because of a prudent fear of violence and of the polarization of opinion or because the administrators shared the loss of nerve of many liberals. (Moreover, the administration was able to tread softly because there was no right-wing attempt to clear the Straight, which could have led to violence in comparison with which an administration-protestor conflict would have been a happy alternative.) Later in the year similar issues concerning "free speech" might have been raised by the Young Socialists' gathering of funds for the NLF or by the Young Friends' collection for medical supplies for both sides. Both collections were permitted at the Straight, however, as there was evidently no law specifically forbidding the advocacy of these acts (after all, we were not at war with anyone) as there was in the case of draft-card burning.

The "Trojan horse" incident

Not only the most serious but the most ludicrous incident of the year raised the slogan of free speech. During a presidential absence, the head of the campus Safety Division confiscated copies of the *Trojan Horse*, the student literary magazine, on the grounds that it was obscene. When the President returned and the university backed out of this dubious venture, District Attorney Richard Thaler blundered in. Hundreds of students surrounded him in his car in front of the Straight, protesting the violation of freedom of the press and the invasion of the campus. More shocking to some citizens of Ithaca than anything in the *Horse* was a faculty-chaplain statement asserting that six-letter words such as "nation" were just as obscene as the four-letter literary favorites. The entire incident was embarrassing to the university, which had generally managed to avoid external intervention. The head of the Safety Division later resigned, only to be hired by the City of Ithaca for its Police Department, and the DA may have become more wary of such exploits as a result of a state court decision acquitting the *Horse* of obscenity. A commission subsequently examined university policy and revised it to leave the prosecution of crimes per se to civil authorities, while according violators neither protection from the laws nor additional penalties. The important qualification that the university would punish acts that interfered with its functioning or which were detrimental to the educational environment (e.g., pot) in essence assured that outside authorities would stay out unless called in, and also reassured those who did not care about the *Horse's* vocabulary but feared the disruption of teaching or of administration.

The right to free speech (or was it freedom of the press?) was also exercised by students who wore buttons bearing the devices "I am not yet convinced that the proctor is a horse's ass" and "I am." When the administration refused to hold its regular open student briefings, because students present were wearing the buttons, a controversy arose as to whether students' "rights" were violated thereby. An assistant of the proctor went so far as to punch one button-wearer on the steps of the Straight. The assistant's contract was not renewed.

Dean Rusk and Dow

The end of the year saw a long-postponed lecture on campus by Dean Rusk. Activists decided to attend the lecture wearing death's head masks. Prompted by the hope of preventing serious disruption, or perhaps by genuine sympathy with the demonstration, President Perkins introduced the speaker, not by praising him, but by trying to appease the protestors; and the Secretary of State of the United States had to accept the conditions of discourse at Cornell and address the hundreds of gaping skulls. Presumably he thought that any attempt to change matters might have made them more embarrassing for him, and refusing to give the lecture would have been cowardice before the bar of the self-appointed conscience of the country, even if its verdict was already in.

This past year saw a continuation of anti-war protests. A visit by a recruiter for the Marine Corps provoked a demonstration at which students urgently exercised their "right to hear" by walking over the prone demonstrators blocking their way. After considerable public discussion concerning the necessity that exercises of the right of free speech not interfere with the rights of others, a demonstration against a recruiter from Dow Chemical was uneventful. Though opposition to the war was as widespread as ever, general sympathy with the more extreme tactics of the anti-war movement faded. In a referendum as to whether Student Government should give $1,000 to the Anti-War Spring Mobilization, the vote was 3 to 1 against, in a turnout several times the size of those for Student Government elections. The next day the *Sun* looked like *Al Ahram* the morning after the Six Days' War. Staff elections in the spring moved the *Sun* from the New Left back to the middle of the road. That spring's mobilization in Washington, partly organized from Cornell, drew far fewer Cornellians than had the previous year's. Extremist talk about bringing the city to a grinding halt, hippie plans to exorcise the Pentagon, and the sight of mobilizers practicing for police brutality and resistance by kicking and dragging one another across the arts college quadrangle alienated students.

Besides the war was now somewhat overshadowed by another issue: race.

The McPhelin incident

Over the past few years, with support of liberal integrationist faculty and the help of interested students, the administration had been successful in raising the number of black students significantly from a handful to about 150. By last year, however, the Cornell Afro-American Society had moved toward a militant Black Power position; it rejected the integrationist hopes and principles that had brought its members to the campus but which no longer squared with national or local conditions or with the aspirations of the most articulate leaders of black youth. This rejection formed the background for the most serious incident in recent Cornell history.

Professor Michael McPhelin, S.J., visiting for the year from the Ateneo University of Manila, taught a large introductory economics lecture course. Remarks about the Western origin of economics, the "achievements of Western civilization," "the economic superiority of European nations," "good human resources," and finally "sickly and perverted games" played by slum children, offended three black students. They complained that Father McPhelin "consistently and subtly, constructed a philosophy of racism; to clarify, we do not mean individual or overt racism, but institutionalized, or covert racism, that type by which attitudes of white superiority are perpetuated." They were shuffled from the vice president for student affairs to the dean of students to the dean of the arts college, and finally to the chairman of the Economics Department, to whom they presented their demands: a black economist to represent the other side, a public apology, and Father McPhelin's dismissal. The chairman attempted to persuade the students "of the difficulties their demands produced in the context of academic freedom and the diffusion of responsibility in the university,"[3] and refused to act. At no point, apparently, were the students informed of the procedure by which the university can rightfully consider a faculty member's dismissal, and they saw no possibility of proceeding further through legitimate channels.

The next day a meeting of the Afro-American Society was held, and the day after that the three students demanded that Father McPhelin let them read to the class a statement of their grievances and demands, including that for his dismissal. When he asked to read the statement himself first, they refused and attempted to read it anyway, throwing the class into disorder; whereupon Father McPhelin dismissed the class. The three students gathered fifty to sixty others at the Straight and proceeded that morning to the Economics Department office, which they occupied. They detained the chairman and three secretaries, until a meeting with someone who could act upon their demands should be arranged. Plainclothes members of the Safety Division tried to prevent the re-entry of several students who had gone for food; in the ensuing scuffle, the

---

[3] I am quoting from the report of the special commission organized to investigate the incident.

police were thwarted. Although the secretaries were soon released, the chairman was detained all day, until the provost and others agreed to arrange a meeting with the dean of the college, and to provide a lecture by an economist of the Afro-American Society's choosing.

It is hard to judge what the administration's response to the seizure alone would have been. On the one hand, university officials did grant one demand; on the other, they claimed not to have given the students any assurances that they would be safe from disciplinary penalties. In any case, the situation of April 4 was speedily and terribly transformed. That evening, Martin Luther King was murdered; and that night, violence broke out across the nation. Students' attention was diverted to what was happening in the cities, the homes of many of them. In Ithaca, several fires and other incidents occurred that night, and a suspicious series of fires on and near the campus during the rest of the term added a note of terror to the atmosphere. White guilt and fear surfaced everywhere. At Cornell, a memorial service for Dr. King was held at which Chaplain Gibbons of Cornell United Religious Work preached the gospel of white guilt, and several black students announced that nonviolence, love and integration had died with their dreamer, that bullets would be met with bullets, and that they would defend their threatened lives.

It was in this context that the McPhelin affair was resolved. After an investigation of the incident by a special commission, the dean of the college acquitted Father McPhelin of "individual or overt" racism, but not of "institutionalized racism," and generously concluded his findings as follows: "My recommendation, Mr. President, is that we as an institution commit ourselves fully and at once to the solution of the great educational and social problems revealed by this incident and that no action be taken against McPhelin" (the term's classes and the Father's stay had ended by then). Evenhandedly, the dean of the faculty, with the concurrence of the vice president for student affairs and the president, decided not to institute disciplinary charges against the students so that the university could begin "coming to grips with the agonies of our society," a phrase repeated by the president in his final statement on the incident.

Despite the mockery which had previously greeted the predictions of the alarmists, the facts remained: disruption of a class, seizure of a departmental office and chairman, and the threatened and actual use of force had gone unpunished and had even received the sympathy and admiration of liberals and administrators for the moral convictions manifested. Although the grievances and background of black militants are very different from those of New Left activists, the groundwork for the Afro-American Society's "bold venture" had been laid by SDS, and the New Left may well try to make further use of it. The particular demands made are not a decisive distinction when the confrontation and unrest they provoke are themselves goals, as they are in the ideologies of both participatory democracy and Black Power. The gymnasium and the Institute for Defense Analysis at Columbia were interchangeable means, not ends; and the fact that Cornell has no Harlem and has already disaffiliated from the Cornell Aeronautical Laboratory is no protection. Furthermore, through supporting black militants, white activists can achieve many of the same effects as through the former imitation of the civil rights movement.

Rumors were rife of fear among those professors teaching potentially controversial subjects, and there was speculation as to what the result might be if a regular Cornell faculty member were to find himself in Father McPhelin's situation. Although the administration had strongly stated its continued attachment to academic freedom, that freedom was diluted by the encouragement of students with grievances to take to dismissal procedures (the dean of the college, however, did warn against this policy), the failure to take disciplinary action in this particular case, and the demand for a general commitment to eliminating "institutionalized racism" masquerading as "Western or middle-class values." Freedom can be impaired by intimidation and even by an aggressively dominant climate of opinion, as well as by oppressive laws. If the defense of the superiority of "white," "Western," or "middle-class" values is to be taboo in the university, then it would seem we must abandon the study of our entire cultural heritage, replete as it is with assertions and justifications of those values, though it regards them as universally true, rather than as "white," "Western," or "middle-class."

Amidst the furor over "white racism" that followed the events of April 4, the Afro-American Society, with the support of some white faculty members who had been liberal integrationists not long before, pressed its separatist demands for an all-black girls' living unit and all-black courses on black subjects. The university acceded to the first demand and the local chapter of the ACLU announced its intention to sue for clear violation of the Civil Rights Acts. At the end of the year, rumor had it that the second would also be effected, though the classes would be all black only through the device of designating them as upper-level courses with admission by consent of the instructor, not in principle.

What is a liberal arts college?

During my years at Cornell, activity expressive of concern with various issues has increased. Students have shown both a greater willingness to challenge authority and a growing contempt for

university rules and for the purposes these rules presumably serve
as parts of an immoral system. The administration has acted either
as if (1) by limited concessions unwelcome unrest can be allayed
until it fades away, or (2) the protests indeed represent unquestionable morality or the wave of the future. The change in student
ethos is, of course, partly the result of developments outside the
university, chiefly the war and the national administration's conduct
and account of it, the draft, especially the abolition of graduate
deferments, and the racial crisis. But one cannot afford to neglect
causes within the university. A university administration cannot
afford to assume that student unrest would disappear with the
resolution of these external problems. Nor should one mistake
superficial problems within the university for basic sources of revolt.
Even granting a host of peripheral demands cannot remedy a
pervasive discontent with the fundamental characteristics of education in the arts college.

These characteristics are determined by the notion that the purpose
of the university is to fill the needs of society, in other words, to
supply trained professionals and technicians and to pursue research
on questions of importance to established institutions. This understanding assumes an acceptance of many things about our society
that serious students frequently cannot grant. It also challenges the
traditional core of a liberal education, the humanities, which
have felt themselves on the defensive for some time. When the
functioning of the university is seen too narrowly in terms of social
needs, the humanities stand on much shakier ground than do the
professional schools, the researching physical sciences, or the consulting social sciences. Social service, of course, does not have to
have this consequence; the nurturing of artistic activity, the training
of rigorous and profound critics and students of our society, or
simply the education of free and civilized men can all be seen
as useful to society. But social utility is generally viewed more
narrowly. Sensitive and thoughtful students hope their education
will address itself to their questions about the leading of their lives
and the ordering of their society, and it is a pity to think that they
can find "relevance" and "meaning" only in Eastern religion, drugs,
and activism while their own culture, once thought to be a series
of responses to personal and political questions, has become the
preserve of scholars and the material for one set of professions
among the many the university prepares for. It would be hypocritical to condemn student activism as irresponsibly premature or
as unaware of the preparatory function of the college years, for
the education offered generally cannot be said to be preparatory for
more than a career — it rarely offers a significant preparation for
citizenship. Recent protests about the war, Black Power, and the
university may have endangered academic freedom or the possibility

of independence and quiet reflection, but the Berkeley protests did serve the useful purpose of drawing serious attention to undergraduate education, and these may do the same, if properly understood. They may work in tandem with the Multiversity to narrow our education or they may help to give us more perspective on its purpose.

8

A different way
to
restructure the
university

IRVING KRISTOL

I HAVE the gravest doubts that, out of all the current agitation for a "restructuring" of the university, very much of substance will come. There are a great many reasons why this is so, among them the fact that practically no one any longer has a clear notion of what a "university" is supposed to be, or do, or mean. We are, all of us, equally vague as to what the term "higher education" signifies, or what functions and purposes are properly included in the categories of "student" or "professor." But, in addition to such basic problems, there is a simple and proximate obstacle: all of the groups — professors, administrators, and students — now engaged in this enterprise of "restructuring" are deficient in the will to do anything, or the power to do anything, or ideas about what might be done.

The faculty

Let us begin with the faculty, since they are indeed, as they claim ("Sir, the faculty *is* the university"), the preponderant estate of this realm. In most universities, it is the faculty that controls the educational functions and defines the educational purposes of the institution. It is the faculty that usually arranges the curriculum, makes staff appointments, etc. It is the faculty that has the moral authority, the mental capacity, and a sufficiently intimate knowledge of the realities of the educational system to operate upon it. Unfortunately, these virtues are far outweighed by an all too human defect — a limited imagination which leads to a lack of objective insight into its own position. What faculty members of our universities fail to see is that any meaningful restructuring will not only have to be done *by* the faculty, but will also have to be done *to* the faculty. And to ask the American professoriat to restructure itself is as sensible as if one had asked Marie Antoinette to establish a republican government in France. Whether or not it coincided with her long-term interests was immaterial; the poor woman couldn't even conceive of the possibility.

Now, I don't mean to suggest that there is anything especially short-sighted or selfish about the American professor. Some of my best friends are professors, and I can testify that they are every bit as broadminded, every bit as capable of disinterested action as the average business executive or higher civil servant. Nor are they particularly smug and complacent. On the contrary, they are all keenly aware of the crisis that has befallen them, while many have long been discontented with their lot and full of haunting insecurities. Nevertheless, they do have one peculiar and notable flaw: being generally liberal and reformist in their political predisposition, they believe themselves able to have a truly liberal and reformist perspective on themselves. This is, of course, an idle fancy. No social group really possesses the imaginative capacity to have a liberal and reformist perspective on itself; individual members of the group may and do — but the group as a whole cannot. Otherwise the history of human society would be what it is not: an amiable progression of thoughtful self-reformations by classes and institutions.

So the beginning of wisdom, in thinking about our universities, is to assume that the professors are a class with a vested interest in, and an implicit ideological commitment to, the *status quo* broadly defined, and that reform will have to be imposed upon them as upon everyone else. If any empirical proof were required of the validity of these assumptions, one need only cast a glance over the various proposals for university reform that have been made by faculty committees at Berkeley and elsewhere. These proposals have one distinguishing characteristic: at no point, and in no way, do they cost the faculty anything — not money, not time, not power over their conditions of employment. They liberally impose inconveniences upon the administration, upon the taxpayers, upon the secondary schools, upon the community. But they never inconvenience the faculty. They never, for instance, increase its teaching load. (On the contrary: after four years of "restructuring" at Berkeley, professors there now spend *less* time in the classroom than they used to.) They never suggest anything that would intrude on those four-month vacations; they never interfere with such off-campus activities as consultancies, the writing of textbooks, traveling fellowships, etc.; they never discourage the expensive — but convenient — proliferation of courses in their specialized areas; they never even make attendance at committee meetings compulsory. This is precisely what one would expect when one asks a privileged class to reform the institution which is its very *raison d'être*. It is rather like asking corporation executives or trade-union leaders or officials of a government agency, all of whom have been given lifelong tenure in their present positions, to "restructure" the institutions and redefine their positions.

I have touched upon this question of tenure because of its symbolic significance. Few professors, in conversation, will defend the present tenure system, whereby senior and middle-level faculty are given a personal, lifelong monopoly on their positions. They will accept the criticisms of it by Robert Nisbet and others as largely valid. They will concede that it could be substantially modified — via long-term contracts, generous severance agreements, etc. — without any danger to academic freedom and with obvious benefits to everyone. They will agree that the "controversial" professor, whom tenure was supposed to protect, is today in great demand and short supply, whereas the mediocre professor is its prime beneficiary. They may even admit that the presence of a tenured faculty is one of the reasons that the university has been — with the possible exception of the post office — the least inventive (or even adaptive) of our social institutions since the end of World War II. They will allow that tenure in the university, like seniority in a craft union, makes for all sorts of counterproductive rigidities. But they will then go on to dismiss the whole issue as utterly "academic." To tamper with tenure, they argue, would produce fits and convulsions throughout their well-ordered universe. Nothing can or will be done, and they themselves could not be counted on to try. Even those economists who argue in favor of a free market for labor everywhere else somehow never think of applying this doctrine to themselves.

So when these same people announce that, to cope with the crisis in the university, they are going to "restructure" the institution, one has the right to be skeptical. To suppose that they actually will do any such thing is probably the most "academic" idea of all.

The administration

Nor is the administration going to "restructure" the university. It couldn't do it if it tried; and it is not going to try because it doesn't regard itself as competent even to think about the problem. University administration in the United States today combines relative

148   IRVING KRISTOL

powerlessness with near-absolute mindlessness on the subject of education.

That statement about powerlessness needs to be qualified in one respect. Though a great many people are under the impression that the boards of trustees are the "real" power structure of the university, this is in fact the one group over which the administration does wield considerable influence. The trustees of a modern university are rather like the boards of directors of a modern corporation. They represent a kind of "stand-by" authority, ready to take over if the executive officers lead the organization into a scandalous mess. (Having little firsthand knowledge of educational institutions, they will then usually make the mess even worse than it was; but that's another story.) They also may — repeat: *may* — intervene in certain broad economic decisions, such as the construction of a new campus, the launching of a major fund-raising drive, etc. But on the whole, and in the ordinary course of events, they solemnly rubber-stamp whatever the administration has done or proposes to do.

And that's about the sum and substance of "administrative power." True, a determined administration can badger and bribe and black-mail the faculty into marginal revisions of the curriculum, just as a determined administration can have some influence over senior appointments. But most administrations are not all that determined — like everyone else, university administrators prefer an untroubled life. And even where they are determined, it doesn't make all that much difference, from an outsider's point of view. Within the institution, of course, even small differences can cause great anguish and excitement.

As for the administration's power over students, that hardly seems worth discussing at a time when the issue being debated is the students' power over the administration. Suffice it to say that, where disciplinary power does exist on paper, it is rarely used; and it is now in the process of ceasing to exist even on paper.[1] In this respect, university administrators are ironically very much in *loco parentis*. They have about as much control over their nineteen- and twenty-year-old charges as the parents do.

There might be something to deplore in this situation if one had reason to think that university administrators could wisely use power, did they have it. But there is no such reason, if what we are interested in is higher education. University administrators have long since ceased to have anything to say about education. By general consent, their job is administration, not education. When was the

[1] "Colleges are not churches, clinics, or even parents. Whether or not a student burns a draft card, participates in a civil-rights march, engages in premarital or extramarital sexual activity, becomes pregnant, attends church, sleeps all day or drinks all night, is not really the concern of an educational institution."—The president of the American Association for Higher Education as reported in *Time*, July 11, 1968.

last time a university president came forth with a new idea about education? When was the last time a university president wrote a significant book about the education of — as distinct from the government of — "his" students? Robert M. Hutchins was the last of that breed; he has had no noteworthy successors. Indeed, the surest way for an ambitious man never to become a university president is to let it be known that he actually has a philosophy of education. The faculty, suspicious of possible interference, will rise up in rebellion.

The university president today is primarily the chief executive of a corporate institution, not an educator. Unfortunately, he usually is also a poor executive, for various reasons. To begin with, he is almost invariably a professor, with no demonstrated managerial experience. More important, there are few meaningful standards against which to judge his performance, as distinct from his popularity. Since most university administrators have no clear idea of what they are supposed to be doing, they end up furiously imitating one another, on the assumption — doubtless correct — that to be immune from invidious comparisons is to be largely exempt from criticism.

Thus, at the moment, all administrations are proudly expanding the size of their plant, their facilities, and their student bodies. An outsider might wonder: Why should any single institution feel that it has to train scholars in all disciplines? Why can't there be a division of labor among the graduate schools? Aren't our universities perhaps too big already? Such questions are occasionally raised at conferences of educators — but, since every administrator has no other criterion for "success" than the quantitative increase in students, faculty, campus grounds, etc., these questions spark no debate at all.

As a matter of fact, university administrators never get much criticism — though, of course, they are convenient scapegoats who are instantly *blamed* for anything that goes wrong. The professors are just too busy and self-preoccupied, and in the ordinary course of events are perfectly content to leave the government of the university to the administration — even when they have a low opinion of the administration. (This has been the story at Columbia these past ten years.) It is interesting to note that, despite the fact that our best economists are all professors, there has been little public criticism from them on the grotesquely conservative way in which universities invest their endowment funds. It was not until the Ford Foundation's McGeorge Bundy made an issue of it that the universities began to bestir themselves. Similarly, it was an off-campus man, Beardsley Ruml, who, some fifteen years ago, pointed out that it was wasteful to leave campus facilities unused for months at a time, because of the vacation schedule. One would have thought that this idea could have passed through the minds of professors of management, or city planning, or something.

An interesting instance of the charmed life of university administrators is a recent report of the Carnegie Commission on the Future of Higher Education. Written by an economist, it delicately refuses to raise any interesting questions and limits itself to arguing for the need of ever greater government subsidies. After pointing out that the deficit in university budgets is largely incurred by the graduate divisions — a graduate student costs about three or four times as much as an undergraduate — the Carnegie report offers by way of explanation of the costliness of graduate education the following: "The conscientious supervision of a student's independent work is the essence of high-level graduate education. . . ."

What this means in practice, as everyone knows, is that the only way a university can attract big faculty names away from other places is by offering them minimal teaching loads in the graduate division, and the only way it can attract the brightest graduate students away from other schools is by offering them attractive (i.e., expensive) fellowships. Whether or not it makes sense for each institution of higher learning to adopt such a competitive policy would seem to be an important problem; but the Carnegie Commission loyally refrained from exploring it. Nor did it show any interest in whether in fact there is "conscientious supervision" in graduate schools, and if so how extensive or effective it is. From casual conversation with graduate students, one gets the impression that such supervision is not all that common, to put it mildly.

In short and in sum: university administrations have neither the power, nor the inclination, nor the stimulus of informed criticism which would result in any serious efforts at "restructuring" their institutions.

The students

And the students? They, alas, are indeed for the most part rebels without a cause — and without a hope of accomplishing anything except mischief and ruin.

In our society and in our culture, with its pathetic belief in progress and its grotesque accent on youth, it is almost impossible to speak candidly about the students. Thus, though most thoughtful people will condemn the "excesses" committed by rebellious students, they will in the same breath pay tribute to their "idealism" and their sense of "commitment." I find this sort of cant to be preposterous and disgusting. It seems to me that a professor whose students have spat at him and called him a "motherfucker" (it happened at Columbia) ought to be moved to more serious and more manly reflection on what his students are really like, as against what popular mythology says they are supposed to be like.

My own view is that a significant minority of today's student body obviously consists of a mob who have no real interest in higher education or in the life of the mind, and whose passions are inflamed by a debased popular culture that prevails unchallenged on the campus. We are reluctant to believe this because so many of the young people who constitute this mob have high I.Q.'s, received good academic grades in high school, and because their popular culture is chic rather than philistine in an old-fashioned way. Which is to say: we are reluctant to believe that youngsters of a certain social class, assembled on the grounds of an educational institution, can be a "mob," in the authentic sociological sense of that term. (We are also reluctant to believe it because many of these students are our children, and we love them regardless of what they do. Such love is, of course, natural and proper. On the other hand, it is worth reminding oneself that members of lower-class lynch mobs have loving fathers and mothers too.)

The really interesting question is: How did they get that way? After all, we do assume that young people of a certain intelligence, provided with a decent education, will be more rational — and therefore more immune to mob instincts — as they near the end of their education than they were at the beginning. The assumption is plausible; but it also patently fails to hold in many instances, and this can only represent a terrible judgment on our system of education.

How is it possible for a Columbia or Berkeley sophomore, junior, or even graduate student to believe in the kinds of absurd simplicities they mouth at their rallies — especially when, before entering college, many of these youngsters would have been quick to recognize them as nothing but absurd simplicities? How is it possible for a radical university student — and there is no reason why a university student shouldn't be radical — to take Ché Guevara or Chairman Mao seriously when, in his various courses, he is supposed to have read Marx, Max Weber, Tocqueville, has been examined on them, and has passed the examination?

When I discuss this problem with my professor friends, I am informed that I display a naïve faith in the power of formal instruction as against the force of the Zeitgeist. And there is a measure of justice in this rejoinder. There can be no doubt that we are witnessing, all over the world, a kind of generational spasm — a sociological convulsion whose roots must go deep and far back and must involve the totality of our culture rather than merely the educational parts of it. It is fairly clear, for example, that many of the students are actually revolting against the bourgeois social and moral order as a whole, and are merely using the university as a convenient point of departure. Whether their contempt for this order is justified is a topic worthy of serious discussion — which, curiously enough, it hardly ever receives in the university. But, in any case, this question ought not to distract us from the fact that those radical students who are most vociferous about the iniquities of the university are the least interested in any productive "restructuring."

On the other hand, not all of the rebellious students are all that radical politically; and it does seem to me that, in these cases, it ought to be possible for a university education to countervail against the mish-mash of half-baked and semiliterate ideologies that so many students so effortlessly absorb within a few months of arriving on campus. My own opinion, for what it's worth, is that the college and the university fail to educate their students because they have long since ceased trying to do so.

The university has become very good at training its students for the various professions; and it is noteworthy that, within the university, the professional schools and divisions have been the least turbulent. But for the ordinary college student — majoring in the humanities or in the social sciences — the university has become little more than an elegant "pad," with bull sessions that have course numbers or with mass lectures that mumble into one ear and ramble out the other.[2]

The entire conception of a liberal education — of the most serious ideas of our civilization being taught by professors who took them seriously — has disappeared, under pressure of one kind or another. The graduate divisions, with their insistence on pre-professional training, have done their part; but so has the whole temper of our educational system over the past decades, with its skepticism toward "great ideas" in general and toward great ideas of the past in particular. I believe that, when students demand that their studies be "relevant," this is what they are unwittingly demanding. After all, what could be more "relevant" today than the idea of "political obligation" — a central theme in the history of Western political philosophy — or the meaning of "justice"? And, in fact, on the few

---

[2] A special word is necessary about sociology departments, whose students play a leading — perhaps critical — role in the current rebellion. Sociology is an odd kind of hybrid: a profession many of whose members are completely unprofessional in outlook, temperament, and intellectual rigor. When I was in New York's City College in the late 1930's, most students majored in sociology because it was the closest thing to a major in current social problems that the curriculum offered — and majoring in such problems was what they really wanted to do. In the end, most of them did become professional sociologists; and if they remained interested in social problems and social reform, their interest was anything but simple-minded. But these days, though the motivation for majoring in sociology is still a heightened concern with social problems, the number of sociology majors is so large, the departments so amorphous, the curriculum so sprawling, that it is quite easy for a student to move through his courses with his passions never being seriously disturbed by a sociological idea.

campuses where such teaching still exists, the students do find it "relevant," and exciting, and illuminating.

But, whether I am right or wrong in this appraisal, the whole issue is, like so many others, "academic." The students think they are rebelling against the university as a "bureaucratic" institution, and they think it so powerfully that they are not likely to listen to anyone who informs them that they are really rebelling against a soulless institution — one that has been emptied of its ideal content. So those who are not set upon destroying the university will be permitted to tinker at "restructuring" it. They will serve on committees that define the curriculum; they will help enforce a dwindling minimum of student discipline; they will be solemnly listened to instead of being preached at.

But you can't reform an institution unless you know what you want; and though our university students have always been encouraged to want the true, the good, and the beautiful, they have never been taught how to think about the conditions and consequences of such desires. To date, most of the reforms sponsored by students have been in the direction of removing their obligation to get any kind of education at all. It is not surprising that harassed administrators and preoccupied professors are quick to find such proposals perfectly "reasonable."[3]

A proposal

So where are we? In an impasse, it would appear. Here we have a major social institution in a flagrant condition of crisis, and not one of the natural social forces involved with this institution can be relied upon to do any of the necessary work of reformation. In situations of this kind, the tradition is for the governmental authorities to step in and fill the power vacuum. And such, I think, will again have to be the case this time.

That last sentence made even me, its author, shudder as it was written. The spectacle of state or federal legislators invading the campus en masse for solemn investigation or deliberation is the kind of tragic farce we can do without. And the idea of state legislators or congressmen trying to impose educational reforms by legislation is as fantastic as it is horrifying. Still, the fact remains that there is a genuine "public interest" at issue here, and there is no one except government who can be asked to defend it. Fortunately, I believe that for once we are in luck, in that the particular circumstances of

---

[3] Jacques Barzun, in his recently published *The American University*, points out that it has long been common in many universities for students, at the end of a course, to hand in written critiques of its form and substance. He also points out that, if one surveys these critiques over a period of time, one discovers that the most recent will be demanding a return to what was rejected by students only a few years back.

the moment permit government to act in an indirect, noncoercive, prudent, yet possibly effective way.

The first such particular circumstance is the fact that the very idea of "higher education" has become so devoid of specific meaning that there is little danger of government, or anyone else, imposing some kind of orthodox straitjacket on the prevailing chaos. There just aren't any such orthodoxies available. Indeed, the very reason we have a crisis in the universities is because all such traditional notions about the function and ends of higher education have, during these past three decades, become otiose.

The real problem at the moment is that no one — not the faculty, not the administration, not the students — has any kind of clear idea of what any "institution of higher learning" is supposed to be accomplishing. It is even beginning to be suspected by many that such phrases as "the university" or "higher education" have acquired different and contradictory meanings, that the vast number of young people now moving onto the campuses are too diverse in their interests and talents to be contained within the old category of "university students," and that the root cause of our distemper is our failure to sort out all these meanings and people, and to make suitable institutional adjustments.

In other words, the situation seems to be such that what we need is a huge injection of pluralism into an educational system that has, through the working out of natural forces, become homogeneous and meaningless at the same time. No one can presume to say what the future pattern of higher education in America should look like. Not until we have far more experimentation — not until we have tried out different kinds of "universities" for different kinds of "students" — can we even hope to know what the real options are. In the ordinary course of events the prospects for this kind of pluralism would be so dim as to be utopian: none of the existing institutions can be counted on to cooperate except in a ritualistic and rather hypocritical way. But this leads me to the second "particular circumstance," which gives the prospect an honest dimension of reality.

This second particular circumstance is the fact that government — especially the federal government — is going to be pouring more and more money into the universities. This is inevitable, and I am willing to persuade myself that it is desirable. But it is neither inevitable nor desirable that the money should flow through the conventional channels — i.e., directly from the public treasury to the bursar's office. Understandably enough, college presidents cannot imagine it proceeding otherwise — higher education is "their" province, and they feel strongly that the money should be "theirs" to expend as administrative discretion and wisdom prescribe. But the citizens of this republic have a claim to assert that higher education is "their" province, too; and they have a right to insist that public monies be expended in such a manner as might overcome the crisis in our universities, instead of deepening it.

What I would therefore like to see — and the idea is one that is slowly gaining favor with many observers; it is not original with me — is something along these lines: (a) state expenditures for higher public education should be frozen at the present level, and all increases in this budget should take the form of loans to qualifying students — these loans being valid for out-of-state institutions as well as in-state ones;[4] (b) federal grants to institutions of higher learning (excepting research grants) should be slowly phased out entirely, and this money — together with new appropriations, which are to be expected — should also be replaced by loans to the qualifying student. This means, in brief, that our universities should have a minimum of direct access to public funds to spend as they see fit, since their vision in this matter has turned out to be too imperfect. It also means that students will have more of the only kind of "student power" that counts: the freedom to purchase the kind of education they want, on terms acceptable to them.

Its effects, both beneficial and risky

There are potential benefits and risks attendant on this proposal, and they merit a listing. But, first, one must face the frequently heard objection to student loans — that their repayment may place too great a burden on a student, especially the student from a poor family, after his graduation. This objection can be surmounted. To begin with, not all students would need loans, and many would need only small ones. There are plenty of well-to-do parents who would still want to pay for their children's education. In addition, repayment plans can be — have been — calculated so as to be proportionate to the student's average income during his working life, and to exempt those whose average income would be below a fixed level; and the burden on both student and taxpayer (for a subsidy would still be necessary, especially for women) could be made perfectly tolerable. If one wished to be more egalitarian, one could augment a loan program with a part-scholarship program for those from low-income families. When all is said and done, however, the university graduate is the prime beneficiary, in dollars and cents, of his education; he ought to be the prime taxpayer for it. There is no such thing

---

[4] Ideally, the entire state budget for higher education should, in my opinion, take the form of student loans. But so radical a measure has little chance of getting through — the state universities would lobby it to death. Besides, so radical a measure is not really necessary. With a ceiling on their budgets and with inevitably increasing costs, the state universities will be constrained gradually to compete for students in terms of the education they offer, as against the low fees they charge, and their position will become a little less privileged with every passing year.

as "free" higher education. Someone is paying for it and, as things now stand, it is the working class of this country that is paying taxes to send the sons and daughters of the middle class — and of the wealthy, too — through state colleges. (Some 60 per cent of the students at Berkeley come from families with incomes of over $12,000.) It is not an easily defensible state of affairs, though we are now so accustomed to it that it seems the only "natural" one.

Now, as to benefits and risks:

(1) A possible benefit that might realistically be expected is that college students would take a more serious and responsible view of their reasons for being on the campus. To the extent that they would disrupt their own education, they would be paying for this out of their own pockets. As a consequence, there would certainly be less casual or playful or faddish disruption. One does get the impression that for many students the university is now, like the elementary and high schools, a place of compulsory attendance, and that the occupation of a campus building is a welcome lark and frolic. If these students were called upon to pay for their frolics, some of them at least might go back to swallowing goldfish. This would be bad for the goldfish but good for the rest of us.

(2) Another potential benefit is that the large state universities, denied the subsidy which permits them to set very low tuition rates for state residents, would find it difficult to grow larger than they are; the college population would probably become more widely distributed, with the smaller and medium-sized institutions in a position to attract more students. This would be a good thing. It is clearly foolish to assemble huge and potentially riotous mobs in one place — and to provide them with room, board, a newspaper, and perhaps a radio station to boot. This violates the basic principles of riot control. We should aim at the "scatteration" of the student population, so as to decrease their capacity to cause significant trouble. I would also argue there are likely to be some educational gains from this process.

(3) An obvious risk is that a great many of the radical and dissenting students would use their money to attend newly founded "anti-universities." And many of the black students would veer off into black nationalist institutions of higher learning. Something like this is bound to happen, I suppose, though to what extent is unpredictable. It would, beyond question, create bad publicity for the whole student loan program. On the other hand, it would take the pressure off existing institutions to be both universities and "anti-universities" — as well as "integrated" and "black nationalist" universities — at the same time. The degree to which such pressure has already been effective would shock parents, state legislators, and public opinion generally were the facts more widely known. Quite a few of our universities have already decided that the only way to

avoid on-campus riots is to give students academic credit for off-campus rioting ("field work" in the ghettos, among migrant workers, etc.). And at Harvard — of all places! — there is now a course (Social Relations 148), which enrolls several hundred students and is given for credit, whose curriculum is devised by SDS, whose classes are taught by SDS sympathizers, and whose avowed aim is "radicalization" of the students.

(4) As a corollary to this last risk, there is the possibility that more new, "good" (in my sense of that term) colleges would also be founded. I'm not too sanguine about this — a fair portion of the academic community would surely look more benevolently on a new college whose curriculum made ample provision for instruction in the theory of guerrilla warfare than one that made a knowledge of classical political philosophy compulsory. Besides, it would be much easier to find "qualified" faculty for the first type than the second. Nevertheless, it is conceivable that the "traditionalists," as well as the academic hipsters, could take advantage of the new state of affairs. And among the students they attract there might be quite a few blacks who are not really interested in studying Swahili or Afro-American culture or "black economics," but who — as things are now moving on the campus — are pretty much forced to do so by their black nationalist fellow students.

(5) The greatest benefit of all, however, is that the new mode of financing higher education will "shake things up." Both university administrators and faculty will have to think seriously about the education of the students — and about their own professional integrity as teachers. This shake-up is bound to have both bad and good consequences. Some universities, for instance, will simply try to reckon how they can best pander to what they take to be student sentiment, and many professors will doubtless pay undue attention to their "popularity" among students. On the other hand, it is reasonable to assume that you can't fool all the students — and their parents — all of the time; and if students are paying for their education, most of them will want to be getting their money's worth.

So, at long last, the academic community, and the rest of us as well, will have to engage in sober self-examination, and address ourselves to such questions as: What *is* this "college" of ours, or this "university" of ours? What *is* the "higher education" we offer? What *do* we parents expect from a particular "institution of higher learning" when we send our children there? The answers will certainly be too various to be pleasing to everyone. But at least they will be authentic answers, representing authentic choices.

It would be ridiculous to expect that, during this period of "shake-up," calm will descend upon our campuses. As I have already said, the roots of the student rebellion go very deep, and very far back. I recall Leo Rosten observing long before Columbia that, so far as he could see, what the dissatisfied students were looking for were adults — adults to confront, to oppose, to emulate.

It is not going to be easy to satisfy this quest, since our culture for many decades now has been plowing under its adults. But I agree with Mr. Rosten that this is what is wanted, and I am certain it will not be achieved until our institutions of higher education reach some kind of common understanding on what kind of adult a young man is ideally supposed to become. This understanding — involving a scrutiny of the values of our civilization — will not come soon or easily, if it ever comes at all. But we must begin to move toward it — and the first step, paradoxically, is to allow a variety of meanings to emerge from our existing, petrified institutions of higher learning.

9

The academic system: a sociologist's view

TALCOTT PARSONS

THE proper position of the academic community in the American society has never been fully settled. The academic system has been part of the wider ongoing society, dependent on it for support and, in some senses, responsible to it. The conception of the "ivory tower," with no responsibilities beyond the pursuit of its occupants' self-defined interests, has never gained wide support. On the other hand, the conception of "academic freedom" has long served as a primary justification for the insulation of the academic community from some of the pressures on it from other sectors of the society. The aim of this essay is to strike a proper balance, appropriate to the situation of academia in contemporary American society. It will, of course, be the statement of an "interested" party, a man whose career has been bound up with the academic enterprise.

A differentiated society

American society is, increasingly, a highly differentiated one. Thus the separation of church and state and the recent clarification of the separation of religion and public education make for a sharpness of differentiation between religious and secular concerns that was not characteristic of the historic past of Western societies. Family and kinship have also become separated from the main functions of economic production and formal education; there are fewer "family businesses" and less inheritance of occupational roles.

It is not surprising that higher education has been involved in this process of differentiation. Education has grown enormously in the last century, both in absolute quantitative terms and in its relative importance in the society. Education is no longer a matter exclusively of teachers and students; the largest proportion of basic research activity is carried out in academic settings, and must be counted as part of the complex of higher education.

This process of differentiation has had a paradoxical consequence: it has increased the autonomy of the system of higher education from particularities; yet it made academia more interdependent generally with the rest of the society. The emergence of "pure" academic concerns has meant an independence from religious ties, which historically have dominated higher education, and from "practical" demands, levied most often by political and economic needs. The autonomy of the academic system is institutionalized in the ideal of academic freedom, the freedom for a class of individuals to devote their *primary* commitments to the pursuit of knowledge in the secular intellectual disciplines, to the transmission of this knowledge and of the skills essential for its pursuit, and to its application to various social uses.

But, insofar as the academic system is a differentiated subsystem of the society, it remains in complex ways interdependent with it. It depends on outside sources for political and economic support, even when its efforts are not of immediate pragmatic "use"; it also depends, in ideological terms, on "legitimation" from the rest of the society. In the former context, it may become vulnerable to the charge of being "useless"; in the latter, to the charge of being "subversive," since no one knows where "free inquiry" may lead.

Membership in the academic system is a full-time occupation for a considerable number of persons, but not for the majority in the system. Students spend but a few years within the fold; for most their adult lives will be spent in other contexts, though without there being, often, a complete break — witness the importance of alumni bodies to the academic world, as well as the life-long psychic identification of being a "Yale man" or a "Smith graduate." The majority of faculty members of professional schools, moreover, are academic men and "practitioners" of their profession concurrently. Thus, clinical teachers in medical schools even *as teachers* are directly engaged in the practice of medicine, for they try to "cure" patients. Hence the academic and the nonacademic worlds are not only interdependent, they are interpenetrating. This is even more evident in the mundane fact that universities require many non-academic goods and services, the purveyors of which (e.g., financial offices) are brought directly into the academic organizations.

Yet, autonomy is an essential condition of the system's ability to function as an agency of creative innovation in the advancement of knowledge and of its application. Medical schools train physicians up to the given level of medical knowledge in order to serve society. But, they also attempt, as a primary obligation, to advance knowledge in medically relevant fields through research. The heroes of their faculties are not only the "good physicians" who do well by their patients, but the great innovators of medical science, the Pasteurs, Flemings, indeed Freuds. The emphasis on innovation is just as clear in faculties of arts and sciences. Though the relation between "basic science" and practical usefulness is highly complex, it surely cannot be said that the latter is the main standard for evaluating scientific contribution. In the social field, such figures as Alfred Marshall, Max Weber, Emile Durkheim, and George Herbert Mead are not honored primarily because they "invented" a practical procedure. This holds even more obviously in the humanities. Two "greats" of the humanistic tradition of my own university, William James and Alfred North Whitehead, are honored much more for their contributions to the stock of fundamental ideas than for any impact on the practical world.

Academic organization as "associational"

The American academic system is, of course, immensely complicated and diverse. There are, in all, about 2,300 institutions of "higher learning." The full universities (about 150) include graduate schools of arts and sciences, undergraduate colleges, and graduate schools of professional training in law, medicine, public health, education, business, public administration, social work, etc. There are liberal arts colleges, independent and denominational professional schools, theological schools, technical schools, and a growing number of junior and community colleges. This diversity of organizational type is matched by a wide range of quality. Few would now dispute that the best American universities are among the finest in the world. Yet, institutions classed as offering "higher" education taper off to levels that sometimes can scarcely compete with the better secondary schools.

A critical feature of the American system is its exceedingly rapid recent growth. Thus, the United States has embarked, in the last third of the century on what, by all historical standards, is an unprecedented program of *mass* higher education. About 40 per cent of the eighteen-to-twenty-one age cohort receives some higher education, a proportion far greater than in any other country, and the percentage is increasing.

Thus, the academic system has entered a phase of "large organizations." But, even within the system, the heads of the academic world do not, through their power (which I define as capacity to make and execute decisions binding on the organization), control a very large fraction of the population, as compared to the "top management" of large corporations and high officials of government. At the primary core of the university, in the organization of a faculty, power is highly decentralized. The main pattern of academic organization is "associational" rather than bureaucratic. It does not stress "line" authority, since basically all full faculty members are formal equals — or colleagues, as the common phrase goes. Indeed, relative freedom from the authority of organizational "superiors" is one of the main aspects of academic freedom.

Not only is power diffused within the academic system; the system as a whole, though of the greatest importance to society, does not wield much power over that society. There is obviously a very important relation, though by no means an identity, between power in our sense and the control of economic resources. The essential point about the academic world is that it is not even self-supporting. It must be heavily subsidized, increasingly from government sources, but very importantly by the private contributions of individuals and foundations. The magnitude of our educational expenditures is not a measure of the academic system's *autonomous* control of its economic resources.

The academic community, especially its more prestigious sectors, has become part of the establishment of American society in the sense of receiving rewards in such forms as respect and opportunity. But this position is not based on the autonomous power position of the academic community, nor on the independent control of economic resources. It derives from the valuation by the general community, including the holders of power and wealth, that what the academic system produces in the form of knowledge and trained personnel is of use in the society.

Conflict situations

The process by which the American system of higher education and research has come to be differentiated from other parts of the society has been marked by considerable conflict. Consideration of these conflicts can open "windows" both on the process itself and on the significance of the system's principal boundaries in relation to its sociocultural environment.

The first conflict concerned the process of secularization, which arose at the time the leading private institutions underwent the transition from college to university. The older colleges had been established under religious auspices and had taken their religious connections seriously. It is perhaps relevant that the emergence of the new university system coincided with the controversies that followed the publication of Darwin's *Origin of the Species* in 1859. Only with the clear establishment in the universities of the dominance of the *secular* intellectual disciplines was their freedom established. This process was facilitated both by the relative liberalism and by the denominational pluralism of the branches of American Protestantism associated with the best colleges — Harvard's Unitarianism is a striking example. It was also facilitated by the fact that the new system of state universities for constitutional reasons was required to be secular. It is significant that all the important new universities — Johns Hopkins, Clark, Cornell, and the University of Chicago — were predominantly secular. Despite the piety of John D. Rockefeller, Sr., the university founded by his donation did not amount to the "establishment" of the Baptist religion in the University of Chicago. Indeed, the separateness, until quite recently, of the Catholic system of higher education gives some indication of the importance of secularization of the predominantly Protestant private sector.

Such a fundamental change could not take place without serious opposition. But the outcome has mainly been one of differentiation and not the development of an anti-religious secularism, as happened in some countries in Europe, notably France. One principal outcome of secularization was a marked diminution in the role of ministers of religion on academic boards of trustees, and their place was taken largely by businessmen. The domination of university boards by businessmen led to a major conflict between the faculties and the trustees over the issue of academic freedom. During this period, the American Association of University Professors was founded (1915) and did much to establish standards of academic freedom and tenure.

The primary issue was the effort of boards of trustees to impose their views on economic policy on the faculty members. For obvious reasons, this affected social scientists principally, especially economists, much as the previous religious controversies had affected especially biologists, geologists, and philosophers, and there were a number of famous cases, such as those of Thorstein Veblen, Richard T. Ely, and Edward A. Ross.[1] The outcome of the conflict was the vindication of academic freedom and tenure, and the establishment

---

[1] Such conflicts often generated equally extreme positions on both sides. A notable example of the antibusiness "muckraking" was Upton Sinclair's *The Goose Step*, which alleged that, in all matters concerning economic policy, American universities followed the financial interests of the business groups importantly represented among donors or on boards of trustees. Thus, the University of Chicago was said to serve almost exclusively the interest of the Standard Oil Company, Harvard of Lee, Higginson & Co., etc. This book appeared while I was an undergraduate at Amherst College, evoking the comment from an "institutional" economist of that period, a great admirer of Veblen (the late Walton Hamilton) that the same, clearly "antibusiness" economics that he was teaching at Amherst, he had learned as a graduate student at Chicago.

of the autonomy of the academic profession, centering on the objective understanding of social and economic phenomena. This autonomy did not preclude participation by the professorate in political action, though the boundaries were hardly well defined.

This phase of the conflict over academic freedom, centering on the views of the business community, shaded later into a phase during which the problem became progressively more political, as sectors of the academic community came under attack from both economic conservatives and patriotic populist quarters. The issues came to focus about "radicalism" and "communism." A great deal of the hostility to the New Deal came to be channeled into these attitudes. The substantial participation of academic people in the New Deal in various capacities, as well as the widespread academic sympathy for it, made the academic world a vulnerable target. During World War II, the fact that the United States was allied with the Soviet Union suppressed this tendency for a time. But with the Cold War it reemerged in intensified form, culminating in the "McCarthyism" of the early 1950's. This attack on the universities in the 1950's can be seen as part of a general "rear guard" movement, involving much irrational emotionalism, staged by those elements in American society that were affected in the most unsettling ways by the great social changes of the time.

The 1960's have seen a very different questioning of the universities. It is an "attack" on the alleged "complicity" of the universities with the establishment, or power structure. Unlike the other three instances, the attack comes, politically speaking, from the left rather than the right. This is indeed a new shift since, in American tradition, the autonomous pursuit of knowledge has always been aligned with left-of-center political forces. There is another important note, however. The pressure from the New Left to "politicize" the universities, however marked by tactics of militant demonstration and the like, is above all an appeal to "conscience," based on a certain presumptive sharing of values. This situation ironically reflects the success of the academic system, for it is that autonomous system that itself has helped generate these values.

The militancy of the radical New Left student groups, with their tactics, not only of demonstration but of sharp "confrontation" and obstruction, has already been a factor contributing to the revival and possibly the strengthening of pressures from the right, not least as manifested by the boards of regents of state universities. Thus both faculties and university administrations have sometimes been caught between the nether millstone of student militancy and the upper millstone of rightist pressure and even intervention. How far the latter is a tendency that is specific to the academic situation, and how far it is part of a more general rightward shift of the American political climate remains to be seen.

Cognitive rationality

The autonomy of the academic system is grounded in a set of values — not only in the general value system of the society, but in the more specific subvalues appropriate to this differentiated subsystem. These may be called the values of *cognitive rationality*, a category parallel to the values of economic rationality that guide an advanced economy.

The focus of cognitive rationality lies in the secular intellectual disciplines. The most distinctive feature of the academic development of the last century has been the attainment of a differentiated autonomy of these disciplines within the university system, institutionalized especially in the graduate schools of arts and sciences and evident in the involvement of these faculties in relatively "pure" or "basic" research. Despite difficulties, this institutionalization has been extended from the "scholarship" of the humanities (which justifies its position), and the "research" of the natural sciences (which has sanctioned its role) to include, in increasing measure, the social sciences. As we have already suggested, this "basic discipline" complex is far from being a closed system. However, its relative integrity is a crucial feature of — and in value terms a primary asset to — the larger system. The entire complex comprises the sphere in which the pattern of academic freedom and the institution of tenure find their most important fields of action.

Academic freedom, in this sense, is the freedom of the members of a select and qualified professional group — and some associated with them, especially students — to devote themselves predominantly to the implementation of the values of cognitive rationality in organizations that are structured and differentiated from others in such a way as to favor this orientation. As with all freedoms in the activistic American value system, there is a correlative obligation to produce, i.e., to "make contributions," in this case to the advancement of knowledge or indirectly through teaching those who can hope to advance knowledge.[2]

It is my argument that the institution of academic freedom estab-

[2] Thus construed, academic freedom comes very close to Max Weber's conception of *Wertfreiheit* (possibly translatable as "value freedom") of science— Weber used the term *Wissenschaft*, which included the humanities and was closer to our "discipline" than to science in the narrower sense. It is important to note that Weber introduced this concept in a polemic context directed against movements urging the "politicization" of academic life that were important in his own time. In particular, these involved the use of the prestige of academic appointments to advocate partisan political positions without distinction between the elements for which scientific expertise could honestly be claimed and those based only on the personal political commitment of the speaker or writer. (See Weber's famous essay on "The Meaning of 'Ethical Neutrality' in Sociology and Economics," in *The Methodology of the Social Sciences*, translated and

lished the *primacy* of the values of cognitive rationality and that this primacy is strongest at the core of the academic system in the functions of research and in the training of academic professionals. The supreme importance of *competence,* of the mastery of knowledge and the techniques of its advancement, goes hand in hand with it. With this value of competence, which makes it a *duty* for those who claim the privileges of academic status to be competent, goes the obligation of *integrity,* which is the commitment to the values of the academic profession. In short, academic freedom is only possible if this value of cognitive rationality, rather than any other, is the core of the professor's academic concerns.

I have spoken of the primacy of the values of cognitive rationality in the academic world — not of their *exclusive* role. It has almost always been taken for granted that knowledge should, so far as possible, be put to practical use. It is surely not desirable, indeed not possible, to draw a rigid line between those who create and evaluate knowledge and those who communicate it to others or put it to practical use. The applied professions constitute the most important institutionalized agencies for the utilization of sophisticated, technical knowledge. In the American system of higher education, especially, the professional schools have become integral to the modern university, with important links to the arts and sciences faculties. With the development of the research function, much of it, including that defined as "basic," is done by members of professional school faculties, many of whom are relatively "pure" scientists or scholars. Furthermore, many members of arts and sciences faculties engage in some kind of "applied" work. The basic legitimacy of such "shading off" from the pure to the applied should not be questioned. However, it is essential that the *primacy* of the academic function be maintained, especially at the structural core of the university.

Historically, the core of the academic system has been "general education," which centers in the undergraduate college. Though some training for the less advanced professions is common at this level, a large proportion of undergraduates are not directly preparing to be professionals, but are "getting an education," after which they go on to postgraduate or professional work. General education in-

edited by Edward Shils and Henry A. Finch (Glencoe, Ill.: The Free Press, 1949).

It is quite clear, especially in the later essay, "Science as a Vocation," that Weber did not mean that the scientist, qua scientist, should have *no* value commitments, but that he should give primacy to the differentiated values appropriate to science, such as concern for the logical clarity and empirical validity of knowledge; that he should not let other values, however valid they might be in other spheres, intervene in the scientific enterprise. Through his conception of *Wertbeziehung* (value relatedness), however, Weber held that such other values could legitimately play a part in the formulation of problems for scientific investigation; but they should not enter into statements of the grounds of validity of scientific propositions.

cludes a great deal of knowledge as codified in the various disciplines, but also involves the development of a kind of a "world view" that is not very far removed from ideology. The function of undergraduate education, far from tending to atrophy in favor of professional training, has conspicuously held its own. And it is clearly in the relatively nontechnical undergraduate teaching in the social sciences that it is most difficult to keep standards of the objective validity of knowledge apart from the teacher's own personal commitments to social policy, as based on values other than cognitive rationality.

The graduate school, though by no means copied directly from Germany, was greatly influenced by German models, especially in the strong emphasis on research. The graduate school did not, however, despite the initial intention of some of its founders, displace the undergraduate college, but was typically added to it so as to make a "university." In the majority of institutions that have graduate schools, most faculty members not only teach graduates and do research, but also teach undergraduates. Even in the most specialized and prestigious institutions (e.g., MIT, Harvard) such undergraduate teaching is regarded with general approval.

The "collegial" pattern

We have been sketching a picture of the most important single type of American academic organization, the "full" university. This is a highly differentiated and pluralistic organization that is multifunctional. It is the main agency of "basic" research in the society, but also of much "applied" research. It is the main agency for training new members of the academic profession itself, the successors of the present generation of researchers, graduate teachers, and undergraduate teachers. It is the main agency for training practitioners of the higher order applied professions. Finally, it is no less a prominent, though far from exclusive, agency for the general education of what is now a very large fraction of each new age cohort of the population.

The university is highly differentiated, yet this differentiation has by no means led to complete separation of the various functions. On the contrary, *all* four primary functions of the academic system — research, graduate teaching, undergraduate teaching, and "application" — are typically performed by most members of faculties of arts and sciences; all except undergraduate teaching are performed by members of professional school faculties.

This pattern ramifies far beyond the full university type to include liberal arts colleges of various levels of quality, the large urban colleges with their strongly undergraduate emphasis (though many are now adding graduate and professional programs), various lower

level professional institutions or programs operating within undergraduate colleges, a fringe of strictly denominational religious institutions, and the like. It is notable that, in recent years, many units
of the Catholic system, which for long was very separatist, have
moved rapidly toward inclusion in the more general academic
system, deemphasizing their purely denominational character.

As relatively autonomous institutions, colleges and universities
undertake a large share of self-government. Faculties, as wholes, as
departments, and as individuals who are both engaged in their own
teaching and research and acting as members of committees, departments, and faculties, play a large — though varying — part in such
government. That their governing responsibility is considerable is
indicated by the fact that, in a pilot study I have been conducting
with Gerald Platt, all classes of respondents wished to reduce the
time and effort given to "administration," whereas this did not hold
for any of their other academic functions.

One further feature of the academic system is particularly important to my argument. It concerns a facet of the institution of academic freedom that derives from the fact that a typical faculty,
especially one of arts and sciences, is composed of specialists
trained in a wide variety of subjects — not only disciplines, but many
specialties within disciplines and many kinds of interdisciplinary
interests. It is a fundamental institutional expectation that there
should be a wide range of autonomy for each faculty member. He
should be constrained by a minimum of supervision by administrative officers or pressures to conformity from peers. The basic structure of the faculty tends to be that of a "company of equals" for
those having full membership, usually protected by "tenure" appointment. Differences of basic rank tend to signal stages of career rather
than of "final" status. The evidence indicates that this "collegial"
pattern is more strongly institutionalized in the more prestigious
reaches of the system.

In this situation, power tends to be highly decentralized, giving
the individual professor a large measure of control over his own
teaching and research. The importance of formal collective decision-
making is relatively minimized. Where faculties and departments
are concerned, decisions ordinarily take place by the democratic
franchise, with each member, including deans and chairmen, casting
one vote. In this type of organization, integration operates far more
through persuasion and influence than through authority and power.
This appears to be another aspect of the "pluralism" of academic
organization, for members are expected to follow a tolerant "live and
let live" policy in their mutual relations, respecting the spheres in
which others claim special competence and interest.

How students fit in

Finally something needs to be said about the status of students. It is sometimes rather intemperately asserted that the academic system should be run exclusively for the benefit of students. This would, however, conflict with the multifunctional character of academia; the relation of students to academia is, in fact, quite complicated.

First, we should note the great variety of different kinds of students as well as the very great numbers of them. They differ by kinds of study, from freshmen in community colleges to the most advanced levels of postgraduate training. They differ in subjects of interest, not only within the range of the intellectual disciplines, but with reference to fields of application. They differ by type and quality of educational institution and by various factors of socioeconomic and family background, as well as by political conviction or inclination.

Insofar as students have in recent years come to play a more active and political role, the center of gravity seems to lie in the undergraduates at our major colleges, particularly in the leading state universities, starting with Berkeley, but conspicuously including Michigan and Wisconsin. The higher quality liberal arts colleges, such as Oberlin and Swarthmore, are also considerably involved, as are some of the Ivy League universities. Graduate students, more in arts and sciences than in the professional schools, are the second most involved group, particularly because of the recent and very immediate impact of the draft, an impact intensified by the war in Vietnam.

Students have long had a status of "membership" in the university that clearly distinguishes them from the customers of a firm in the usual market context. Students must be "admitted" to a college or graduate school; they graduate to become "alumni," which is by no means a status of negligible importance. Their membership constitutes a presumptive status of a "citizenship" in the academic community. Its content is now involved in a process of transformation, the main direction of which is clearly toward more egalitarian relations, though just what shape it will take and how far the changes will go remains problematical. A first aspect of the change is a diminution of the role of college and university administrations as standing *in loco parentis*. Students are thereby coming to be treated, in their "private" lives, more as responsible adults and less as "wards" of the institution. This process has been going on for at least half a century; in the more "advanced" sectors, it probably does not have very much further to go. Its importance is accentuated by the vast growth of coeducation among the college population and by the prevalence of marriage among graduate students and some undergraduates.

There seem to be two other major contexts of change, both involving student-faculty relations far more than the one just mentioned. These concern the teaching-learning process and the "government" of the institution, respectively. They are closely interdependent, but distinct. With respect to the first, the faculty seems to have two bases of superiority or "precedence," and correspondingly of responsibility, that cannot be shared in a completely egalitarian fashion with all students. The first, particularly salient in the academic sphere, concerns the superior competence gained by their technical training and experience. If there were no substantial differences on this score, it would be difficult to legitimize the process of formal education at all. The alternative to some form of institutionalized faculty "precedence" would seem to be a "populist" ideal of complete equality of all participants.[3]

To assert the necessity of faculty "precedence" is not to impugn the student's academic freedom, which is the freedom to be instructed so far as possible in what is objectively known, and in the methods of enhancing knowledge, with a clear recognition of what questions are legitimately controversial as distinguished from those for which answers seem to be established. The student's academic freedom also includes the basic right to question what he is taught within the framework of orderly procedure. This right becomes particularly important in areas relating to social and political policy, where scientifically established answers are rare and partial and where the right to differing opinions is institutionalized in the political structure.

The second basis of the precedence of the faculty member over the student is a consequence of the former being typically a teacher and researcher on a career basis, not just for the several years of studentship. His personal commitments give him a far larger stake in the academic enterprise than has the average student. Hence he is entitled to a larger "say" than is the student.

Academic government

This topic shades into that of the government of the academic institution. There are at least four principal entities involved, namely trustees, administrations, faculties, and students. They are interrelated in a manner somewhat analogous to the separation of powers

---

[3] Ignoring these considerations would readily lead to a pattern analogous to the old idea of "producers' cooperation" in industry, namely government by pure egalitarian democracy with respect to all important decisions by all members involved in any capacity. No society in which a socialist regime has held power has closely approached this pattern of industrial organization. Perhaps the closest approach is the early Israeli kibbutz, a very small unit (not more than about two hundred adults) with assured markets and outside underwriting. Cf. S. N. Eisenstadt, *Israeli Society* (New York: Basic Books, 1968).

in governmental affairs, though the lines are differently drawn. Faculties have a role somewhere between the functions of the judicial and legislative branches of government, participating in both. As the groups most thoroughly committed to academic values, they bear the largest responsibility as judges of the standards of the system and are the most important, though not the sole, determiners of the "educational policies" that implement these standards. Students and alumni play a role in some respects parallel to those of constituencies in relation to political office-holders. But the "judicial" role of the faculty substantially modifies the "pure democracy" of the constituency type relationship.

Though administrations and trustees clearly must have certain kinds of authority over both faculty and students, it is (or should be) limited by the academic freedom of the other two groups. The definition of these limitations, especially with reference to faculties, have been rather fully worked out in the course of the controversies over academic freedom and tenure during the last fifty years.

The core problem of student status is in the faculty-student relationship. This relation of teacher to student is one of the two central functions of the academic system — the other being research. ("Service" to the community is a third function and one that is rising in importance.)

From one point of view, the faculty-student relation is an extension of "socialization" begun in the family. It is inherently an asymmetrical relationship because those being socialized must learn and internalize cognitive content, patterns of value, etc. Although asymmetrical, however, socialization cannot be treated as a one-way process of inculcation, but as a reciprocal process of interaction. Though ideas in such fields as child training and progressive education have probably not yet stabilized, this has been a prominent note in American educational thought. It has often been closely associated with a realization of the importance of what is sometimes called independence training. Indeed, higher education may be considered an extension and culmination of independence training. But independence is not gained simply by letting a student go on his own. There is a didactic process, including lectures and assigned readings. These serve both to economize the scarce resources of time and energy of students and instructors, and to expose the student to the instructor as a potential role model. In this sense, lectures are important in letting the more eminent faculty members reach much larger numbers of students than is possible in tutorial and seminar contexts. At the same time, there should be, and increasingly has been, a considerable element of independent student work that comes to a focus in projects done under guidance. The broad trend surely has been to cultivate in students the capacity to approach and solve problems independently, rather than to require the passive ingestion of masses of codified information.

We have stressed that students are, by the definitions of their roles, participating members in the academic system. But, the justification of the student's obligation to recognize faculty precedence remains. The matters of competence and of commitment and responsibility cannot simply be declared irrelevant; long training and experience and previous achievement, as well as career commitment, must "count." Besides, the higher up the educational ladder a person goes, the more *specialized* becomes the role complex into which he is being socialized. If he undergoes additional training in some field, academic or professional, his role becomes more specialized, and he must respect the standards of competence and integrity of that field. In this setting, the academic freedom of the student, properly sub-classified for the immense variety of different classes of students, appears to be part of the academic freedom of the system as a whole, and is entirely consistent with faculty precedence. It should not be forgotten that modern students have much freedom of choice. Subject to realistic possibilities, they can choose the institution at which they study. They can choose among the various fields for an area of specialization or for areas among which they can distribute their attention. There is generally a considerable elective component in choosing among courses and instructors. Finally, student initiative, though unevenly distributed, can considerably affect the more detailed conduct of courses.

The participation of students in the government of the academic enterprise poses a somewhat different problem. We have stressed the importance of the decentralization of power in the academic system. Such decentralization implies that a particularly important location of the student's autonomy must lie in his relations to his instructors *taken individually.* However, this assumes the giveness of two basic sets of conditions, namely the framework of educational policy and the composition of the faculty through the process of appointment. Probably the crucial contemporary questions of student power arise in these two areas.[4]

In this context, two elements are clear: faculty members have career stakes in their professions and often long-term stakes in their particular institutions, and they have a greater competence in many, though not all, academic matters. Students are usually present for only brief periods, not exceeding a few years. A strong case can be

---

[4] A particular area of recent tension, of course, concerns procedures for student discipline in matters other than academic standing as such. Here the problem concerns, on the one hand, a balance between faculty and administration roles and, on the other, the mode and extent of student participation in decisions. No satisfactory, simple, and general solution seems to be in sight, but structural and procedural improvements are urgent.

made for student representation in many fields touching the government of universities, but it would seem patently silly for students
as temporary members of the academic community to have governing power *equal* to that of faculties, to say nothing of a fully democratic pattern of "one member one vote," with every freshman having
the same voice as any senior faculty member.

The problem of the balance between what we have treated as the
primary functions of the academic system and functions that impinge
on its boundaries should be considered in somewhat the same light.
We have suggested that faculty members should have considerable
freedom to take on political commitments and activities outside the
core functions of their roles, but this cannot go so far as to make
educational institutions into instruments of particular political
causes. The same principle applies to the student component of
academic freedom; student power cannot supersede faculty power.
Without a faculty, and its autonomous core position, a university is
nothing.

The academic system and pluralism

The functional and structural pluralism of the academic system
clearly have a direct bearing on the character of its relations to its
social environment. As a differentiated subsystem of the society, it is
the source of several different kinds of outputs that in various ways
are important in other sectors of the society. But it is also dependent
on the rest of society for what we have called support. By and large,
the system does not and should not command, in its own right, the
economic resources essential to its functioning. Equally, academics
are not men of power who command the primary decision-making
positions in government or in the large organizations of the society.
Indeed, I would argue that their proper functions would inevitably
be corrupted if they did. Even within the academic system the men
of power should (as on the whole they do) play roles facilitating,
rather than controlling, the primary academic functions themselves.

The academic system can secure the necessary support because
on the whole, despite many imperfections, it is committed to the
implementation of a set of values that, without having the same
primacy in the rest of the society, are widely shared — i.e., knowledge and higher education in its various forms are very widely
considered to be intrinsically good. This commitment to admired
values, then, is one of the main factors responsible for the high level
of influence of the academy in the society at large. The academic
system is also an open system. This openness is structured in the
generally pluralistic and mobile character of the society as a whole.
Both student bodies and professional personnel have become immensely more variegated and in a sense cosmopolitan than was true

of earlier generations. The present American system is very far from
the late nineteenth-century British system, which was primarily
concerned with the education of a small sociopolitical elite of students. Correspondingly, it cannot subsist on the narrow support of a
small establishment.

These circumstances essentially make the academic system an
integral part of the generally pluralistic society, with its egalitarian
strains and its commitments to equality of opportunity as well as
equality of basic citizenship rights, its universalistic legal system
and supporting moral sentiments, its modified version of free enterprise, and its liberal political system. Hence, with respect to both
its values and its interests, the academic system has a high stake in
the pluralistic, liberal character of the main developmental trends
of American society. Its own value patterns define the commitments
of its members not only to their primary functions, but also to their
main internal relational patterns. Thus, academic discussion, in the
classroom, the seminar, or the department or faculty meeting is
governed on the whole by the same kind of procedural rules that
govern parliamentary procedure — though they do not usually have
to be so highly formalized. Indeed, similar patterns are involved in
the conduct of written academic discussion and controversy. There
is recognition of a general right to be heard, which precludes monopoly of speaking time and interference with the free speech of
recognized participants in discussion. As in the political arena, there
is a presumption of a plurality of legitimate viewpoints, hence of the
legitimacy of dissent from any "established" viewpoint, whether that
of the teacher, a majority in any particular meeting, or a dedicated
minority. These *procedural* institutions are deeply embedded in our
liberal, pluralistic society, including its legal and political systems,
and the academic system certainly shares a stake in them. But there
are various ways in which this academic stake in the liberal system
may be understood, and these do not impinge equally on all parts
of the differentiated pluralistic academic system. In particular, I
should like to discuss two different contexts of the definition of
freedoms and responsibilities.

Academic freedom

The institutionalization of academic freedom requires that the
relation between collective responsibility (e.g., of a university as a
corporate entity) and the responsibilities and freedoms of individuals or collective subunits must be more carefully articulated than
is the case for some other types of social organization. I have emphasized the extent to which power and responsibility are decentralized and autonomy is emphasized in academic faculties. Thus the
individual academic man, though he must negotiate over the sub-

jects he will teach, tends to have very considerable autonomy — the more so the higher the standing of his institution — with respect to detailed subject matter and, to a high degree, his teaching procedure, and the evaluation of student performance. In research, his autonomy extends even further. The university faculty or administration does *not* take corporate responsibility for detailed decisions in these areas. It appoints what it considers to be "good men," gives them broad mandates, and leaves the rest to them within a very free regulatory and corporate framework. Similar things can be said about departments, which certainly enjoy a good deal of autonomy.

Clearly, the same principles should extend to the freedom of members of the academic community with respect to the functions that stand at, or slightly beyond, the boundaries of strictly academic obligations. This freedom is, indeed, very generally institutionalized with respect to "outside" functions, ranging from performances benefiting other parts of the academic community (especially disciplinary and other associations) to "service" functions of various kinds. But there is a crucial distinction between the scope of the freedom for members of an academic collectivity to act *as individuals* and the implications of directly parallel corporate action taken by the collectivity as a whole. This seems to me to be an *essential* distinction, grounded in the structure of the academic system, not merely an "adventitious" liberty that academic people enjoy as citizens.[5] The right of the academic individual publicly to take "partisan" position seems to me to be grounded *both* in his rights as a citizen and in the institutions of academic freedom. He also has the right, in a sense that needs to be carefully defined, to involve the name of his educational institution. It is clear that the institution is not necessarily in a corporate sense committed. At the same time, members of its faculties are often identified as such when they participate in public matters, and their general position of influence in the society is inseparable from such memberships, current or even past.[6] The essential normative requirements seem to be two: (1) the persons involved should make clear that they speak as individuals, not as spokesmen for a corporate commitment of their institution; (2) they should make clear the degree to which they claim professional expertise as a grounding for their position.

Corporate positions *are* justified in political contexts where the

---

[5] Thus it has seemed to me and many others quite proper for members of university faculties, identifying themselves as such, to sign statements of dissent from government policy, e.g., in Vietnam, whereas it would be a very different matter for a university to take a corporate position on the same issues, e.g., by vote of its board of trustees or its faculty of arts and sciences.

[6] Listings such as those in *Who's Who in America* or *American Men of Science* always note this information as well as special honors, publications, etc. These data are essential to the "identity" of the individual; they define *who* he is.

interests of the educational institution, the academic system, or relevant sectors of them are at stake. Thus, I can see no objection to university administrative officials testifying, as some recently did, before a congressional committee in opposition to the new draft regulations, which may seriously depopulate the graduate schools, as well as involving many inequities. Similarly, corporate academic opposition to special teachers' oath legislation is justified. On a more general level, universities can legitimately act, collectively, to defend themselves from a political movement or regime that threatens their autonomy or the academic freedom of their members. It is widely felt, retrospectively, that the German universities corporately — not just the members of their faculties individually — should have fought much more vigorously against the threat of the Nazi movement in the early 1930's.

Another context is of a somewhat different character. The modern, highly differentiated type of society, far more than simpler societies, develops a very wide range of functional interchanges among its different sectors. These interchanges make appropriate outputs in some sense "impersonally" available to those with an interest in using them. The prototype is perhaps economic production for a market, where the producers of goods have no personal contact with their ultimate consumers and generally do not know even who they will be.

Though the direct beneficiaries of the teaching function stand as individuals in structured relationships with their teachers, a crucial part of the output of the academic system is communication, especially through the printed word, but also through radio and television, with recipients who may not be individually identifiable or predictable. The general term "broadcasting" may be used for this type of communication. The broadcasting situation raises two sets of questions of responsibility.

One set concerns the academic man's freedom to publish and otherwise to broadcast. The main academic system must be firmly committed to maximal individual freedom in this respect, subject only to laws of libel, obscenity, and the like, and such informal standards of professional dignity and taste as are conventional. Any involvement of the university as a corporate entity, even at the level of *nihil obstat,* to say nothing of requiring *imprimatur,* is clearly to be considered intolerable. The principle of academic freedom involved here is the same as that in teaching and of expressing political and other opinions "as an individual."

Academic responsibility

The other problem area concerns the order of *responsibility* that can legitimately be imposed either on individuals or on corporate entities for the uses to which their broadcast outputs are put. In the case of economic products, it is clear that they may turn out to injure someone or be put to criminal uses. With increasing consistency, the law has taken the position that, if manufacturers use reasonable care in providing for safety and control, they cannot be held responsible for injuries incurred in the use of their products. Certainly, for example, the manufacturers of an automobile cannot be held liable for its criminal uses. It is entirely possible that research outputs also may be put to antisocial uses of many different kinds. Furthermore, much applied research takes place in fields over which both political controversies and moral dilemmas exist, most obviously in the design of weapons of war. Thus, the first nuclear fission was achieved as part of a deliberate effort to develop an atomic bomb. It required the contributions of the highest level physical scientists, and plunged them, along with others, into serious conflicts of conscience. The possibility of the antisocial use of disciplined knowledge is most conspicuous in such areas, and perhaps in the medical fields, but is by no means confined to them. In particular, the "subversion" of what are felt to be essential belief systems and value commitments is an ever-present possibility in the efforts to develop and apply new knowledge.

Understandably, the academic attitude has been predominantly on the side of freedom of "broadcasting." Most academic men would neither have favored suppressing the teaching of, or publication about, evolution because of its alleged antireligious consequences nor condoned the dismissal of Veblen because of his antibusiness ideas, etc. With the growth of the "power" of knowledge, however, the situation is sometimes reversed. It is perhaps not surprising that some within the academic fold, who become aware of this "power," come to advocate the imposition of severe restrictions.

We have noted the tendency of some politically oriented groups — at the present mainly those on the left and prominently including students — to try to enlist the academic system in the service of political causes, often ones propounded by militant minorities near one end of the political spectrum. The advocates of a cause sometimes pressure the academic community to forbid its members to engage in activities, e.g., research work, which in their opinion will, or even might, produce results injurious to their cause. An example would be, as in the case of the nuclear physicists, the improvement of weapons that might make the conduct of disapproved wars more effective. Such positions are often supported by allegations that there is a sharp polarization of moral legitimation between a corrupt "establishment" and a morally pure opposition. There is a "demand," then, that the academic community disassociate itself radically from a maleficent "establishment" to avoid the guilt of "complicity."

It is my view that the same principles of academic freedom that have justified the assertion of independence from certain types of religious orthodoxy, from conservative business pressure, and from political pressure from the right, also justify resistance to current pressures from the left to restrict the freedom of academic activities to the kinds of work that *this* group views as morally justified. However, it is important to reemphasize the distinction between individual and corporate involvement. The strongest strictures should be directed against restrictions on individuals' freedom to do work that, certainly indirectly, but sometimes directly, serves interests that the political militants may condemn. Institutions should be more conservative in making commitments to specific organs of government and, especially, political parties or other partisan groups. But even there something can be said for preserving ranges of institutional freedom. Thus, I approve heartily of the Harvard policy of not accepting research grants or contracts on a corporate basis, if the output of the research is expected to be "classified," though members of its faculty are free to engage in such work "as individuals." However, I should not wish to argue that it is basically illegitimate for Harvard's neighbor, MIT, to accept such connections. The essential principle seems to be to resist pressure for either the individual or the corporate entity to bind itself to particular "outside" interests, whether "establishment" or antiestablishment.

Teaching and research

This essay has argued that the problem of the relation of the American academic community to politics should be approached in the light of the nature both of its own internal structure, as it has developed in the last century, and of the special ways in which it has been differentiated from, but integrated in, the society as a whole. The underlying assumption is clearly that the broad pattern of interrelation has on balance benefited both academia and society.

One of the prime conditions of the "health" of the academic system has been its differentiation as a subsystem, both from the previously dominant systems of cultural commitment, notably religion, and from the primary operative sectors of the society, notably economy and polity. Its autonomy as a system, thus achieved, has not eliminated its symbiosis with — hence, in certain crucial respects dependence on — these other systems. The crucial point about this symbiosis is that the legitimation of the system of higher education derives broadly from the same institutionalized pattern of values as does legitimation for most of the principal institutions of the wider society. This is true with particular clarity for those aspects of the value system that stress equality of citizenship rights, equality of opportunity, the other basic constitutional freedoms (with their correlative obligations), and social progress through individual and collective achievement.

In a very broad sense, the members of the academic profession are, to varying degrees, given a privileged status, relatively free from direct obligations to contribute to the functions of the ordinary workaday world, but carrying obligations to devote themselves primarily to the process of knowledge. It is essentially this specialized function of being more concerned with the future resources of the society than with its current "problems" that provides the normative basis for establishing priorities for the academic system as a whole among its primary constituent activities. It is my view, which some will dispute, that the first priority should go to the research function, the advancement of knowledge, with the highest evaluation falling to relatively "pure" or basic research. (This is not to say that every academic man should be *primarily* a researcher or that every institution should primarily emphasize research. Indeed, quite the contrary: the *combination* of research with the teaching and service functions is an especially salient characteristic of the American academic system.) Research, and the training of graduate students for research, does not require the largest amounts of the system's resources, especially of manpower. For reasons of scarcity, these functions are concentrated only in a small sector of the system, and it is the most prestigious.

The teaching function clearly holds the second priority, but, as we have stressed, falls into three primary subsectors, namely graduate teaching of future academic professionals, graduate teaching of "applied" professionals, and undergraduate teaching that emphasizes "general education." In terms of the subvalues of the academic system itself, the first has the highest priority. However, the other two are particularly crucial for the wider society; they constitute forms of "output" that are very essential to the genesis of societal support. Seen in this context, the service function should have the lowest priority among the three main functions, though its importance is not anywhere nearly negligible. The teaching of research requires a component of apprenticeship, so that teacher and student are cooperatively *doing* research. Similarly, the teaching of professional practice requires actual performance of the functions of practice, again with students in apprentice roles. Something similar can be said of general education. In the more general cultural areas, the spirit of rational evaluation of the cultural tradition, of history, of the state of society, and of human relations to the environment should be active and alive. Good teachers of undergraduates in these spheres convey some of this spirit to their students, often in settings of controversy. This evaluative spirit then penetrates into the spheres of "application" of knowledge in the more or less professional senses, e.g., health, education, law, and the like, especially into matters of public policy and the social and cultural issues of the day.

It is almost impossible to draw a sharp line between the more conventional professional forms of "service" and such evaluative functions with reference to cultural, political, and ideological matters, especially when the latter may shade into active advisory functions to public authorities, political movements, and the like. *Qua* academic man, the first obligation seems to me to be as clear as possible about how far "advice" can be grounded in genuinely valid knowledge and about where it rests on more subjective and "partisan" elements. To my mind, this includes the recognition, certainly in the cultural and sociopolitical fields, that orientations with respect to such "problems" heavily involve values *other* than the cognitive rationality that has primacy in the academic system. These non-academic value components are sometimes well integrated with academic values as part of the more general societal integration of values — in the main, such integration exists in the health fields — but they are often much involved with social and political conflict, hence with various forms and degrees of opposition to some institutional status quo. In this situation, I would hold that the members of the academic profession, in their respective fields of competence, are obligated to inform the public, including their own students, both about the state of knowledge bearing on the questions at issue, and about how such knowledge is intertwined with noncognitive values and with the emotional commitments of various groups. I find no way to exempt members of the academic profession from this obligation to what Weber called "scrupulous intellectual honesty," even though it necessarily bears unevenly according to fields of competence and the motivational involvements of individuals and classes of them. Indeed, if the academic system were to withdraw from this obligation, it would be repudiating a very important part of its obligation to "contribute" to the welfare of society, which very generally includes enhancement of welfare through fundamental change.

An "engine of change"?

The process we have just been discussing — the clarification of the relevance of cognitively rational evaluation to cultural, political, and social issues of the day — should be conceived as reciprocal inter-action, not as one-way "instruction" by faculties and their members. The interaction should certainly include discussion of the internal structures and the functions of the colleges and universities, and the nature of their relations with other groups and interests in their social environment. If the values of cognitive rationality are to play an effective role in this reciprocal discussion, however, two conditions need to be fulfilled. First, *competence* must have an opportunity to make itself felt as an essential factor in clarifying the role of valid knowledge. Second, there is the underlying importance of strict observance of the *procedural forms* of intellectual discussion.

The above considerations concern an important "interface" between the academic system and the more turbulent aspects of society as a whole. They involve a kind of "dialectic" relation in that the academic system is differentiated from the rest of the society, and to a degree "withdrawn" from the more immediate social pressures, while the results of its activities constitute major influences *on* the society, not least on its processes of change.

The academic system is not primarily an "engine" of change (or reform) in the sense either that government strove to be in the New Deal or, more extremely, that Communist governments attempt to be in undertaking the radical restructuring of their societies. In a "lower key," however, a strong and prominent academic system is by no means a bulwark of the status quo, but very much a source, through many channels, of impetus to societal change. The development of the secular intellectual disciplines, which now lie at the core of the academic system, has been intimately involved with the three "revolutions" that have underlain the emergence of modern society — the industrial revolution, the democratic revolution, and the educational revolution. Indeed, it is the focus of the present phase of the educational revolution.

Such considerations indicate that both the values and the concrete interests of the academic system give it a primary stake in maintaining a balance of differentiation within and integration in what is, in the broadest sense, a liberal, legally ordered, and pluralistic society. In this general sense, it is structurally congruent with the main outlines of such a society; the two are for the most part mutually supportive, though not without very considerable strain and conflict. One such conflict centers around the questions of which involvement of "outside" interest within the academic community should be considered legitimate. There seems to be a considerable range of permissible variation in these respects. Thus some institutions may prefer not to have ROTC programs, an issue that seems to be parallel to that of contracts for classified research. Whether or not recruiters for outside agencies, such as the armed services of industrial firms, should be allowed to use campus facilities seems to be a similar question. General policies about such questions seem legitimately to be somewhat negotiable, with the presumption that students as well as administrations and faculties should have a voice in the decisions — though not usually the one deciding voice.

The academic sanctuary

Within the academic community itself, the most important issue seems to me to be the maintenance of the procedural norms that are so essential to the implementation of cognitive values. Our general theme of the differentiatedness of the academic system implies that in some respects it should be considered a sanctuary. Its relative removal from the manifold pressures of the outside world makes possible certain special freedoms, not basically different in kind from those outside, but higher in degree. With all reservations made for the ultimate importance of verification, one critical focus of academic freedom is not only the freedom to, but the encouragement of, "playing with ideas." Such "play," which may be carried out in deadly earnest, requires some immunity from immediate confrontation with consequences or objections, before the fuller implications of the new ideas can be explored. The basic spirit of tentativeness, therefore, as contrasted with "commitment," must be granted unusual tolerance. Where some elements within the community feel passionately committed or opposed to the idea of a course or action, this should not be permitted to infringe the freedom of others to question or express dissent from their position. The academic way of dealing with such conflicts is discussion under procedural rules, not "confrontation." The latter has a tendency to "escalate" conflicts. The limiting case of such escalation is the attempt to place more or less definitely physical constraints on freedom of opposition. This can range from keeping a person in a room to which free access is barred (as in the case of the Dow Chemical recruiter at Harvard in October 1967) to "shouting down" a disapproved spokesman in a meeting and denying him the opportunity to speak.

I have suggested that a number of the questions about what interests should or should not be allowed to participate in the academic community or use academic facilities may appropriately be regarded as negotiable, with a presumption that the patterns of acceptance and rejection need not be absolutely uniform for all institutions. However, there is a certain relation between different types of cases that press for universalistic standards. Thus, rules that allow students to invite "controversial" speakers to the campus must also be related to the demand of faculties and administrations that student groups accord the basic "civil liberties" of the academic community to everyone allowed on the campus, even speakers who are strongly disapproved of. Beyond such obvious matters of reciprocity, it seems to me that its special relation to the principles of freedom of thought and communication place on the academic community a *special* obligation to maintain freedom of discussion scrupulously in its internal operations. Tolerance of intellectual opposition should be *greater* inside the academic community than in the society at large. Hence, the precedents of the legitimacy of civil disobedience and various forms of "confrontation" in the outside political arena become dubious when applied to the inside affairs of academia.[7]

---

[7] Student militants often claim that the "system" is so rigidly bound by its vested interests that *only* the tactics of confrontation and internal civil dis-

The currently militant movements are clearly *selective* among what, from a wider and longer point of view, are the "most important" issues. Thus the sometimes passionate devotion of the Old Left to Marxism and the leadership of the Soviet Union is generally absent in the New Left. The symbol of "capitalism" as the focus of evil seems to have been more or less fully replaced by "power structure" and "establishment." The intensity of "commitment" on such issues, when combined with such sharp selectivity, tends strongly to impose a presumptive polarization between those who fully share the intense commitment and those who do not. The latter are defined as enemies of the movement, even when, as is sometimes the case, they share evaluations, though less intensely.[8]

The legitimation of such polarization of commitment takes the form of "absolutizing" a selective value, by claiming an either/or consequence. Thus discrimination on the basis of color becomes an absolute evil, while other discriminations, e.g., on the basis of social class, become altogether secondary if not trivial. The effect is to lower the *level of generality* in the definition of the value pattern to which a commitment is demanded and exclude from the "moral community" those who share the implicit source — e.g., the valuation of basic equality — but who are unwilling to make such an exclusive commitment to *one* — however important — and not to others.

Precisely because the academic system develops *generalized* cultural and societal resources, it cannot be institutionally committed to the *exclusive* legitimacy of any particular and specific value "commitments" — however pressing such an immediate cause may seem to be. Individual persons can express such "absolutist" views and participate in such movements, again subject above all to procedural norms. But the academic system *as such* cannot be committed to such exclusive positions on the level of its own self-definition without betraying its larger trust as the guardian of the main cultural tradition of our society. It cannot, as a system, be "enlisted" in the "war" against what are regarded as the salient contemporary evils. Against such "demands," it must maintain the position of pluralism.

---

obedience can have any reforming effect. This may be true in certain cases— I do not claim absolutism for my position. But the above analysis merely makes clear that the cost of such tactics in disruption is high and should only be undertaken when the urgency is great. Of course, if a group wishes to overthrow the "system" as such, that leaves little more to be said.

[8] It is well known that the bitterest hostility of the Community movement in its "effervescent" phase was reserved for the moderate and "democratic" socialists.

INDEX

academic freedom, 165, 166, 168, 170, 171, 182; and autonomous university, 159–161; and business community, 163–164; corporate vs. individual, 174–178; and secularization of higher education, 162–163
academic standards and Black Studies, 31–32, 35–36
activists, *see student activists*
Ad Hoc Faculty Committee, Columbia, 83–86
administration, university, 142–143, 147–150
Afro-American Society, Cornell, 140, 141, 142
alienation: and childhood upbringing, 63; and dynamics of change within individual, 62–63; and parental influence, 61–62
American Association for Higher Education, 148 n.
American Association of University Professors, 163
American Society for Aesthetics, 20
American University, 153 n.
Amherst College, 163 n.
amnesty, 82, 84, 102
Antioch College, 17, 53, 128
Anti-War Mobilization, 135
Anti-War Spring Mobilization, 139
Architect Renewal Committee for Harlem (ARCH), and Columbia gymnasium issue, 125–127

Associated Students, San Francisco State College, 25–26
Association of African and Afro-American Students, Harvard, 24
Atomic Energy Commission, and university research, 8–9
Authoritarian Personality, 54
authority, moral, of university, 101

Barzun, Jacques, 153 n.
Bell, Daniel, 67–107
Bennington College, 17
Berkeley student movement, 54, 73, 102, 128, 131, 137, 144, 146, 151, 155, 169; and active violence, 21; ambiguity of aims, 5–6, 19; Board of Educational Development, 12–13; Committee on Participant Education, 12–13; differences from other student movements, 3–5; and educational experiments, 11–13; educational vs. political issues, 6–9; effect on university, 9; and experimental college, 13; Free Speech Movement, 3, 7, 9–10, 11, 13; free-university movement, 9–11; Herr Committee, 14; and liberal arts curriculum, 13–14; and radical tradition, 54–55; report of Select Committee on Education, 11–14; and student participation in university policy, 15–17; and university reform, 9–11; "Vietnam Commencement," 7

and social differentiation, 159–161; and societal change, 57, 180–181; sociology, 152 n.; student career problems, 66; student opinion of, 20–21; student participation, 15–17; vs. student radicals, 17–19; student status, 169–170; students, as agents of restructuring, 3, 6–9, 16–21, 89, 90, 104, 143–144, 150–158; as surrogate, 7–9; and trustees, 148

Veblen, Thorstein, 163, 177
"Vietnam Commencement," Berkeley, 7
Vietnam War, as student movement issue, 4–6, 19, 21, 46, 51, 53, 61, 66, 67, 71, 73, 75, 80, 81, 94, 96, 135–136, 139, 175 n.

Weber, Max, 165 n., 169, 180
white students, and Black Studies, 30–31
Wisconsin, University of, 54, 55, 102, 128, 169

Yale University, and Black Studies program, 23–24, 33
Young Americans for Freedom (YAF), 52